The Mail&Guardian

A-Z of South African Politics

The Mail&Guardian

A-Z of South African Politics

The Essential Handbook

2004

Edited by
Paul Stober & Barbara Ludman

First published in 2004 by Jacana Media (Pty) Ltd.
5 St Peter Road
Bellevue, 2198
Johannesburg
South Africa

© *The Mail&Guardian*

All rights reserved.

ISBN 1-77009-023-1

Cover design by Disturbance
Proofread by Owen Hendry of Wordsmiths
Printed by Formeset Printers
Set in Bembo 11/13
See a complete list of Jacana titles at www.jacana.co.za

Contributors

Justin Arenstein, Julia Beffon, Maureen Brady, Matthew Buckland, Matthew Burbidge, Nawaal Deane, Judith February, Drew Forrest, Philippa Garson, Julia Grey, Yolandi Groenewald, Ferial Haffajee, Karen Heese, Ufrieda Ho, Lisa Johnston, Nicole Johnston, Ronald Monwabisi Kete, Jaspreet Kindra, Matuma Letsoalo, Barbara Ludman, Thebe Mabanga, Fiona MacLeod, Khadija Magardie, Noko Makgato, Mmanaledi Mataboge, Nicola Mawson, Marianne Merten, Thandee N'wa Mhangwana, Fikile-Ntsikelelo Moya, Trish Murphy, Roshila Pillay, Vicki Robinson, Ciaran Ryan, Pat Schwartz, Sam Sole, Paul Stober, Rapule Thabane, Thomas Thale, Mike van Graan, Wisani wa ka Ngobeni.

Acknowledgements

Thanks to Hoosain Karjieker, David Macfarlane, Sewela Mohale, and visiting intern Shreya Mukherjee at the *Mail&Guardian*; to Mike Martin, Maggie Davey, Chris Cocks, Bambi Nunes at Jacana; Owen Hendry of Wordsmiths; and to the Electoral Institute of Southern Africa and the Independent Electoral Commission for the information on election results set out in an appendix.

Contents

Introduction

Politics in South Africa dates quickly. And so we present the *Mail&*
Guardian's fourth *A-Z of South African Politics* to help you navigate a
fascinating country, but one whose politics can sometimes seem
overwhelming.

In 1994, when Anton Harber introduced the first edition, he wrote that
"South African politics used to be simple. There was right and wrong,
black and white, the powerful and the disempowered, the oppressed and
the oppressors, the voters and the disenfranchised ... [now] the country
boasts a bewildering array of personalities, organisations, institutions, ideas,
issues, debates, conflicts and events, many of them new and unknown."

After ten years, the "bewildering array" is more bewildering. And the
previous editions have quickly become historical documents, as people
have moved: into government and out of it; from the political seats into
the civil service; from politics into business; from business into the
academy. The political network is new; it's more female, younger, and
more African.

The *A-Z of South African Politics* is a tool to understanding who matters
and why.

It's written, and edited, by authorities in their field, which gives the
book the inside track and that under-the-skin feel that is a staple on the
CV of *Mail&Guardian* writers and contributors. Started 19 years ago, the
newspaper has always been unashamedly political, and the practice
continues even as interest in and passion for political writing has been
replaced by the era of showbiz writing and what Jeremy Seabrook has
called the "banal cult of celebrity".

It is a challenge – and a service to democracy – to make politics sexy
and compelling. An apathetic nation is a dangerous nation, for it is then
when tyrants rise. Look to the United States to see the lesson of plump,
middle-class apathy, or to Zimbabwe to see what can happen when
freedom is taken for granted.

There are no celebrities in this book – though Reserve Bank governor
Tito Mboweni and Gauteng premier Mbhazima Shilowa are jollers of
note. Each profile is tackled dispassionately but with an eye always on the
quirk, for the extraordinary, for sparkling leadership and for those with an
ability to say and think that which is unpopular.

Since the last edition, new politics has happened quickly. Patricia de Lille has been a perennial through the editions; this time she is a leader of a new entrant – the Independent Democrats.

Social movements had not yet made a significant mark in 1999 – they feature now. And Zackie Achmat, the leader of the Treatment Action Campaign who is globally recognised as an activist of note, makes his debut in the series. We welcome him and look forward to other young leaders making their mark in civil society.

In 1994, South Africa's politics was consumed by domestic affairs – this year's edition reveals the extent to which the country has been absorbed into the maelstrom of African politics.

The trend Phillip van Niekerk noted in the 1999 edition has been completed – the African National Congress has (mostly) shrugged off the identity of liberation movement to become a party of government. There is another identity worth shrugging off now and that is our self-definition as "post-apartheid South Africa". The end of transition should by now be nigh. And this should also signal an end to excusing government practices and delivery less than we dared dream of in 1994. There can be no patience with slovenly civil servants or corrupt politicians – often excused because this is still a state in transition.

We should look now for national self-confidence and for shoulders to the wheel. Unless South Africa deals effectively with joblessness and poverty, the next edition could be very different – more tenuous, less stable and hopeful.

As with the three previous editions, this one would not have been possible without co-editor Barbara Ludman who has been the midwife of each. With an exacting eye for detail and a slavish commitment to deadline (which I wish was a more generalised quality across the newsroom) she is the quintessential independent journalist. She ensures the integrity of the publication.

Her co-editor Paul Stober, a contributor to the previous editions, has brought an incisive understanding of the body politic to this edition. In an era when political journalism is based, too often, on what outside and often ill-informed analysts say, he is an acknowledged expert who has been covering South African and international politics for more than a decade. It's been good to have that eye on this edition.

Ferial Haffajee
Editor
Mail&Guardian

I

Profiles

Achmat, Adurrazack

National Chairperson, Treatment Action Campaign

Zackie Achmat and his organisation, the Treatment Action Campaign, have become symbols of HIV and Aids activism in South Africa.

Despite a solid struggle background, Achmat has not shied away from taking issue with the new government for its failure to provide free anti-retroviral drugs to people with Aids. The lessons learned as an African National Congress activist have served the 42-year-old gay film-maker well.

He was raised in a Muslim community in Cape Town and started his political life at 14 as one of the leaders of the 1976 anti-apartheid school boycotts. Between 1976 and 1980 he was repeatedly detained by the security police, which prevented him from completing high school.

In 1980 he turned to underground work and was active in promoting the ANC – from organising the first mass ANC funeral in the Western Cape to publicising the Freedom Charter in huge murals spray-painted onto walls all over Cape Town.

He became well known for his work at the National Coalition for Gay and Lesbian Equality and, as its director, took cases to the newly formed Constitutional Court that saw the decriminalisation of sodomy and the granting of equal status to same-sex partners in respect of immigration. He also campaigned for the retention of the clause in the Bill of Rights prohibiting discrimination on grounds of sexual orientation.

He learned he was HIV-positive in 1990, but it took some time before he moved on to the HIV and Aids campaign. He felt that the struggle against HIV and Aids was woefully disorganised and directionless, and his work focused on ensuring that all people with Aids have access to free treatment.

Achmat himself refused to take anti-retroviral treatment, even after his HIV morphed into full-blown Aids, until the government drew up a national treatment plan giving everyone who needs them free access to the drugs. First on the list was pregnant women, and the TAC will go down in history for its triumph over the Health Ministry when, in 2002, the Constitutional Court ruled that the government is obliged to provide free anti–retroviral treatment to HIV–positive pregnant women to prevent the transmission of the virus to their unborn babies.

The TAC has also taken on international drug companies, accusing them of profiteering and pressuring them to grant licences so that generic drugs can be produced for developing countries.

Achmat and the TAC have won international and local acclaim. They have been nominated for the 2004 Nobel Peace Prize. Achmat was featured as one of the 35 heroes of 2003 in *Time* magazine, and the TAC won an MTV Free Your Mind Award in Germany. Locally, *ThisDay* newspaper named Achmat Person of the Year for 2003, and the Tshwane University of Technology honoured him with its Communicator of the Year award. In 2004, a panel of judges convened by the *Financial Mail* named him Politician of the Decade.

Achmat has become a symbol of HIV and Aids activism, but he does not work alone. Without the dedication, hard work and legal expertise of Aids Law Project director Mark Heywood and his colleagues, the campaigns would never have got off the ground.

Date of birth: 21 March 1962

Balfour, Ngconde

Minister of Correctional Services

If Ngconde Balfour thought the Sports Ministry was tough, wait until he's had a few months in his new post. There are nearly 200 000 men and women in 241 South African prisons with a capacity of just over 111 000 – and that's just the beginning of the challenges he'll be expected to sort out. They include warder corruption, recidivism, the plight of children held with adults, pervasive gangsterism – and more.

His bulk – Balfour is known to enjoy a good meal, or several – was the subject of good-hearted jibes from President Thabo Mbeki when the new Cabinet was sworn in. Noting that Balfour is a heavyweight, Mbeki joked "now he told me he is going to sit on all those wrongdoers" – and the crowd erupted in laughter.

Perhaps Balfour should have tried that method when championing transformation in sport. He had a tough time, with cricket banning the quota system, rugby still battling to bury the ghost of racism, and football riddled with scandalous officiating on the field and indecision in the boardroom. But he is likely to find Correctional Services an even harder ball game.

The only real experience he takes to his new post is the time he spent as a political detainee because of his involvement with the Azanian Students Convention and, later, the United Democratic Front.

Balfour's experience in sport, however, is extensive. The fact that he held a BA sport and recreation management degree from the University of Fort Hare, and a Graduate Diploma in sport and recreation from Victoria University in Australia, may have helped him acquaint himself with the Ministry of Sport. So has his experience as a former national director of rugby development, head of sports administration at the University of the Western Cape, and international director of the Cape Town 2004 Olympic bid.

As sports minister, Balfour was generally poor – though there were signs during his last year in charge that he had got over his habit of talking first and thinking later. From his uncritical backing of Hansie Cronje when reports first came out of India of the South African cricket captain's involvement in match-fixing, to his ham-fisted attempts to bully rugby administrators into line, Balfour was a loose cannon.

But his genial nature, and the unimportance of sport in the wider context – no matter what sports fans believe – meant that the consequences of his errors were not too serious.

It is open to debate that winning a contest against rugby supremo Louis Luyt on whether government could overrule sports bodies constitutes fair preparation for facing down rioting prisoners.

Date of birth: 23 August 1954

Balindlela, Nosima
Premier, Eastern Cape

The appointment of Nosima Balindlela as the new premier of the Eastern Cape has been greeted with some alarm, given her uninspiring record as Education MEC. Sceptics also question whether she will be able to heal long-standing divisions in the ruling party, improve the province's notoriously poor socio-economic service delivery record, and sort out its ill-managed finances.

Balindlela's promotion from the lowly provincial portfolio of Arts, Sports and Culture is clearly part of President Thabo Mbeki's drive to empower female politicians – she is one of four female premiers in South Africa. But it may prove a poisoned chalice. The provincial administration has been so dogged with problems that last year, a presidential task team led by the Minister of Public Services and Administration, Geradine Fraser-Moleketi, was deployed to clean it up.

At least Balindlela should not have to worry about former premier Makhenkesi Stofile breathing down her neck – he has been pre-emptively shifted to the national Cabinet as Minister of Sport.

Balindlela's own record in government leaves much to be desired. Appointed Eastern Cape education minister in 1994, she was fired by Stofile after overspending her budget by about R2-billion and presiding over a fall in the province's matric pass rate to 44%. Later, she was brought back to the provincial cabinet as MEC for Arts, Sports and Culture.

The province has become a byword for maladministration. The Public Service Accountability Monitor, an independent organisation based at Rhodes University, has 576 reported cases of misconduct, corruption and misgovernment in the province on its database, involving misappropriated or unaccounted-for funds totalling R6,946-billion.

The departments concerned report that 210 (36%) of these have been resolved. However, the Monitor believes that, on the strength of available information, only 41 (7%) have been satisfactorily resolved, which includes the relevant legal provision and disciplinary action. It says only R324,28-million (4,67%) of the missing public funds has been recovered or accounted for.

The provincial Health Department is likely to be a thorn in Balindlela's side. It is investigating several employees for allegedly attempting to steal close to half a million rand.

Financial audits conducted by the Auditor-General's Office show that between 1996 and 2003, only 11,7% of the Eastern Cape's provincial budget was adequately accounted for. The Auditor-General issued audit disclaimers for an amount of R110-billion, of a total budget allocation of R129,5-billion, over that period.

Over the past two years, however, there have been signs of improvement. In 2001/2002 the province adequately accounted for 17,7% of its budget, rising to 59% in 2002/2003.

And Balindlela's first move as premier was to separate Finance, which is now a free-standing portfolio, from Economic Development, which she has merged with Arts, Sports and Culture.

Balindlela is a flamboyant figure with strong religious convictions. She wakes up at 3 am every morning to meditate. While Education MEC she dressed in school uniform, and while Arts and Culture MEC, in traditional Xhosa attire.

Born in Hermanus in the Western Cape, she and her family were forcibly moved to Middeldrift in the Eastern Cape. After obtaining a teacher's diploma, she completed a BA at Fort Hare University and went on to post-graduate studies at British and American institutions. Between 1973 and 1994 she taught at various schools and teachers' colleges, as well as lecturing in education at Fort Hare and the University of Transkei.

In the late 1980s she was active in the United Democratic Front, which led to her dismissal from two of the institutions where she taught.

She is enormously popular among grassroots African National Congress members in the province.

Date of birth: 28 November 1949

Benjamin, Jean

Deputy Minister of Social Development

Jean Benjamin is no stranger to politics. She was expelled from the University of the Western Cape in the 1970s for protesting against apartheid. Now, she faces a different kind of struggle: how to ensure equality amongst South Africa's poorest citizens.

The Department of Social Development has come under fire recently from NGOs who claim that welfare grants are not available to all who qualify for them. Regardless of where the blame for bad administration may lie, be it with another inefficient department or even with corrupt officials in her own department, Benjamin has a difficult task ahead.

Achieving an honours degree in psychology in London after fleeing South Africa to avoid a subpoena as a state witness in a terrorism trial in 1973 indicates a certain amount of tenacity, which she will need in copious quantities in her new portfolio if she is to become involved in weeding out the R1,5-billion fraud in the social grant system.

She returned to South Africa in 1980 and immediately re-entered the political fray. Not only was she an activist, but also sang at political rallies. Her love of music became evident prior to her first term in Parliament, when she opened a jazz club. Jean's Jazz Gallery was doomed to failure, however; the pressure of being an MP meant that there was no time to run a club, although she still relaxes by listening to jazz and dancing.

Benjamin obtained a PhD in social psychology in 1996, ironically from the institution that banned her at the start of her political career. She has served on several political, parliamentary and UWC committees, as well as lecturing in social psychology at UWC. She became an MP in 1997 and has authored three language-based publications.

Benjamin is one of ten women deputy ministers, moving into her position after being chairperson of the members' interest sub-committee of the National Assembly rules committee.

Date of birth: 24 November 1955

Botha, Ntombazana

Deputy Minister of Arts and Culture

The former deputy minister of provincial and local government is a good candidate to fill the gap left by her predecessors, Brigitte Mabandla – whose warmth endeared her to all sectors of the arts – and Buyelwa Sonjica, who was well liked and respected during her year in the post. Botha also has strong people skills, which were in evidence at provincial and local government.

A hard-working deputy, she also shares Mabandla's strong interest in the status and welfare of women. In her former post, Botha started the Women in Local Government programme, aimed at helping female councillors overcome past disadvantages and take a leadership role in development at local government level.

Botha has obtained credits towards a BProc degree, a sign of ongoing interest in the law which started with her first job as book-keeper and paralegal. From 1991 to 1997, when she entered Parliament, she was coordinator for the Lawyers for Human Rights' paralegal training project at regional, provincial and then national level.

Born in East London, Ntombazana Gertrude Winifred Botha helped establish the United Democratic Front in the Border region of the Eastern Cape in 1983. She served as vice-chairperson of the Eastern Cape NGO Coalition in 1996 and 1997, and joined Parliament in July 1997.

The church is a strong feature in her public life. She obtained a number of qualifications through church leadership programmes at the Andover Newton Theological School in Boston. And – relevant to her new post – she has coordinated the East London choral music festival since 1999.

Date of birth: 21 July 1943

Buthelezi, Mangosuthu

Certainly one of the most controversial personalities ever in South African politics, Buthelezi – Zulu prince, founder of the Inkatha movement and

Inkatha Freedom Party, erstwhile home affairs minister – resumed open confrontation with the African National Congress in 2004 after years of reconciliation.

In the interest of national unity, former president Nelson Mandela had made Buthelezi home affairs minister in 1994. He retained the position under President Thabo Mbeki in 1999, but only by default. Buthelezi had been offered a deputy president's position – but only, he said, if the IFP gave up the KwaZulu-Natal premiership. The party rejected the deal, and Mbeki kept Buthelezi on in Home Affairs.

Throughout the ten years they continued in the Government of National Unity, Buthelezi and other IFP ministers served under – and, sometimes, alongside – the ANC. But in 2004 Buthelezi entered into a "Coalition for Change" with the Democratic Alliance in an attempt to keep control of KwaZulu-Natal, just in time for the 2004 provincial and national elections.

This led to bitter exchanges between the IFP and the ANC, with the ANC accusing Buthelezi of moving to the right. Buthelezi and Mbeki also clashed in court after Buthelezi, who had had a torrid and frustrating several years at Home Affairs, insisted on presenting an immigration Bill which Mbeki opposed. The two clashed in court.

Buthelezi eventually lost the case and, more importantly, his post when Mbeki announced his Cabinet after the elections. He now sits on the opposition benches without a solid government position for the first time in years.

Buthelezi has been leader of the IFP since its formation as the Inkatha movement in 1975. All speculation of a successor has come to naught, and even now it is not clear who will succeed him. IFP spokesperson Musa Zondi has discouraged speculation around him, saying it might jeopardise his chances.

After the IFP performed dismally in the 2004 elections, winning only 6% of the vote, Buthelezi offered to resign in an IFP national council meeting.

But his supporters are believed to have urged him on. It is believed that among the youth wing there is widespread unhappiness with his continuing leadership, but they are reluctant to speak about their convictions in public.

Buthelezi started his political career by joining the ANC Youth League in the late 1940s at Fort Hare University, where he met political activists such as Robert Sobukwe, founder of the Pan Africanist Congress, and ZK Matthews, who went on to become an ANC president. Buthelezi was expelled after student boycotts, and completed his degree in social sciences at the University of Natal.

In 1953 he took up his position as chief, and in 1970 was appointed head of the KwaZulu Territorial Authority, becoming chief minister of the homeland in 1976.

The Black Consciousness Movement of the 1970s branded him a homeland collaborator, though he consistently declined to accept independence for KwaZulu or enter into political deals with the government until Nelson Mandela was released from prison and the ANC unbanned.

He founded Inkatha in 1975 with the blessing of the ANC, but his relationship with the movement deteriorated after the late 1970s when he criticised the ANC for the armed struggle and for calling for sanctions against apartheid South Africa.

Date of birth: 27 August 1928

Chaskalson, Arthur

Chief Justice of South Africa

As president of South Africa's first Constitutional Court and the country's chief justice since the positions were amalgamated in November 2001, Arthur Chaskalson has played a groundbreaking role in shaping the court and the country's constitutional jurisprudence. His influence over every aspect of the court's work in this formative period has been immense, and he will, say observers, "be a very hard act to follow" when he retires – which will be, at the latest, when he reaches age 75 in 2006.

During the 1990s his experience in constitution-making helped to prepare him for his future role in the Constitutional Court. He assisted in the drafting of the Namibian constitution, joined the African National Congress's constitutional committee (as an expert and a non-member of the ANC) and served on the technical committee on constitutional issues, appointed by the Multi-Party Negotiating Forum in May 1993 to advise on constitutional matters and to participate in the drafting of the interim Constitution.

Johannesburg-born Chaskalson is a graduate of the University of the Witwatersrand (BCom 1952; LLB cum laude, 1954) where he complemented his studies with a position on the university's soccer team, also playing in the Combined South African Universities team in 1952.

He was admitted to the Johannesburg Bar in May 1956 and took silk in July 1971. During his career at the Bar he appeared as counsel on behalf of members of the liberation movements in several major political trials, notably the Rivonia trial. He also acted in major commercial disputes.

In 1978 he was one of the founders of the Legal Resources Centre, a non-profit organisation which sought to use law to pursue justice and human rights in South Africa. Chaskalson left a lucrative practice to become the first director of the LRC in November 1978 and remained there for 15 years, acting in several landmark cases that changed the lives of millions of South Africans burdened by the yoke of apartheid's race laws.

He was a member of the Johannesburg Bar Council from 1967 to 1971 and from 1973 to 1984; chairman of the Johannesburg Bar in 1976 and again in 1982; a member and later convenor of the National Bar Examination Board (1979-1991), and vice-chairman of the General Council of the Bar of South Africa (1982-1987).

He has been a member of the board of the Faculty of Law of the University of the Witwatersrand since 1979, and was an honorary professor of law at that university, a member of the board of the Centre for Applied Legal Studies, a member of the National Council of Lawyers for Human Rights, and chairman of the Rhodes Scholarship Selection Committee for South Africa.

He has been a member of the Judicial Service Commission since 1994, during much of that time its chairman, and has been joint honorary president of the General Council of the Bar of South Africa since 1994.

In 1985 he was elected an honorary member of the Bar Association of the City of New York in 1985, only the second South African (the first was Jan Smuts) to be honoured in this way.

He has also been vice-chairman of the International Legal Aid Division of the International Bar Association; is a commissioner of the International Commission of Jurists (elected in 1995) and a member of the Academy of Science of South Africa (elected 2001). Since June 1999 he has been a member of the Permanent Court of Arbitration, having been selected by South Africa to be one of its four members on that court.

Date of birth: 24 November 1931

Dandala, Reverend Hamilton Mvumelwano

General Secretary, All Africa Conference of Churches

Reverend Mvume Dandala, renowned church leader and peacemaker in South Africa, now extends these roles to the continent at large as general secretary of the most influential ecumenical organisation in Africa – the All Africa Conference of Churches.

After serving for seven years as presiding bishop of the Methodist Church in Southern Africa, Dandala, then president of the South African Council of Churches, was appointed in September 2003 to lead the Conference, a Pan-African body of 169 Christian churches with a presence in 39 countries and an estimated membership of 120-million Christians across the continent.

As leader of the Conference, which is based in Nairobi, Kenya, Dandala's duties are diverse, ranging from addressing human rights and poverty to mediating in wars and conflicts; from fighting hunger and disease, especially HIV/Aids, to helping refugees in Africa.

The high esteem in which Dandala is held in South African social and political circles is underscored by the fact that his induction as general secretary of the Conference was attended by, among others, President Thabo Mbeki, Cabinet ministers and senior government officials, including Reverend Frank Chikane, Archbishop Desmond Tutu, and many business bigwigs.

Dandala has taken to his new role in Africa with much zeal. In the opening statement of a three-day interfaith regional peace summit for the Horn of Africa, East and Central Africa in March 2004, he called for peace on the continent, urging Africa's religious leaders of diverse faiths to influence their governments to appreciate that the continent needs leaders who genuinely embrace peace and are focused on uniting communities.

His skills in mediating conflict, as evidenced in the role he played in helping to quell the political violence of the 1980s and early 1990s in Port Elizabeth, Johannesburg and on the East Rand, are still much sought after. His contribution to peace in South Africa was recognised in 2001 with the award by President Thabo Mbeki of the National Order of the Baobab in Silver. The award also acknowledged his invaluable work with the Peace Secretariat in the Eastern Cape.

Dandala, who was born in the rural town of Mount Ayliff in the Eastern Cape where his father was a minister, has been a member of the Methodist ministry since 1970, and served in various positions while rising through the ranks to become presiding bishop in 1997. He has an MA from Cambridge University, an honorary professorship from the University of Pretoria, and an honorary doctorate from the University of Transkei. He was the first black person to be appointed prior of the Order of St John, a position he continues to hold.

Date of birth: 26 October 1951

Johnny de Lange

Deputy Minister of Justice

The new deputy justice minister has a gift for putting up the backs of what one might consider his constituency. In 2003, for example, as chairperson of Parliament's portfolio committee on justice and constitutional affairs, he angered top judges when he suggested that they were underworked and overpaid.

When the judges accused him of undermining the independence of the judiciary, he compounded the insult: "The shrill, hysterical tone and content of the statement is most unusual and, one would venture, unbecoming to members of the judiciary," he said.

Even as an ordinary MP, Johnny de Lange was never one to show any semblance of tact. In 1999 he called Democratic Party (as the Democratic Alliance was known then) leader Tony Leon a chihuahua, which he described as an "arrogant little dog". Leon, never at a loss for words, retorted that De Lange was a bullfrog.

He didn't restrict his ire to judges or the Opposition. In February 2003, while still chairperson of Parliament's justice committee, De Lange angered his own comrades when he told members of the rules committee that the presiding officers, who were then National Assembly Speaker Frene Ginwala and National Council of Provinces Chairperson (now Education Minister) Naledi Pandor, had used Finance Minister Trevor Manuel's name to put forward their own agenda on Parliament's budget.

Ginwala demanded he withdraw the allegation or substantiate it. De Lange said he would first consult with the Finance Minister. Ginwala then adjourned the sitting. De Lange eventually apologised, although not everybody was happy with the extent of the apology or its apparent sincerity.

Lawyers are others who have incurred De Lange's wrath. He is said to have told off Pretoria lawyers after they complained that they had not been consulted when the Justice Department opened a new deeds office in Nelspruit.

For the lawyers, the new office meant that Pretoria firms that had hitherto benefited from the conveyancing jobs brought to their town had to share the cake with emerging attorneys in Mpumalanga and, in some cases, watch as ordinary local people accessed the deeds office without the help of lawyers.

De Lange's appointment is a promotion and acknowledgement of his hard work and an opportunity to help to implement the many Bills and Acts he helped to enact.

Born Johannes Hendrik de Lange in 1958, he was a United Democratic Front leader in the Western Cape in the 1980s and, as an advocate, defended accused in a number of political trials.

De Lange is a founder member of the National Association of Democratic Lawyers, for which he was director of the legal education, research and training project from July 1993 to March 1994. He also served as a member of the Goldstone Commission of Enquiry into Violence in Crossroads, Cape Town.

Date of birth: 15 January 1958

Didiza, Thoko

Minister of Agriculture and Land Affairs

Thoko Didiza has won a lot of hearts and minds in her four years as Minister of Land Affairs and Agriculture. Under her stewardship, the Agriculture portfolio has grown, and though white farmers are still hesitant to trust her totally, she has gone to great lengths to build a relationship with farmers' unions such as AgriSA.

Her handling of the Land Affairs portfolio has been more controversial, and the slow pace of land reform has made her term very difficult. It is only in the past two years that land restitution has accelerated dramatically, but she is still struggling to convince organisations such as the National Land Committee and the Landless People's Movement that land reform is being done at the right pace.

The amendments to the Restitution of Land Rights Amendment Act, which give her the right to expropriate land from difficult farmers, are in danger of souring her budding relationship with AgriSA, which fears that the Act will give her too much power.

Didiza's agricultural policy is centrally focused on using land reform to promote black commercial farmers. But she has often been criticised for neglecting the millions of poor and landless people who either have no interest in commercial farming, or lack the necessary skills and capital.

She started off her career in government as deputy minister of agriculture in 1994 and handled the difficult job with great success. When she was appointed she admitted she knew little about farming, but her ability to adapt and learn has served her well.

She was originally appointed in 1994 under National Party Minister of Agriculture Kraai van Niekerk. Some in the African National Congress felt that the job should have gone to Derek Hanekom, who had developed the party's agricultural policy. Instead Hanekom was appointed Minister of Land Affairs, and he and Didiza clashed regularly.

When the NP left the government in 1996, Hanekom received the additional portfolio of Agriculture as well. But he lost his Cabinet position after the 1999 elections, and Didiza was appointed as his successor.

When she took office, Didiza started cleaning house. Hanekom and his appointees believed in policies which emphasised uplifting the rural poor and giving impetus to small-scale farming, but Didiza prioritised the creation of a black commercial farming class.

Her early term in office was branded by the exodus of mostly white senior officials who had worked under Hanekom.

The result was the shelving of key programmes initiated by Hanekom, most notably land redistribution projects and land tenure legislation.

But two years into her term, Didiza took the issue of land restitution by the horns. In the last eight months of 2003 there was a 197% increase in the number of hectares restored to claimants under the land restitution programme. This achievement is a result of prioritising rural claims, and not merely relying on "chequebook restitution", where the community receives no land, only money.

It remains to be seen whether the department will meet its target of distributing a third of the country's white-owned and state-owned land by 2015.

Her biggest success last year was the department's budget expenditure. It spent 98% of its budget, with 79% of this going to land reform. Officials credit the improvement, which increased by 58% from last year, to Didiza's management.

Commercial farmers were encouraged by the way Didiza fought at the World Trade Organisation's talks in Cancun, Mexico for the scrapping of government subsidies in developed countries. These subsidies make the goods of farmers from the United States and the European Union unfairly cheap on world markets.

She has, however, come in for flak on the Communal Land Rights Bill, intended to secure the tenure of people living under traditional leaders. It has been criticised for putting too much power in the hands of traditional leaders, and granting the minister too much power. Didiza says she will be able to protect communities' interests better this way.

Thoko Msane Didiza was born in Hammersdale. She matriculated at the famous Ohlange High School in Durban, established by ANC founder John Dube, then completed several diplomas in personnel training, public relations, journalism and financial management. She worked as legal secretary at Mafuka Mbuli and Company, receptionist at the Diakonia Ecumenical Church Agency, and national deputy general secretary of the South African Council of the Young Women's Christian Association.

She started her political career as a member of the ANC Youth League and was one of only two members of ANCYL that made it on to the party's national executive committee at the 1997 Mafikeng congress.

Date of birth: 2 June 1965

Dlamini-Zuma, Nkosazana

Minister of Foreign Affairs

When President Thabo Mbeki made Nkosazana Dlamini-Zuma his inaugural Foreign Minister in 1999, the writing was on the wall. Not only had he put his most trusted lieutenant in the portfolio most close to his heart, but he effectively placed his bets on her as a future president too.

Since then, Deputy President Jacob Zuma has come under a serious political cloud, thereby exponentially increasing his former wife's chances as a future president when Mbeki ends his second and final term in 2009. It is not a terribly well-kept secret that this is the outcome Mbeki desires; whether the rank and file will fall in behind him is a political wild-card.

As Foreign Minister, Dlamini-Zuma has not done a bad job when considering the mess that previous incumbent Alfred Nzo bequeathed her. Nzo had no foreign policy; his bacon was saved only by the global stature of former president Nelson Mandela, who was South Africa's walking foreign policy as he brought charm but no real strategy to a series of high-profile geopolitical adventures.

That changed under Mbeki, whose passion is foreign affairs: in effect, the Presidency makes foreign policy and the department carries it out. In this, Dlamini-Zuma has the stature of a deputy president.

Quickly Mbeki and Dlamini-Zuma brought direction and impact to foreign policy.

The continent became the priority, as signaled by Mbeki's early African Renaissance projects. Links with the South are the next priority, with Brazil and India targeted as key partners. Next are relations with the G8, notably with the United States, Britain, the European Union and Canada.

The African Renaissance evolved into a fully fledged and funded policy. It is given policy and practical expression through New Partnership for Africa's Development (Nepad) plan to develop the continent. The Nepad secretariat, under Wiseman Nkuhlu, reports to Dlamini-Zuma.

She spent her first term giving life to Mbeki's other legacy dream – the African Union, the political structure through which Nepad will be implemented. Now three years old, the AU is still a baby, but it is a recognised union with its own commissioners, a peace and security council, and a Pan-African parliament.

The jury's out on whether it will become a talk-shop like its predecessor the Organisation of African Unity, but Dlamini-Zuma's role in nurturing the infant union will be a considerable part of her legacy. She has grown visibly in the role, learning not only the French language, but also a spot of Francophone-African chic. Her look is a far cry from the schoolmarmish image she projected as South Africa's first health minister.

African politics and South Africa's role in it are clearly Dlamini-Zuma's passions, though she is also building quick links with India, Brazil and other giants of the developing South. The country's stature has grown since 1994, and the key conurbations of the West, like the G8, the EU and the US, regularly seek South Africa's counsel on major issues including aid and trade policy, African union, and – with less success – an approach on the festering sore that is Zimbabwe.

Dlamini-Zuma has been instrumental in maintaining South Africa's dogged support for Zimbabwean President Robert Mugabe. Annoyed by media criticism, she has dug in her heels over Zimbabwe, refusing to countenance any criticism even when realpolitik has called for it. This has damaged both her standing and South Africa's as a moral beacon in the region.

Feminist Mbeki may well be part of the president's identity as a modern African leader. He has among the highest number of female Cabinet members in the world. It may also be that he is getting the country used to female leadership, so that he can anoint his own successor. Time flies. When he leaves the stage in less than five years' time, Mbeki will need a loyal lieutenant to ensure his African dreams materialise, and there is none more loyal than Dlamini-Zuma.

A native of KwaZulu-Natal, she studied medicine at Natal University's medical school, during which time she also served as vice-president of the South African Students Organisation. She went into exile and completed her medical degree at the University of Bristol in the UK. Zuma also served as an ANC doctor in Swaziland before returning in the early 1990s.

Date of birth: 27 January 1949

Du Toit, Dirk Cornelius

Deputy Minister for Agriculture and Land Affairs

Du Toit has been an MP since 1994. Intimately involved in the drafting of the Constitution in 1996, he was appointed in 1999 as deputy minister to new Land and Agriculture Minister, Thoko Didiza.

Known for his brilliant legal mind, Du Toit is often employed in fine-tuning Bills associated with his department. He worked on both the Amendment to the Restitution Act of 2004 and the Communal Land Bill when problems emerged after consultations with interest groups.

Overall he is not seen as a big mover or shaker inside his department. But the Deputy Minister has taken the issue of land reform as a personal challenge. Of all the issues he has dealt with, land reform remains his pet project and he is running up his bonus miles, personally trying to attend every land handover ceremony that he possibly can.

Dirk Cornelius du Toit holds a BA, LLB from the University of the Free State and a doctorate from the University of Leiden in the Netherlands. He served on the national council of the Democratic Party before joining the African National Congress.

He was appointed legal adviser of the National Education Health and Allied Workers Union in 1992, and served as assistant secretary of the executive council of the then Southern-OFS region of the ANC. He became a member of the Bloemfontein central branch of the ANC, and was deployed in the Central West region.

Date of birth: 19 September 1943

Erwin, Alec

Minister of Public Enterprises

It is significant that Alec Erwin's appointment as Minister of Public Enterprises has been warmly welcomed by the Congress of South African Trade Unions, with the organisation identifying the minister as a "product" of the labour federation.

This is understandable – anyone who has engaged with the 56-year-old Erwin is likely to be struck by how much he has retained this progressive identity, along with his intellectual roots. Having read for an honours degree in economics and lectured at the universities of Natal and York in the late 1970s, Erwin also played a prominent role in shaping South Africa's labour movement under the auspices of the Federation of South African Trade Unions, the forerunner of Cosatu.

Between the late 1980s and early 1990s, Erwin was the national education officer of the National Union of Metalworkers – a role he had played at Cosatu – as well as an executive member of African National Congress regions and branches.

His appointment to Public Enterprises suggests that government now sees a strategic role for parastatals – it is unlikely to succumb to calls for a large-scale privatisation exercise. Instead, Transnet, Eskom and, to a lesser degree, Telkom are likely to be used to drive growth by providing the investments and infrastructure the economy is dying for.

Erwin's strategic brain and appreciation for the role of the private sector has also meant that he's built up strong relations with business. He is a man the sector trusts, even though it may not always agree with him.

While he may not have to sell too many state assets, he is likely to have to do a public relations exercise with a private sector which has come to equate commitment to privatisation as commitment to a market-driven economy.

Erwin also played a key role in formulating policy positions prior to the ascent of the ANC to power; specifically in relation to Cosatu's Economic Trends Group, the Industrial Strategy Project, the Macro-Economic Research Group, and the Reconstruction and Development Programme. With the advent of democracy, he was appointed deputy minister of finance, and then promoted to minister of trade and industry in 1996. It was late in the day that he joined the Communist Party – only in 1991, when some of his colleagues, long-time members of the SACP, were turning their backs on the party.

Along with his strong struggle credentials, Erwin has developed a high profile in international relations, especially in trade negotiations. Erwin was appointed president of the United Nations Conference on Trade and Development between 1996 and 2000, and has played a key role in representing developing countries' interests in trade rounds, having earned respect for his competency, diplomacy and integrity in tough trade negotiations. He was integral in concluding South Africa's Free Trade Agreements with the United States, the European Union and the South American trading bloc, Mercusor, as well as the establishment of the G20, a group of developing countries which lobby for fair trade. He is tipped as a future director-general of the World Trade Organisation; it is possible that he could become Africa's first.

In his term, Erwin was more a trade than an industry minister. His passion for the former was not matched by his ardour for the latter. The opening up of the economy has meant that exports now count for a significant proportion of gross domestic product. Exports grew by 30% in 2002.

The motor industry scheme has contributed significantly to this success, though attention is now turning to the job-creating impact of such plans.

He came to the black economic empowerment party late, only finalising policy and legislation in 2003, to the chagrin of not only black business, but reportedly the President as well.

The long-term 11 spatial development initiatives have attracted investment of R113-billion, though only five are working as well as planned. These are the Maputo Development Corridor, the Fish River SDI, the West Coast Investment Initiative, and the Wild Coast and Lebombo initiatives.

The failure to adequately support small, medium and micro enterprises was acknowledged by the minister himself, and support institutions Khula and Ntsika have proven disappointing.

Whatever Erwin's leadership failings, however, the depth of his experience and personality are likely to ensure that he remains respected and in a prominent position on the national and world stage.

Date of birth: 17 January 1948

Fakie, Shauket
Auditor-General

The Auditor-General has found himself repeatedly the target of long-standing litigation by one of the unsuccessful bidders in the controversial multi-million rand arms acquisition deal, Richard Young.

Although his office declared the deal above board in November 2001 – and so did the Public Protector and National Prosecuting Authority – Fakie was long embroiled in a legal battle over the release of tender documents to Young. He was also accused by Young of having "edited" the final report of the Joint Investigation Task Team (which included his office, the Public Protector and the National Prosecuting Authority) after it emerged that there had been several drafts. Fakie has dismissed such claims, but subsequently said that there were some weaknesses in the team's report, even though he stood by it as the "best we could have done under the circumstances".

Ironically, it was Fakie's office which early on raised doubts over the correctness of the way sub-contracts were allocated in a 2000 review of the procurement package submitted to Parliament's standing committee on public accounts, the watchdog on government spending. This followed the first corruption allegations raised by Patricia de Lille, then a Pan Africanist Congress MP, in late 1999.

All the wrangling over the arms deal has largely overshadowed the other work of the Auditor-General: vetting national and provincial government departments and municipalities to ensure they correctly spend, and account for, their budgets. In future the Auditor-General's office will also scrutinise government's delivery performance, although that project will take seven years to get fully off the ground.

The Auditor-General is not a popular post; it tends to focus on shortcomings within public finances. But various initiatives by the office under Fakie's guidance have produced streamlined auditing procedures and buy-in from officials.

The Auditor-General is one of South Africa's key watchdog institutions and the only independent body to provide a check on financial impropriety at all levels of government and its public entities, established under Chapter 9 of the Constitution to "strengthen constitutional democracy" alongside the Public Protector, Gender Equality Commission, the Human Rights Commission, Independent Electoral Commission, and Commission for the Promotion and

Protection of the Rights of Cultural, Religious and Linguistic Communities.

The Auditor-General's hand will be strengthened by pending public audit legislation expected to be passed by the National Council of Provinces in 2004 to replace the 1995 Auditor-General and 1992 Audit Arrangements Acts. The new law will give the office more oomph, including the power to search and seize documents indicating wrongdoing. This power was missing during the arms deal investigations.

Under the proposed law, he would be able to exclude "sensitive cases" or "confidential, secret details" on written request from the relevant minister from his reports, although he would be compelled to indicate to Parliament that this had been done. And the relevant MPs could make provisions to view such details.

Fakie was appointed Auditor-General from 1 December 1999, as successor to Henri Kluever, after rising through the ranks of the office he joined as provincial auditor for Gauteng in 1995. Three years later Fakie was promoted to deputy auditor-general and chief executive officer. In this latter capacity he led the implementation of employment equity in an office which had so far remained largely white and male.

Fakie, who holds a BCom and BCompt Honours degree from the University of South Africa, qualified as a chartered accountant in 1986 in South Africa and 1988 in Australia. For 17 years he worked as chartered accountant and also was member of various industry organisations like the Association for the Advancement of Black Accountants in Southern Africa.

The Auditor-General's office has served several terms as external auditors to the World Health Organisation. Fakie himself was appointed external auditor for the United Nations Industrial Development Organisation for a two-year term from July 2002.

Date of birth: 19 August 1953

Fraser-Moleketi, Geraldine

Minister of Public Service and Administration

The minister is determined to turn her hulking department into a well-oiled machine. This is a portfolio that needs tough leadership – and Fraser-Moleketi is one of the more tough-minded members of the Cabinet.

In the past, opinions of Fraser-Moleketi were coloured by one's ideological stance. Three years ago she was criticised by those on the left as a union-basher, a South African Communist Party stalwart who had sold out to economic conservatives in the government. But she was hailed by those concerned with better services and more value for taxpayers' rands, rather than lifelong job security for public servants.

Today it seems that civil service unions have worn her down and she has worked with labour, albeit incredibly slowly, to implement restructuring agreements for the public service.

Fraser-Moleketi is industrious and clear-minded, despite her fondness for opaque process-speak, and her reformist endeavors have been complicated by the past and present use of the state sector for racial redress and the ruling party's delicate relations with labour. But her insistence that working for an African National Congress government does not mean sheltered employment represents an important conceptual shift for her.

Fraser-Moleketi's upbringing was steeped in politics. She grew up in Klipfontein where her grandmother was a trade unionist and an uncle was involved in the Unity Movement. Her studies at the University of the Western Cape were interrupted in 1978 when she went into exile in Zimbabwe.

She completed a three-month military training course in Angola before attending special commanders' training in the Soviet Union in 1982. She returned to Zimbabwe to serve in the leadership of the SACP and was seminal to its relaunch in South Africa in 1990. Over the next two years she served as personal assistant to SACP general secretary Chris Hani and SACP chairperson Joe Slovo. In December 1991 she was elected to the SACP central committee and politburo – and a decade later, she was purged from the SACP leadership amid accusations of undercutting socialist ideology in her quest to streamline the public service.

In between, she served as Minister of Welfare when the National Party pulled out of the Government of National Unity, and in 1999 the mantle of Minister of Public Service and Administration settled on her shoulders.

Fraser-Moleketi's passion extends to the messier task of weeding out corrupt officials in the public service. She headed up an interim management team to stabilise the Eastern Cape, which has been riddled with corruption mostly in the departments of education, health, roads and public works and social development. She is also the chairperson of the public service anti-corruption strategy – a role that presents a conflict of interest, because the strategy is managed by the Public Service Commission, an independent monitor of the public service. Also last year, the minister led a negotiation process on the African Union Convention on Combating and Preventing Corruption as well as the United Nations Convention against Corruption.

Fraser-Moleketi's challenge will be to forge an effective link between bureaucracy, particularly at a local government level given South Africa's service delivery challenges, and building trust among South Africa's citizenry in the public service, notorious for being ruptured by corruption and maladministration.

She is married to Jabu Moleketi, deputy finance minister.

Date of birth: 24 April 1960

Gabriels, Ebrahim

President, Muslim Judicial Council

His recent election to a second term as president of the Muslim Judicial Council, the faith-based body representing the nearly 1,1-million strong Western Cape Muslim community, is an indication of faith in Ebrahim Gabriels's leadership abilities. A graduate of the Islamic University in Medina, Saudi Arabia, Gabriels has managed, during his tenure as president of the MJC, both to appease the largely conservative religious elements in the community and to pave the way for popular Muslim participation in what may best be termed "the rest of South Africa".

The reputation of the MJC has changed from that of a "dial-a-fatwa" religious organisation to one more diverse, and vocal. Under Gabriels's leadership, the council has been repositioned as another non-governmental organisation with views on issues ranging from the war in Iraq to HIV/Aids. Previously, the nearly 60-year-old organisation could be described, at best, as being the place to call to find out if a particular brand of chips was halaal (religiously permissible) or to locate a Muslim marriage officer.

At the helm of the MJC, as well as heading the United Ulama Council (a body comprising other regional religious forums), Gabriels has been seen as providing leadership, "rhetorically and spiritually", to the Muslim community. He is said to have a more liberal and "moderate" interpretation of Islam than that of his predecessor, the late Sheikh Nazeem Mohamed. This was illustrated at the height of "Pagad-fever", community enthusiasm for the activities, often violent, of People Against Gangsterism and Drugs, when Gabriels took what was regarded as a contrary stance to that of the community, calling for regard for the rule of law and opposing vigilantism.

According to its website, the MJC "advocates cooperation with government and other faith-based organisations concerning religious matters in the general interest of society". Under Gabriels, the MJC has provided sound-bytes on a range of subjects, including previously held "taboos" like domestic violence and HIV-positive Muslims.

Gabriels pioneered the "ten years of democracy khutbah" concept, introducing the notion of Muslim participation in social activism into the Friday prayer lecture. In this way, the MJC is integrating itself into the wider community, a move also illustrated by Gabriels's presence on the Religious Leaders Forum convened by President Thabo Mbeki.

Unfortunately, Gabriels's views on the treatment of women have not undergone any major revolutions. During the South African Law Commission's study into the recognition of Muslim marriages, the United Ulama Council, which he heads, expressed its displeasure at women being given the right of divorce, and at restrictions on polygamy. Earlier this year, a high-profile executive member of the MJC said on a television talk show that the way women dressed contributed towards the high incidence of rape in the country. But as far as "dinosaurdom" goes, Gabriels's MJC gives cause for optimism.

Gigaba, Malusi
Deputy Minister, Home Affairs

The appointment of African National Congress Youth League president Malusi Gigaba as Deputy Home Affairs Minister was not universally welcomed. Ambitious and ferociously loyal to the national leadership of the ANC, he has launched attacks on the media and "deviants" from the party line, including the Congress of South African Trade Unions. Under his leadership, the Youth League has shown little independence from its parent body. Rather than helping South Africa's youth, facing the three deadly afflictions of poor education, HIV/Aids and unemployment, its primary concern seems to have been to provide national visibility and business opportunities for its top dogs. Many of its members – including Gigaba, who first went to Parliament as an ANC MP in 1999 – serve in the government. The league has its own investment arm, which has come under fire for enriching a few leaders and creating conflicts of interest.

He, however, has insisted that the youth have a right to benefit from the fruits of freedom – in every sector.

Gigaba has led the league through a transition from a radical youth organisation to what he calls "developmental politics" wherein youth participate in various ways in government at all levels.

His pairing with new Home Affairs Minister Nosiviwe Mapisa-Nqakula means there is likely to be much more consensus on policy direction. Gigaba and Mapisa-Nqakula have been identified by the leftists in the ANC as being in Mbeki's circle.

Born at Eshowe in KwaZulu-Natal, Gigaba has an MA in social policy, majoring in urban affairs and policy, from the University of Durban-Westville. After joining the ANCYL and the South African Communist Party in 1990, he moved swiftly up the ranks. He served as youth league regional chairperson in Durban and as KwaZulu-Natal provincial secretary, becoming national president in 1996. He has served three terms as president, but is expected to step down when the league holds its congress in August 2004. At its last congress in 2001, members ruled that the he should serve the ANCYL in a full-time capacity and recalled him from Parliament. In 2004 the league's national executive committee reversed the decision.

Date of birth: 30 August 1971

Gillwald, Cheryl

Deputy Minister, Correctional Services

If one day South Africa establishes a super ministry in charge of the criminal justice cluster, it would be wise to study how Cheryl Gillwald, while still deputy minister of justice and constitutional affairs, succeeded in getting different components and units in the Department of Justice to work as an oiled machine.

Under Gillwald, the Justice Department developed a board, similar to the board of a corporation, with the department acting as the holding company. The various divisions of Justice, including the Masters of High Court, Magistrates Commission, the National Prosecution Authority and others, were "subsidiaries" represented on the board by their heads and senior managers.

It may be a unique way of doing government business, but it is not altogether foreign for Gillwald. Educated in Johannesburg, she earned a BCom in personnel management at what was then the University of the Orange Free State, and promptly went into business, soon becoming director of finance and administration for transport and construction companies in Harrismith. By the early 1990s, she was director of two Free State companies, one of them a plant hire firm.

When the African National Congress appointed her to Parliament in 1994 (the Senate, first, and three years later, the National Assembly), she gave up active involvement in the business world. However her business background presumably came in handy when she devised her plan of action at the Department of Justice, and could be useful for her new posting to a department in desperate need of organisation.

At the time of writing, Correctional Services Minister Ngconde Balfour and Gillwald were said to be in discussions about what her role would be at Correctional Services.

At the Justice Department, she was concerned with factors affecting women and child abuse. It was Gillwald who drove the project at Justice to establish special courts to deal with the prosecution of sexual offences. If her dedication to the welfare of women and children follows her to the new department, then it is reasonable to expect that her attention will fall on the plight of children in detention and mothers with babies in jail.

Date of birth: 13 December 1956

Goldstein, Dr Warren
Chief Rabbi-Designate

South Africa's chief rabbi-designate will be a mere 33 years old when he takes over the spiritual leadership of the country's frequently fractious Orthodox Jewish community from current Chief Rabbi Cyril Harris at the end of 2004.

Upbeat as he is about it, it will not be an easy task. Already he has come under fire from some of the elders of the increasingly hidebound community for, of all things, not wearing a beard. It will take some doing to win them over.

But Goldstein has much going for him. This lawyer-turned-rabbi has a reputation as a formidable Jewish scholar, and his doctoral thesis (from Unisa) tied his two passions together under the title "Remoralising Legal Systems: Insights from Jewish Law", dealing as it does with Jewish law's relevance to human rights and modern constitutional law.

Goldstein, a fourth-generation South African, proclaims his dedication to South Africa, its Constitution and the concept of the African Renaissance and to South Africa's "unique" Jewish community. Confident and creative, he sees his youth not as an obstacle to success but as an advantage, viewing himself as one of a new generation of young Jewish leaders "committed to the future and success of the New South Africa". "South Africa," he has said, "is a young democracy; young people are making an impact on our new society ..."

An unshakeable supporter of Israel, "an affirmative-action state to protect a vulnerable people from genocide and persecution", he sees no contradiction in "loving South Africa, being devoted to South Africa and pouring one's energies into making the New South Africa a successful country, while at the same time being connected to the land of Israel and the Jewish people".

He is co-author with Mandela grandson Dumani Mandela of an exchange of letters published as African Soul Talk (subtitled "When politics is not enough") and exploring the soul, the purpose of life, religion, morality and spirituality. In the prologue to the book, the pair conclude that "the way to nation-building in South Africa is through spirituality and common values" and that "politics divides people". He nonetheless, if an interview in the *Mail&Guardian* is anything to go by, is astutely political about avoiding direct answers to awkward questions.

Pretoria-born Goldstein is the son of High Court Judge Ezra Goldstein. He is currently spiritual head of the Sunny Road synagogue in Glenhazel, Johannesburg.

Date of birth: 21 June 1971

Gordhan, Pravin

Commissioner: South African Revenue Service

It takes money – a lot of money – to run a modern state, and the South African Revenue Service has lately become very good at finding it. Every year since 1994, the revenue service has collected more than the ever-rising target set by the minister. For the 1994/95 tax year, the minister set a modest target of R109,7-billion and Sars collected R113,7-billion. For 2002/2003, the target was well over twice that figure – R280-billion – and Sars came through with R281,5-billion.

Some of that success is due to good financial planning by the Treasury and by Sars, including predictions of economic growth and fluctuations in the exchange and interest rates – i.e. setting realistic targets. But efficiency also plays a part, and the commissioner can take some credit for that.

Nothing in Pravin Gordhan's background prepared him for shaking money out of South Africa's hard-pressed corporate and individual taxpayers. He qualified as a pharmacist at the University of Durban-Westville and worked at King Edward Hospital in Durban. But repeated detentions for his activities in support of the Natal Indian Congress and the Durban Housing Action Committee – it became part of the South African National Civic Organisation – made extended periods of employment impossible. Building South African Communist Party structures in the 1980s, he also coordinated campaigns against the tricameral parliament, and was involved in the founding of the United Democratic Front. The role he played in the African National Congress's Operation Vula led to his arrest in 1990 and a charge of treason.

He was granted amnesty a year later, in time to participate in multi-party negotiations: he chaired the management committee at the Convention for a Democratic South Africa.

In Parliament, he was elected chair of the constitutional committee and was a senior member of the Constitutional Assembly.

In 1994, the International Monetary Fund reported "widespread frustration within both the trading community and the Customs administration itself with the inability of Customs to adequately monitor and control trade flows. To a significant extent, this situation has arisen from South Africa's complex trade regime ..." which was a polite way of noting that a decade of sanctions-busting had resulted in extremely porous borders. International crime syndicates were moving in, worsening the situation.

When Inland Revenue and Customs and Excise were combined into the South African Revenue Service in 1997, Gordhan was drafted as deputy commissioner to help drive the transformation process. A year later he was named commissioner.

Transformation at Sars encompassed a wide range of operations, from trying to make the staff component more accurately reflect the population – it still doesn't – and instituting a grading system with job descriptions, to increasing computerisation. Key was the adoption of a flatter structure which devolved authority and accountability throughout the organisation.

A programme called Siyakha (we are building) includes upgrading infrastructure on the country's borders, for example establishing anti-smuggling teams, and working closely with countries in the Southern African Development Community.

Another part of Siyakha is tax collection, and it encompasses both a velvet glove and an iron fist. Here's the interesting way Sars literature describes its success in using that fist: "significant increases in the total revenue contribution of corporates through sector-specific enforcement action".

The velvet glove includes bringing tax collection to the people, with taxpayer service centres set up to answer queries, processing centres for administration, for example assessment and registration, and separate compliance centres for audits and investigations.

Siyakha has been rolled out in KwaZulu-Natal and the Western Cape, and was on its way to Gauteng in mid-2004.

Up until last year, the biggest contributor to the nation's coffers was personal income tax, followed by VAT, and then corporate tax. The good news is that in 2003, it shifted; and now it is corporates that bear the heaviest burden.

Quite a lot of Gordhan's energy has been focused on Customs, and although illegal goods do get through, the situation has so improved that the commissioner has been elected chairperson of the World Customs Organisation every year since 2001.

The commissioner, meanwhile, has decided to acquire an academic stamp on the work he's been doing: he's studying towards a post-graduate diploma in economics at the London School of Economics.

Date of birth: 12 April 1949

Hanekom, Derek

Deputy Minister, Science and Technology

Derek Hanekom has reversed the usual order of political life. In 1994, he was made a minister; ten years later, he's been made a deputy minister.

His first ministry was Land Affairs; Agriculture was added two years later when the National Party left the Government of National Unity, and the NP agriculture minister, Kraai van Niekerk, stepped down.

Hanekom was perhaps better suited to the first posting than the second. He played a key role in developing the African National Congress's initial land reform policy, and as land affairs minister he got restitution and redistribution moving as early as 1995. When his controversial Extension of Security of Tenure Act − granting tenure to farm labourers − was adopted in 1997, he broke into a jive in Parliament, and one newspaper called him the "Minister of Toyi-toyi".

Still, Agriculture seemed a natural ministry for a former farmer who spent the four years from 1990 as coordinator of the ANC's agricultural desk. But his focus appeared to remain largely on supporting the rural poor, and he did not survive long in President Thabo Mbeki's first Cabinet. His deputy, Thoko Didiza, who shared the president's interest in building a black commercial farming sector, took over both portfolios.

Relieved of the burden of office, Hanekom took on the tasks of an ordinary MP, serving mainly on the agriculture and land affairs portfolio committee. He also enrolled for an MA in agricultural economics at the University of Pretoria.

A Capetonian, Hanekom served three years in prison in the 1980s for leaking information to the ANC about South African Defence Force support for the Mozambican rebel movement Renamo. Although the official charge was illegal possession of secret state documents, Hanekom and his wife, Patricia Murray, had turned their farm into a transit point for ANC recruits en route to exile. After his release he lived in exile in Zimbabwe, working on development projects and coordinating the Popular History Trust, returning to South Africa in 1990.

Date of birth: 13 January 1953

Hangana, Nomatyala

Deputy Minister, Provincial and Local Government

Nomatyala Hangana leaves behind a Western Cape housing department in shambles. Many in the province privately express disappointment that the former chairperson of Parliament's housing committee did not rise to the challenge when given the chance to put policy into practice.

In her defence, the problems, caused in large part by obstinate officials and opaque procedures, were already there when she arrived in late 2001.

But it was during her term that Auditor-General Shauket Fakie issued a negative audit finding due to large-scale underspending, a problem confirmed in the forensic audit Hangana finally ordered.

Findings by auditors in early 2003 revealed financial irregularities and poor management controls, construction work signed off despite the lack of compulsory site visits, and houses built smaller than the size that had been agreed. And housing remains the Western Cape's Achilles heel; the backlog is estimated at 350 000 units.

Hangana had been redeployed to the province from Parliament, where she had served since 1994, after the African National Congress-New National Party provincial government took control at the end of 2001. Her appointment was possible under a special provision of the provincial constitution, which allowed for the appointment of two extra MECs who were not members of the provincial legislature, but served as public representatives elsewhere.

Politically Hangana is closely linked to the ANC Women's League, having served repeatedly in the league's Western Cape and national structures. In August 2003 she was re-elected to the national executive committee and also serves on its national working committee.

Originally from the Eastern Cape – she went to school in the rural Debe-Nek area near King William's Town – she obtained a paralegal diploma in 1984, then worked at the Legal Resources Centre in Cape Town before moving on to the Athlone law firm then run by Bulelani Ngcuka and SM Matana.

Date of birth: 12 April 1956

Hendricks, Benedicta Lindiwe

Deputy Minister, Trade and Industry

The new Trade and Industry Minister is fortunate that his deputy, Lindiwe Hendricks, has been in the job since 1999; she can contribute continuity in the broadly defined area where both will be working, whether protecting South African interests in international trade negotiations or encouraging the formation of enterprises at home.

As deputy, Hendricks has been responsible for small business development – not yet one of Trade and Industry's major successes – as well as economic empowerment, consumer affairs and other areas aimed at poverty alleviation and the creation of employment.

A lawyer, Hendricks earned both a BProc degree and an LLB from the University of Fort Hare, served articles, and established her own firm of attorneys in Durban. While in Parliament, she was a member of the justice and constitutional development committees and the joint standing committee on intelligence.

Because of her pioneering work in initiatives like the South African Women Entrepreneurs Network and women in everything including mining, technology, science and business in general, it is easy to categorise Hendricks as a custodian of peripheral issues at the department. Although expectation in her staff circle was that she would be promoted to a full minister, not necessarily in Trade and Industry, her retention as deputy minister was greeted with no sense of surprise.

It is easy to forget the central role she played at the negotiation of the European Union trade agreement. She is also active in seeking out trade opportunities in places like Saudi Arabia. Yet for all that, she remains identified with projects like Thombo IT academy in Port St Johns, in the Eastern Cape, sponsored by the American company Cisco.

A lawyer by training, she is widely praised for her ability to interpret legalese for a struggling entrepreneur who is unaware of a departmental incentive. She is described as a hands-on, driven individual who believes in implementation.

Date of birth: 29 July 1957

Holomisa, Patekile
President, Contralesa

Patekile Holomisa straddles the many often contradictory worlds of contemporary South Africa with relative ease.

A lawyer by training and trade, the inkosi of the sub-clan of the abaThembu nation presides in a system that is believed to impose a leader on a community purely on the basis of genealogy while he himself sits in a democratically elected Parliament as an African National Congress MP.

He perceives the contradiction as ignorance of traditional customs. For example, there are rare times when amakosi are elected – when there is no outright heir to a throne, or an existing one is deemed unsuitable. Whether men and women are allowed to ascend the throne differs from one community to the other.

Holomisa has turned his tenure as MP and president of the Congress of South African Traditional Leaders of South Africa into a personal crusade to ensure that traditional and customary values are respected and protected. This is where his Business Day newspaper column, which he uses to strike down misconceptions, comes in handy.

The two worlds of Holomisa – a cousin of United Democratic Movement leader Bantu Holomisa – have often collided.

As a United Democratic Front activist in the 1980s, he had to get permission from the then banned and exiled ANC before he could take up the throne of the Eastern Cape tribe as well as his seat in the Transkei bantustan.

And as a committed traditionalist and fiercely independent-minded man, Holomisa has had to take account of party protocol when the contradictions between Western-type politics and time-honoured traditions have forced him to make a political choice.

Though at times he acts like a Western politician, often he takes on a more chiefly aspect.

In 2003, for example, he called iNkosi Maxhobayakhawuleza ka Sandile of the Amarharhabe to ask him to take issue with a Johannesburg-based family belonging to Maxhobayakhawuleza's tribe for the "sacrilegious" act of allowing television cameras to film their son's rite of passage to manhood.

In his column, Holomisa wrote: "Africans are very quick and eager to adopt foreign value systems which undermine their own. Yet they seem not to recognise the fact that the religious rituals and practices of the Muslims, the Hindus, the Jews and so on are not subjected to public scrutiny and thus ridicule."

In April 1996 the ANC charged him with violating the party's code of conduct for its public representatives when he challenged the party-sponsored Local Government Transition Bill and publicly called for a boycott of local government elections.

In opposition to the Bill, Holomisa aligned himself with other amakhosi, such as inkosi Mpiyezintombi Mzimela, who leaned towards the Inkatha Freedom Party.

An ANC disciplinary hearing initially found him guilty but the decision was overturned on appeal.

Holomisa has often defended traditional authority from the accusation that it is an affront to gender equality because it allows men to be polygamous and often disinherits women and children.

"It's a well-known fact that men tend to want more partners than women do. Customary law legitimises that," he told the Sunday Times. "It makes honourable people of women. You can't just be a mistress. You have to have your own home with your own children and so on, if a man declares his love for you. The other system promotes divorce, because when you fall in love with another woman you're required to divorce the one you have and marry the other. That is a kind of serial polygamy."

With regard to the rules of inheritance, he added: "In order to protect the assets of the family you have to have somebody who will not become a member of another family."

He is married to Bukelwa Nolizwe, daughter of Kaizer Matanzima, former chief minister of the Transkei.

Date of birth: 26 August 1959

Jordan, Zweledinga Pallo

Minister of Arts and Culture

Pallo Jordan is the first African National Congress political heavyweight to be appointed to head up an Arts and Culture portfolio at either national or provincial level since 1994. This, together with the final separation of Arts and Culture from Science and Technology, in whose shadow the sector had languished both politically and in terms of funding, is welcome news for the beleagured cultural community since the stature and public profile of Jordan will help to assert the sector on the national canvas.

Jordan is the son of two academics and he himself has acquired a number of degrees in South Africa, the US and Britain, including a post-graduate degree from the London School of Economics. His father was a novelist and a linguist who began his academic career at the University of Fort Hare and went on to become the first African member of staff at the University of Cape Town in 1946.

Pallo Jordan was elected to the National Assembly in April 1994 in position number five on the ANC list, and was appointed as minister for posts, telecommunications and broadcasting. He later served as minister for environmental affairs and tourism. The new appointment marks his return to the Cabinet after a five-year absence.

Jordan is regarded as one of the Tripartite Alliance's key and most independent thinkers. In an open letter responding to Jordan's piece "The crisis of conscience in the SACP" in which he criticised the "spirit of intolerance" and "petty intellectual thuggery" of the South African Communist Party's leadership, Jeremy Cronin writes, "Let's just say it's refreshing to have intelligent, robust debate within the ranks of our national liberation alliance."

During a Media Freedom Day speech last year, Jordan stated that "democracy ... is about the right ordinary people have to participate in society's decision-making processes".

It is this intelligent, robust debate and commitment to democracy that have been eroded in the cultural sector, and Jordan's appointment has been widely welcomed as key to realigning public policy and its outcomes with the interests of arts and culture practitioners.

Date of birth: 22 May 1942

Kasrils, Ronald

Minister of Intelligence

In 2004 Ronnie Kasrils was appointed to President Thabo Mbeki's second Cabinet as Minister for Intelligence Services, reconnecting him to a life-long association with security-related matters interrupted by his five-year tenure as minister of water affairs and forestry.

Kasrils's appointment was something of a surprise, although he was rumoured to have coveted the job for some time. He has experience in the field, having been a member of Umkhonto we Sizwe (MK), the African National Congress's military wing, from its inception in 1961, and having served as chief of MK intelligence from 1983 to 1987. At the time, he received specialist intelligence training in Moscow and also completed a brigade level officer's course in the Soviet Union.

From 1987 he was involved with the ANC's secret plan – known as Operation Vula – to establish an underground leadership corps inside the country. The implementation of Vula was significantly devalued by the unbanning of the ANC in 1990 by President FW de Klerk. However the exposure of the Vula network by apartheid's security police later that year led to the withdrawal of Kasrils's temporary indemnity. He went to ground and remained on the run until June 1991 when negotiations between the ANC and the De Klerk government resolved the status of Vula operatives.

It was during this last period as a fugitive that Kasrils was described by police as "armed and dangerous", a soubriquet he took for the title of his highly readable 1993 autobiography.

While on the run, Kasrils, a long-time member of the South African Communist Party, also took pleasure in taunting his trackers, popping up at public events before disappearing again, thus earning himself another nickname – the Scarlet Pimpernel.

Such bravado was part of the "Yeoville boykie" style that Kasrils appears to have retained, notwithstanding the fact that some of his more severe comrades regarded it as egotistical or, worse, undisciplined. Critics say a weakness for flattery, which is open to manipulation, may be a problem at the intelligence ministry, where Kasrils succeeded the more incisive and independent Lindiwe Sisulu.

Nevertheless, Kasrils is a canny and popular politician. In 1994 he was appointed deputy minister of defence in the Mandela government, where, together with the late Joe Modise, he played an important role in charming the old-guard generals and smoothing the integration of liberation fighters and an apartheid defence force built on *swart en rooi gevaar*.

By the time the controversy around the democratic government's R30-billion arms procurement programme broke early in the first Mbeki presidency, Kasrils was safely ensconced in the calmer glades of Water Affairs and Forestry.

His time there was relatively unremarkable, with the department under the firm hand of one of the mandarins of the democratic bureaucracy, director-general Mike Muller. Nevertheless Kasrils showed a willingness to listen to criticism, and later in his term began revisiting the affordability and sustainability of water schemes parachuted into poor communities. He also launched a belated campaign for basic hygiene, something the Health and Education Departments should have done long before.

Unlike some other communist members of Cabinet who found their ministerial duties pitted them against the party, leading to their ejection from SACP executive structures, Kasrils has retained his membership of the central committee.

By contrast, his relationship with South Africa's Jewish community has been considerably more fraught.

A grandson of immigrants from Latvia who fled the tsarist pogroms, Kasrils has outraged mainstream South African Jewry by his outspoken support for the Palestinian cause and condemnation of Israeli government policy. His rhetoric may have to make way for the greater discretion demanded by his new post.

Date of birth: 15 November 1938

Kgoali, Joyce

Chairperson, National Council of Provinces

For almost two years Joyce Kgoali has run the African National Congress parliamentary caucus, the first woman to do so. She was named chairperson of the National Council of Provinces after the 2004 elections.

If the career paths of her predecessors is anything to go by, then she's headed for bigger political office. She replaced Naledi Pandor, who is now Education Minister; Pandor replaced Mosiuoa Lekota, who became Defence Minister.

The NCOP was established under the 1996 Constitution to give provinces a direct say in the legislative process. Each of the nine provinces names permanent delegates to the council, which can hold hearings on proposed laws which impact on provincial powers.

It has been a long-standing bugbear of NCOP leaders that the Council is largely ignored in the public discourse. However, the parliamentarians themselves at times treat the NCOP as a stepchild. It has been used to bring last-minute amendments to Bills or to stop legislation to correct mistakes discovered after the National Assembly has approved the Bills.

Kgoali left school without completing standard 8 because of financial constraints. Her first job at Bond Clothing in 1969 started her on a career as a trade unionist in the clothing and textile sector.

Workers there were unhappy about "the cruel treatment of black people, like having to take breakfast in a dirty and unhealthy shed that looked like a pigsty", she told Sephadi, the ANC's parliamentary newsletter. By 1993 Kgoali was organiser for the South African Clothing and Textile Workers' Union.

Following the 1994 democratic elections, she joined the Gauteng legislature and some months later was sent to the Senate, at that time Parliament's second house before it was reconstituted as the NCOP.

In the midst of the political wrangling around then-Gauteng premier Mathole Motshekga, Kgoali was redeployed to Gauteng in 1997. She served a stint as transport and public works MEC, but was dropped from the provincial cabinet when former trade union leader Mbhazima Shilowa took over as premier.

For almost two years Kgoali remained in the provincial legislature, serving in the ANC Gauteng structures, until she was again redeployed, to the NCOP – this time as whip for Gauteng.

Back at Parliament her political star was clearly on the rise. She became a member of the political committee, a powerful team in charge of keeping MPs in line with ANC national working group decisions.

By May 2002 Kgoali, then also elevated to the Gauteng ANC executive committee, was the first woman ANC parliamentary caucus chairperson.

The next year she was elected to the ANC Women's League national executive council, after years of active participation in the league's Gauteng structures.

Date of birth: 13 January 1950

Kubheka, Mangaliso

National Organiser, Landless People's Movement

Mangaliso Kubheka, national organiser of the Landless People's Movement, is never far from the front page of a newspaper when land reform is the issue. Many white farmers in South Africa appear to believe he is the devil reincarnated.

Here's another view of the 54-year-old former chemicals worker from Newcastle in KwaZulu-Natal: a land activist who fights for the poor and the 26-million landless. Kubheka firmly believes that no one is listening to the voices of the poor calling for land, and that he and his organisation are speaking out for them.

But at the end of 2003 one of his controversial quotes got him into trouble. The Freedom Front Plus laid a charge with the South African Human Rights Commission, which found that Kubheka had uttered hate speech by allegedly threatening to create a people's army to attack farmers who abused their workers. Kubheka denied that he had made this statement, although it had been quoted widely in the media.

He was in the news again that year when he took a Belgian land activist to visit one of the farms where he alleged farm workers' rights were being abused. The two activists ran into trouble with the farmer herself, and she accused Kubheka of assault. The Belgian land activist later wrote a scathing piece on land reform in South Africa for a European publication.

Kubheka was born in 1950 on a farm, De Wet Stream, near Newcastle. He hails from a long line of labour tenants working on farms in the area, and grew up in this environment. He felt his first injustice as a farm worker came when his work in the field was deemed more important than his education; thus he only went to school at the age of nine. Because he was a late starter, he had not finished his schooling by the time he was an adult, and never wrote matric, something that he is quite bitter about.

He moved to Johannesburg where he worked in a chemical factory for two decades. It is here that he came into contact with politics and joined the African National Congress. After violence broke out between the ANC and Inkatha Freedom Party in the early 1990s, he returned to Newcastle where he farmed with his cattle on his birth ground, De Wet Stream. But when the farmer sold the farm in 1999, he and his family faced eviction from the new farmer. It is this action that mobilised Kubheka into a revolutionary land activist.

Kubheka's organisation, the Landless People's Movement, was formed in July 2001 by leaders of landless people's organisations against a backdrop of growing frustration with the slow pace of land reform. The National Land Committee has strong links with the LPM, and was closely involved with the launch of the LPM. But the major difference between the two organisations is that the National Land Committee is a non-governmental organisation and the LPM is a social movement, or a "people's organisation". The LPM draws its mandate from its members and is structurally de-linked from the NLC. But it is also fair to say that at this point the LPM depends on the NLC's support.

The movement opposes farm evictions and violence by farmers towards their labourers. It claims to have a big following, but has never supplied specific numbers about its members. Critics say the movement's support is limited to the Eastern Cape, with only patches of support in other provinces.

The organisation is also unpopular with the government, and the ANC has denounced the organisation as a group of hooligans.

Kubheka called on landless and poor people to boycott the 2004 elections, and on Election Day 60 LPM members were arrested for allegedly contravening Electoral Act regulations by demonstrating too close to a polling station. The members of the Gauteng LPM branch had been demonstrating in Thembelihle, an informal settlement in Lenasia, south of Johannesburg, as part of the organisation's "No land, no vote" boycott campaign. Three LPM members were allegedly brutalised by the police during their time in the cells, indicating that the organisation is not the flavour of the month with the establishment.

The LPM also played a major role in the social movements march at the World Summit, which overshadowed a parallel rally backed by the ANC and addressed by President Thabo Mbeki.

The movement has demanded a national summit to discuss the "fundamental constraints" that caused land reform to fail.

Langa, Pius

Deputy Chief Justice, Constitutional Court

Pius Langa's extraordinary career path has taken him far from his first job as a "learner sorter" in a factory. A member of the first Constitutional Court, he succeeded the late Ismail Mahomed as deputy president of the court when Mahomed was appointed to head the Appeal Court in Bloemfontein. Serious, hard-working and devoted to the concepts of equal rights and opportunity for all, he has contributed considerably to the establishment of the Constitutional Court as a serious force for justice.

Despite a long history of allegiance to the African National Congress, he gave the Judicial Service Commission an undertaking that if he was appointed to the court he would resign from the party because "I think it is very important to be neutral and to give that perception of neutrality". The court, he maintains, must be perceived as "fiercely independent". He also believes it is important that the judges of the Constitutional Court be known to what he calls "the people out there", and that the public should have faith in the judges who are selected.

The second of seven children of a minister, Pius Langa brings to the court a humanity that comes from personal experience of hardship. His education almost came to an end when he was 14 years old because his parents could not afford to pay his school fees. A bursary enabled him to go to secondary school where he studied for his junior certificate, after which he left school to take a job in order to help his family. Determined to matriculate, he studied privately, completing his matriculation studies in one year instead of the normal two.

It was another ten years before he was able to start studying law, which he did by correspondence through Unisa while working in the civil service as an interpreter-messenger, prosecutor and magistrate. After completing two law degrees (by the age of 38) he left the civil service to go to the Bar in Natal, and was soon involved in many political trials. He took silk in January 1994.

Active in many community and educational organisations, he was founder-president of the National Association of Democratic Lawyers and one of the founders of the United Democratic Front and the

Release Mandela Campaign. He was also a member of the reception committee that prepared for the return of leaders from prison and exile.

He represented the ANC at the Convention for a Democratic South Africa where he was a member of the technical committee charged with identifying discriminatory and repressive legislation. Although he was not a member of the technical committee that drafted the Constitution, he was on the constitutional committee of the ANC that prepared drafts for the negotiators, critically assessed the drafts of other political parties, and produced an ANC draft bill of rights.

Date of birth: 25 March 1939

Lekganyane, Barnabas Edward

Bishop, Zion Christian Church

Barnabas Lekganyane was only 12 years old when he became spiritual head of Southern Africa's largest church, the Zion Christian Church (ZCC).

Assuming the hereditary mantle of "holy prophet" from his late father, Lekganyane began to refine the ZCC's interpretation of Christian and animist African teachings into a more coherent spiritual vision.

The teenage prophet broke with tradition and stayed at school in the tiny Limpopo village of Boyne long enough to obtain his standard 9 certificate, before enrolling in the All Africa School of Theology in Witbank, where he earned his pastoral qualification in 1975, just before his 21st birthday.

Armed with formal education to complement his spiritual upbringing, Lekganyane immediately assumed administrative control of the church and launched an expansion programme that has seen the ZCC grow to an estimated eight million members in four Southern African nations. Tens of thousands more claim membership in smaller splinter Zionist churches that draw their rites and inspiration from the ZCC.

The ZCC's moral authority, and the devotion of its congregation, have seen all the major and many fringe South African political parties court the church. Lekganyane has, however, refused to align the ZCC with any one party, and has instead repeatedly used his influence to press for greater moral leadership.

In 1994, on the eve of the country's first tumultuous democratic elections, he put the African National Congress's Nelson Mandela on stage at the ZCC's Easter celebrations, along with the Inkatha Freedom Party's Mangosuthu Buthelezi and the New National Party's FW de

Klerk – and then got all three men to call for peace and tolerance. The Easter pilgrimage has since become an election-year tradition for the nation's political leaders.

But for the estimated two million ZCC members in their distinctive khaki, green and yellow uniforms, it is an annual trek; they descend every Easter on the church's dusty holy city of Moria outside Polokwane for a week of song, dance, and baptisms in local holy rivers and hot springs.

The gathering, believed to be Southern Africa's largest religious festival, draws people from as far afield as Zambia and Malawi. Smaller pilgrimages, of ZCC faithful ferried in by hundreds of buses, are staged to celebrate the ZCC New Year in September, as well as at Christmas.

The New Year celebrations showcase the church's most Africanist ceremonies, celebrating the first rains and appealing for good harvests. The ZCC's synthesis of Christian and African belief includes a reverence for the ancestors; exorcism of water spirits and earth demons; faith healings; and the use of sanctified water to treat both physical and spiritual ailments.

Witchcraft and unsanctified spiritualists remain abhorrent, however, with the faithful urged to commune with the ancestors only through church prophets or seers. They also forswear alcohol, drugs, pork and other "unclean" food identified in the Old Testament, and only buy tea or salt blessed by the bishop himself.

The hard working, "clean living" ethos and religious fervour of ZCC followers dates back to the conversion of the church's founder, Engenas Barnabas Lekganyane, in Lesotho in 1910. The first Lekganyane and a small band of fellow prophets developed their Africanist interpretation of Christianity at the knee of African American preacher Edward Lion.

Lion, who settled in the Basotho kingdom in a bid to return to his African roots, established the embryonic Zion Apostolic Faith Mission before sending Engenas Lekganyane and other prophets to seed their own churches in Botswana, South Africa and Zimbabwe.

Lion's own mission eventually withered away, but all three of his ZCC offspring are the fastest-growing Christian denominations in their countries.

In South Africa, not even the splintering of the ZCC when the current leader's uncle, Bishop Edward Engenas, elevated their patriarch to sainthood and established the Church of Saint Engenas has slowed growth. In fact, followers of Saint Engenas religiously attend the ZCC's Easter pilgrimage alongside their orthodox brethren. All that distinguishes them is their "dove of peace" icon, worn instead of the ZCC's silver star on a green felt backing.

Bishop Barnabas Lekganyane is the oldest of four children – his brother and two sisters pursue lives outside the church hierarchy. Amongst the ZCC's highest-profile followers are former Limpopo premier Ngoako Ramatlhodi, the Balobedu Rain Queen Modjadji, and Limpopo tycoon Masingita Nkuna.

Date of birth: 31 May 1954

Lekota, Mosiuoa Patrick "Terror"

Minister of Defence

Mosiuoa Lekota has walked a familiar career path in the African National Congress – from student activist to prisoner to high-ranking leader.

Defence Minister since 1999, and ANC national chairman, he is now regarded as a potential ANC deputy-president; he has the political credentials and the gravitas for such a move. Some suggest he may even contend for the presidency of the party when President Thabo Mbeki steps down in 2009.

Born in the Senekal district of the Free State, the first of seven children of working-class parents, he matriculated in 1969 from a Catholic mission school, St Francis College in Mariannhill, KwaZulu-Natal. He earned the nickname "Terror" as a striker while paying semi-professional soccer.

In 1972 he enrolled for a social science degree at the University of the North, but was expelled because of his activities in the students' representative council and the Black Consciousness-inspired South African Students Organisation. Between 1974 and 1975 Lekota was permanent organiser for Saso, following the exile of Ongopotse Tiro, later killed in Botswana by an apartheid hit squad.

Lekota was sentenced to imprisonment on Robben Island from 1974 to 1982 for conspiring "to commit acts capable of endangering maintenance of law and order". He had helped organise pro-Frelimo rallies at Turfloop in support of Mozambique's independence struggle.

He was one of many Black Consciousness political prisoners who, once on Robben Island, embraced the non-racial ethos of the Freedom Charter. The United Democratic Front was launched at the time of his release, and he was elected national publicity secretary.

In June 1985, Lekota and 21 other UDF leaders were charged with treason at Delmas. Three years later, he and four other accused – including Popo Molefe, who would become North West premier – were convicted and sentenced to 12 years in prison, but in 1989 they were released after the appeal court reviewed their sentences.

In 1990, when then-president FW de Klerk unbanned the ANC, Lekota moved rapidly up the ranks. Appointed convener of the ANC in southern Natal in 1990, he served as the party's chief of intelligence. In 1992 he was elected onto the ANC election commission. He secured election to both the party's national executive committee and national working committee, and after the 1994 election became Free State premier.

As premier, Lekota clashed with key leaders of the provincial ANC, and in 1997 was removed by the national leadership for the sake of unity in the province. Redeployed as National Council of Provinces chairperson, he trod water for a while. But his popularity in the national ANC remained unimpaired, and he was elected national chairman of the ANC at the party's Mafikeng conference over Steve Tshwete, seen as Mbeki's preferred candidate.

Lekota's rehabilitation was complete when he succeeded Joe Modise as Minister of Defence in Mbeki's 1999 Cabinet. He presided over the final stages of the amalgamation of the former South African Defence Force, the former homeland armies and the liberation movement armies (the ANC's Umkhonto we Sizwe and the Azanian People's Liberation Army, the military wing of the Pan Africanist Congress) into the South African National Defence Force. The integration process, set in motion by Modise, has been largely successful, although there are still complaints of racism in the military, and occasional, but serious, outbreaks of violence apparently linked to continued discrimination.

Under Lekota's leadership, the SANDF has played an increasingly important role in peacekeeping operations and rescue missions on the African continent.

However, there are some blots on his ministerial record. In late 2001, after official investigators had presented their report on the propriety of South Africa's multi-billion-rand arms deal to Parliament, he played a key role in whitewashing the report as a vindication of the government. This was despite the fact that it fingered numerous state officials for wrongdoing and was critical of Modise. In 2003 he became the first cabinet minister since 1994 to be penalised by Parliament for failing to disclose financial interests. However, the open way he dealt with the revelations – he admitted fault and apologised – enabled him to survive the disclosures virtually unscathed.

Date of birth: 13 August 1948

Leon, Tony

Leader of the Opposition

The Democratic Alliance leader has been widely credited with "taking the party out of Houghton" and turning the DA's ailing forerunner, the liberal Democratic Party, into the official Opposition.

And it is to this that his supporters point to fend off persistent criticism of Leon's caustic, combative style and, in the run-up to the 2004 election, the DA's lurch to the right with the absorption of old Nats and even ex-Conservative Party members.

A youthful, but already hard-line, politician, Leon took over the DP reins at a low point in the party's fortunes; it had garnered only 1,7% of the vote in the 1994 elections. Yet despite holding only seven seats in Parliament, the party became a loud and effective voice there.

Determined to broaden his party's support base, Leon aggressively pursued votes, even in New National Party strongholds like Boksburg, which succumbed in various by-elections.

And it paid off. According to Opinion '99, a report by the Institute for Democracy in South Africa, by May 1998 Leon had become the most recognised leader among white South Africans, although he only held seventh spot among black voters.

In that poll, on the back of a "Fight Back" campaign, the DP won enough votes to oust the NNP as second-largest in the country, with 38 National Assembly seats. It was a high point for Leon, who began to style himself as "Leader of the Official Opposition".

From 1999 Leon manoeuvred to make inroads into black and Coloured communities. The party's short-lived marriage with the NNP meant that, by the time it crumbled, Leon and the DA had a foothold in the former partner's Coloured support base.

But "Fight Back" continued to be seen as "Fight Black" among black South Africans. It has been a lasting voters' verdict; in 2004 the DA, by its own admission, fell short of gaining the black support it had anticipated.

Keenly aware of the backlash, Leon used his leader's prerogative to bump up black faces in the party's public representatives lists, which had been overwhelmingly white.

And he has tried hard to shake his dislike of slogans like "Viva!". Ahead of the April 2004 poll, he was known to throw out the occasional "Amandla!" to assembled DA supporters on hundreds of sorties into rural villages and townships and across the Cape Flats. Leon has also learnt Afrikaans.

But the DA under Leon may have reached the limits of its support. It got nowhere near the 30% it had predicted for itself in conjunction with its allies, chiefly the Inkatha Freedom Party. The DA received some 12,3% of the vote, although that was 3% more than the 9,5% it scored in 1999.

Leon's political roots go back a long way. At the age of 18 he became an organiser for the then Progressive Federal Party, one of the many manifestations of the Progressive Party as it absorbed other liberal-leaning parties. A year earlier, he had helped out in party founder Helen Suzman's 1974 election campaign. "She was my idol," Leon said in a recent press interview.

He was representing Yeoville in the Johannesburg City Council – an election he had won by 36 votes – when Suzman retired in 1989. Although Suzman had chosen a different successor for the Houghton parliamentary seat she had held for 25 years, Leon fought for it, and won. But he held back on his ambitions in favour of the older Zach de Beer, an industrialist who went on to become South Africa's ambassador to the Netherlands. Instead Leon became an adviser to the party in negotiations at the Convention for a Democratic South Africa, which hammered out a post-apartheid settlement.

The son of Judge Ramon Leon, he has also found a temporary home in the law. After completing a law degree at the University of the Witwatersrand in 1985, he was admitted as an attorney and served as a law lecturer at his alma mater.

But the brash and hard-talking Leon chose to pursue politics as a career. He is known to thrive in the cut and thrust of parliamentary politics. And he has not pulled any punches in criticising the African National Congress's performance in government, from crime and HIV/Aids to black economic empowerment and the ANC's position in support of Zimbabwe President Robert Mugabe.

This has incurred the wrath of the ruling party, which has frequently countered Leon's attacks on policy by describing him and the DA as "racist" and "untransformed". It was Essop Pahad, spin doctor in the Presidency, who in 2002 unearthed Leon's glowing tributes to the apartheid military, written for the South African Defence Force mouthpiece Paratus during his military service in the early 1970s.

The ANC takes pains to ignore Leon and the DA, despite the DA's Opposition status, but Leon takes his role as Leader of the Opposition seriously. When Mbeki launched a weekly newsletter on his party's website, for example, Leon soon followed suit with his own weekly letter.

His call for the return of the death penalty appears to be a response to sentiments at the grassroots as the party which, under his leadership, increasingly resembles a European conservative political party. This has been noticed by the old liberal establishment, whose criticism – indeed, sense of betrayal – he has dismissed.

With no indication of a successor in the wings, Leon now presides over a party seemingly torn between conservatism – public support of the death penalty by senior leaders – neo-liberal economic values – privatisation alongside a lean state – and humanitarianism, typified by its call for a R110 basic income grant.

Date of birth: 15 December 1956

Mabandla, Brigitte

Minister of Justice

The arrival of Brigitte Mabandla, an academic lawyer, in the Justice Ministry was expected a decade ago.

Her appointment in 1995 as deputy minister of arts, culture, science and technology came as a surprise. She had been a member of the African National Congress's negotiating team at the Convention for a Democratic South Africa, and had been working at the Community Law Centre of the University of the Western Cape, where she had founded projects on the rights of women and children. Clearly, her interest was in human rights and the law. Arts and Science seemed odd portfolios for someone who had no background in either.

But she soon learned. On her departure from Arts and Science in 2003, she was praised by one of the two Inkatha Freedom Party ministers she had worked with, Ben Ngubane, as a person with "a very broad understanding of arts and a great sense of the role of women in science". He credited her with having integrated and united the arts fraternity across the racial and cultural divide.

The arts fraternity is too fractious to be united, either completely or for long, but she managed to be well-liked by most; one artist described her as a "large, overwhelming, warm African earth mother".

She left the department to take up a post as minister of housing – a second detour. Mabandla spent only a year in that job, but during her watch the housing subsidy was raised and tied to the rate of inflation, so that it will go up annually.

The Justice Ministry is clearly where Mabandla belongs. And although her acknowledged strengths – her intelligence, personal warmth and ability to work with people of all kinds – have been useful in her earlier posts, she can finally, in this one, make use of her legal training.

Mabandla left South Africa in the 1970s and earned an LLB degree at the University of Zambia. She lectured in law in Botswana until she became legal adviser in the ANC's Legal and Constitutional Affairs Department in Lusaka.

Among the Bills she will be piloting through Parliament is the Child Justice Bill, dealing with a topic close to her heart. She is on the boards of several trusts concerned with the welfare of children, including the Grassroots Early Childhood Education Project and the National Committee for the Rights of Children.

Date of birth: 23 November 1948

Mabudafhasi, Rejoice Thizwilondi

Deputy Minister, Environmental Affairs and Tourism

Many environmentalists were surprised when Rejoice Mabudafhasi, Deputy Minister of Environmental Affairs and Tourism since 1999, was not promoted to minister in the 2004 Cabinet. She had all the right credentials and experience – and is a woman to boot.

Born in 1943, Mabudafhasi has been a teacher, unionist, activist, detainee and African National Congress stalwart in Limpopo. As deputy during Valli Moosa's time as minister of environmental affairs and tourism, she played a strong role in dealing with "brown" issues like air pollution, occupational health, waste and sanitation.

When environmental justice activists gathered in protest outside Thor Chemicals near Pietermaritzburg or polluting industries in Durban South, it was Mabudafhasi who went to talk to them – and sometimes join them in their protests. She has empathy and good communication at a grassroots level, and would perhaps not wield the same influence with conservative white tourism operators as it is hoped her new minister, Marthinus van Schalkwyk, will.

This is not to suggest she is a lightweight in Parliament. She has been an MP since 1994; and has been a member of the portfolio committees on safety and security, environmental affairs and tourism, labour, agriculture, and water and forestry. She also sits on the boards of various local and international organisations charged with environmental protection.

Date of birth: 23 May 1943

Madala, Tholakele Hope (Thole)

Justice, Constitutional Court

Thole Madala, one of the original members of the Constitutional Court, was the first black Supreme Court (now High Court) judge in the Eastern Cape and the fourth in South Africa. Born in Kokstad, he matriculated at St John's College in Umtata and taught at the Lovedale Institution, Alice, and in Swaziland before taking up law in 1972 at the University of Natal, Pietermaritzburg, where he was instrumental in the establishment of a legal aid clinic to assist the indigent and underprivileged.

Madala lectured at the University of Transkei, initially full-time, but later on a part-time basis while practising as an attorney. He was admitted as an advocate in 1982, handling numerous human rights cases. Together with other lawyers interested in the protection of the rights of the underprivileged, he established the Umtata Law Clinic. As an attorney, he became chairman of the Transkei Attorneys Association.

He was a founder member and director of Prisoners' Welfare Programmes, an association established in 1985 to provide legal, financial and educational assistance to political detainees, prisoners, ex-prisoners and their families. He was also chairman of the Society of Advocates of Transkei, representing it on the General Council of the Bar of South Africa.

Madala took silk in 1993, was elevated to the Bench in 1994, and in October 1994 was appointed to the Constitutional Court. In 1995 he received an award from the Black Lawyers Association Legal Education Centre in recognition of his contribution in the area of human rights.

Date of birth: 13 July 1937

Madlala-Routledge, Nozizwe
Deputy Minister of Health

The newly appointed Deputy Minister of Health is not one to shrink from confrontation or challenges. As deputy minister of defence from June 1999 she was a controversial appointment at a time when the South African National Defence Force was undergoing transformation. Even she was surprised to have been given one of the most powerful positions in the defence force while making no secret of the fact that she is a pacifist, a feminist and a Quaker.

Madlala-Routledge was born in 1952. She graduated from Fort Hare with a degree in sociology and went on to study for a diploma in medical technology, working as a laboratory technician for six years before resigning to participate in the struggle through a position with the Natal Organisation of Women. She has been a member of the South African Communist Party since 1984.

She has a passion for women's rights and has worked to promote them both locally and internationally, chairing the Parliamentary Women's Group until her appointment as deputy minister, and helping to draft the Reconstruction and Development Programme policy on the Empowerment of Women. Her work with gender organisations led to her election as chairperson of the African National Congress Parliamentary Women's Caucus, and she co-authored South Africa's report to the United Nations for the 4th World Conference on Women, held in Beijing in 1995.

Madlala-Routledge is rumoured to be the new and unofficial "Aids minister" because of her effectiveness in ensuring that the defence force introduced a comprehensive prevention and treatment plan for HIV-positive officers. She also opened the first HIV/Aids clinic at 1 Military Hospital in Pretoria, encouraging members of the SANDF to be tested.
Date of birth: 29 June 1952

Mahlangu-Nkabinde, Gwendoline
Deputy Speaker, National Assembly

From debates over genetically modified foods and asbestos to the protection of dolphins, Mahlangu-Nkabinde has dealt with it all as chairperson of Parliament's environmental affairs committee for the past eight years. With a reputation as a no-nonsense and fair chairperson, she has rolled up her sleeves to get to grips with what is widely seen as a Cinderella portfolio, despite dealing with issues of major importance.

Perhaps most controversially, the environmental committee under her reign passed the legislation that banned the thin plastic bags which had been freely given away by supermarkets and thrown away with such abandon that then-Environmental Minister Valli Moosa referred to these bits of plastic festooning trees and pavements the length and breadth of the country as "our national flower".

Her intimate knowledge of matters environmental has gained her support from environmental lobbyists. And, during many a National Assembly debate, fellow parliamentarians have often paid tribute to her dedication and even-handedness. And those qualities will stand her in good stead as deputy speaker.

Mahlangu-Nkabinde played a key role in preparations for the 2001 World Summit on Sustainable Development. On the international front she headed Globe Southern Africa, a global organisation of legislators aimed at fostering cooperation on international environmental issues.

She initially planned to enter the legal profession, but her studies towards a BProc degree at the then University of Zululand were interrupted by the 1976 student protests. She took up various teaching positions in high schools in and around Pretoria until 1981, when she started working at the South African Breweries operations department in Ga'Rankuwa. Her grassroots political activism brought her into regular contact with leaders like Winnie Madikizela-Mandela and Adelaide Tambo.

Mahlangu-Nkabinde has been involved in the African National Congress Women's League for some time, and also serves on the ANC's national executive committee. She has been an MP since 1994, and served as whip for two years before being appointed committee chairperson in 1996. Since 1999 she has also been active in the Inter-Parliamentary Union, an international organisation representing 130 parliaments with the aim of fostering dialogue and entrenching democracy.

Date of birth: 16 August 1955

Mahlangu, Mninwa Johannes

Deputy Chairperson, National Council of Provinces

Mahlangu seems to have found his niche as the NCOP's deputy after holding a number of key parliamentary posts over the past ten years. He was re-elected as NCOP deputy chairperson for a second term in May 2004.

A few months earlier he was one of five MPs who represented South Africa at the inaugural session of the Pan-African Parliament in February 2004.

He went to Parliament in 1994. In August 1999 he was made chairperson of committees, in charge of the smooth running of all the National Assembly's portfolio committees.

In 2002 Mahlangu also headed a committee assembled to select South Africa's second Public Protector. It picked then NCOP deputy chairperson Lawrence Mushwana – much to the opposition parties' dismay that a senior member of the African National Congress should head the anti-corruption institution, established under the Constitution, to "investigate any conduct in state affairs ... that is alleged or suspected to be improper or to result in any impropriety or prejudice". In a somewhat ironic twist, Mahlangu replaced him.

In the 1980s Mahlangu served in the Lebowa homeland government before making the jump to the ANC. A quietly-spoken man, widely known as "MJ" in the corridors, he has risen steadily through the ranks. Among the ANC's internal structures he served on the key political, governance and deployment committees.

After a one-year stint as clerk in the Ndebele Tribal Authority, Mahlangu taught at high school for five years before going on to sell furniture for a living. Religion appears to have played a key role in his public life: he was a preacher for the Bantu Free Church in the 1970s, and obtained a qualification in religious studies from Damelin, where he also studied photography.

He obtained a BA degree from the US-based University of Fairfax in 1995, and is currently studying for a diploma in economics from the University of London.

Date of birth: 8 October 1952

Makwetla, Thabang

Premier, Mpumalanga

Thabang Makwetla was sworn in as the new premier of Mpumalanga on April 30 this year, bringing an end to the unpopular reign of Ndaweni Mahlangu.

There had been long-standing speculation that Makwetla was being groomed for the premiership. However, his appointment is said to have shocked Mahlangu, who reportedly cancelled his appointments and switched off his cellular phone on learning that he had lost his position.

Makwetla, a former African National Congress youth leader of the 1976 generation, is considered a dynamic choice for premier and is destined for a major role in South African politics. He was transferred to the Mpumalanga legislature from the national Parliament, where he had held the senior post of ANC caucus chair, as part of an effort to clean up corruption and infighting in the province. In July 2001 he was appointed to the provincial post of Safety and Security.

At the time, he said the ANC leadership in Mpumalanga lacked sufficient "political maturity" and that the desire for personal advancement was to blame for infighting. His challenge as premier lies in fulfilling his promises to root out the cronyism and graft still endemic in the province.

Makwetla was born in Middelburg in the then Eastern Transvaal in May 1957. He joined the ANC and its military wing, Umkhonto we Sizwe, in 1976 and went into exile in the same year, living in Angola, Botswana, Lesotho and Zambia. He eventually returned to South Africa after the ban on the ANC was lifted in 1990.

He became one of the youngest members of the ANC national executive committee in 1990. Elected to Parliament in 1994, he served on various parliamentary committees, including the standing committee on public accounts.

Makwetla has his work cut out as Mpumalanga premier. This large province – comprising about 6,5% of South Africa's land mass, and home to three million people – was cobbled together from the formerly "white" Eastern Transvaal, parts of the Gazankulu, Lebowa and Bophutatswana homelands, and the entire bantustans of KaNgwane and KwaNdebele. The homeland ethos of corruption, self-seeking and incompetence is deeply entrenched, and Mpumalanga is regarded as one of the ANC's problem provinces.

However, it is not as poor as other poorly governed regions. It has a well-developed transport and communications network and an international airport. The backbone of this is the Maputo development corridor, touted as the key to the region's future economic expansion. The regional economy is based on manufacturing (26%), mining (20%), electricity generation (20%), tourism (8%), and agriculture and forestry (8%). Mpumalanga's gross geographic product represents about 8,4% of the country's total output, and is about seven times larger than that of neighbouring Mozambique. Its growth rate is estimated at 3,4%, one of the fastest in South Africa. This is evident in its capital, Nelspruit, where more and more retail development is being shoe-horned into the city centre.

Makwetla has made a quick start to cleaning up the provincial government by omitting former premier Ndaweni Mahlangu and former provincial public works minister Steve Mabona from his cabinet. Mahlangu, whose premiership was marred by his controversial defence of lying politicians at his first media conference, was also criticised for reinstating Mabona in his cabinet, despite the fact that the latter had previously been fired for corruption linked to the issuing of illegal drivers' licences in the province. Mahlangu also drew fire for delaying action against former provincial health minister Sibongile Manana, notorious for claiming anti-retroviral drugs were a plot to poison poor people and for failing to tackle alleged corruption in the provincial health department.

Date of birth: 19 May 1957

Mangena, Mosibudi

Minister of Science and Technology

Mosibudi Mangena was an inspired choice as the country's first Science and Technology minister. As deputy minister of education, he concerned himself with promoting mathematics and science education in schools. And in his first address – at the launch of the 2004 National Science Week only days after his appointment – he stressed the need to attract more young people and more women into science. "The continued challenge of our national science system remains the frozen demographics in the science and technology work force, both with respect to race and gender," he said. "The only way to overcome this challenge in a sustainable manner is to create the necessary feedstock for the system."

Towards that end, he stressed the ties between his former department and his current one, listing areas of collaboration already in progress, including upgrading the skills of educators in maths and science and arranging supplementary tuition and curriculum support in these areas.

Mangena is president of the Azanian People's Organisation; before the two organisations merged in 1994, he was chairperson of the central committee of the Black Consciousness Movement of Azania. He had joined the South African Students Organisation in 1971, at the University of Zululand. A year later he moved to Pretoria and was elected national organiser of the Black People's Convention. Members of the BCM were continually harassed in the 1970s; Mangena was repeatedly detained and eventually banned, and he went into exile in 1981. He earned BSc, Honours and MSc degrees in applied mathematics from Unisa, returned to South Africa in 1994 and was elected Azapo president.

Azapo boycotted the 1994 elections but stood in the 1999 poll, and gained a single seat in the National Assembly, which went to its president. When Mangena was chosen to be deputy education minister, he resigned his seat and was replaced by current Azapo president Pandelani Nefolovhodwe.

Date of birth: 7 August 1947

Manuel, Trevor

Minister of Finance

Trevor Manuel is one of the pre-eminent members of the new generation of young politicians who have steered the South African ship of state since the country's "independence" election in 1994. Manuel has served continuously in the African National Congress-led government since that date, first as trade and industry minister, and since 1996 as Finance Minister. Having risen through the ranks of the United Democratic Front in the 1980s – he began political life as the general secretary of the Cape Areas Housing Action Committee, and became a UDF executive committee member in 1985 – he is also the most senior "internal" leader in President Thabo Mbeki's Cabinet.

Just a year after the 1990 unbanning of the ANC, he became the head of the party's economic planning department and a member of its national executive committee. He has remained an NEC member ever since.

Manuel's activist background may give the wrong impression – by temperament he is more an administrator and back-room strategist than a rabble-rouser. It should not be forgotten that he was trained as a civil engineer.

Given President Nelson Mandela's and Mbeki's anxiety to keep foreign investors and the local business community on side, his technocratic bent, fluency and personal charm made him a natural choice as South Africa's first finance minister of colour. Despite some early gaffes – he once notoriously deplored the influence of "amorphous" markets – he has come to command the respect and liking of South Africa's business leaders. He also comports himself with ease and confidence in international forums, having served on the Ministers' Council of the Southern African Development Community and on the International Monetary Fund's joint board of governors, as well as chairing the IMF's development committee. The length of his tenure reflects both his competence as a minister and the desire of successive post-apartheid presidents to project an image of stability in his sensitive portfolio.

Manuel has been Mbeki's key instrument in conveying to world markets and multilateral institutions the ability of an African government to run a tight macro-economic ship. His fiscal philosophy, with both its successes and shortcomings, should be seen as flowing ultimately from the president, himself technocratic and managerialist in economic matters. For a number of years in partnership with his efficient and intellectually agile director-general, Maria Ramos, Manuel made the Finance Department (now the Treasury) one of the most effective state departments. Among the department's achievements was the streamlining of the South African Revenue Service, which under its energetic new commissioner Pravin Gordhan has significantly raised state revenue by closing loopholes and improving efficiencies. Another important innovation was the shift to multi-year budgeting, which has helped create a more predictable macro-economic environment. From the outset Manuel emphasised the need to balance budgets, contain state borrowing, curb the public service wage bill and keep a tight rein on inflation. One of his most important achievements was to force budget compliance on wasteful and inefficient provincial governments – a delicate task, given the constitutional separation between different tiers of rule and perceptions in some quarters that the ANC is overly centralist in its instincts.

Justifying his fiscal conservatism, he frequently points to the fact that South Africa came through the emerging market upheavals of the late 1990s relatively unscathed. Although the economy has grown slowly in the past decade – by about 2% a year – it has become increasingly resilient.

One remarkable sign of this has been the stabilisation of the rand after shedding 40% of its value against the dollar in late 2002. Manuel's problem – indeed, the central difficulty of the Mbeki government – has been that macro-economic stability has not delivered foreign direct investment on anything like the scale required to roll back the country's high unemployment rate (about 40%, according to the broad definition).

At the same time, there is evidence that Manuel's macro-economic stringencies, combined with other state policies like privatisation, the restructuring of the parastatal sector and the precipitous dropping of tariff barriers, has had the effect of destroying formal jobs. This led to protracted and acrimonious conflict between the Mbeki government and the Congress of South African Trade Unions, with Manuel being cast as the "neo-liberal" villain of the piece. While unionists were demanding a more active state role in tackling unemployment, he fuelled his unpopularity by loudly insisting it was not the government's responsibility to create jobs.

From 2000 onwards, however, there were tell-tale signs of a shift in Manuel's fiscal style. After contractionary budgets between 1996 and 1999, he moved to expand government spending, with more generous allocations for social welfare and job creation, particularly through an increased outlay on municipal infrastructure. The 2004 Budget symbolically provided for a small increase in the deficit, as well as earmarking some R20-billion for an expanded public works programme. The official rationale for the policy adjustment was that South Africa had faced an economic crisis inherited from apartheid in the early years of ANC rule, requiring tough stewardship, and that the government could relax the reins now that macro-economic stability had been achieved. A more plausible explanation is that pragmatism started to override ideology as the 2004 general election approached and the need for trade union support bulked larger. The budgetary changes were coupled with a government about-turn on HIV/Aids, a virtual standstill on privatisation, and the suspension of public attacks on Cosatu leaders as "ultra-leftist" and "counter-revolutionary".

Manuel has displayed many admirable qualities during his eight years as Finance Minister, including the strength – essential for good leaders in a democracy – to risk unpopularity for the public good. Given the seniority of his portfolio, the length of his tenure and his support in the ruling party, he would be a candidate in most other countries to succeed the incumbent as president. However, the fact that he is Coloured rather than African makes this inconceivable. There are already signs that he is preparing to move out of government, it is rumoured to a top position at one of the Bretton Woods institutions. His successor will almost certainly be his current deputy and former Gauteng finance minister, Jabu Moleketi, who was significantly elevated to the national Parliament after the 2004 election.

Date of birth: 31 January 1956

Mapisa-Nqakula, Nosiviwe

Minister, Home Affairs

Nosiviwe Mapisa-Nqakula is one of the African National Congress's rising stars — a status confirmed in 2003 when she beat the favourite, fellow Umkhonto we Sizwe veteran Thandi Modise, for the position of president of the ANC Women's League. Mapisa-Nqakula replaced Winnie Madikizela-Mandela, who resigned all her positions after being convicted of fraud.

President Thabo Mbeki has given Mapisa-Nqakula one of the senior Cabinet posts as a way of re-affirming his commitment to empowering female politicians. Formerly deputy minister of home affairs, she has replaced Inkatha Freedom Party president Mangosuthu Buthelezi, who was dropped by Mbeki after repeated clashes between the two leaders in the run-up to the 2004 elections.

Mapisa-Nqakula's seniority in the organisation was also underlined when she was chosen to chair the 100 000-strong ANC rally at the FNB stadium when the party wound down its election campaign in April 2004. The rally was the biggest of its kind since former president Nelson Mandela addressed ANC supporters after his release in 1990.

Mapisa-Nqakula has taken to her new position with a vigour that intends to clean up everything that was wrong in the system.

She has ordered a policy audit that will look at whether any Home Affairs regulations are inconsistent with the Constitution, or whether the problems in the department are due to the way regulations have been applied by officials. This became necessary after Home Affairs was taken to court in several instances by aggrieved citizens. That review will also determine whether any regulations have a negative effect on service delivery.

With that, the department is looking to improve its turnaround time for applications for ID documents and passports. She also plans to work on backlogs in the immigration section; the department has been slow in processing the asylum applications of thousands of people living inside the country with temporary permits.

In terms of its new organogram, the department will end up doubling its current staff to boost its delivery capacity. In the process of recruiting new staff, Mapisa-Nqakula has emphasised the need for a new generation of female leadership in a department that has traditionally been male-oriented.

A qualified teacher, she started her political career as a founder member of the East London Domestic Workers Association in 1982 before skipping the border in 1984 to undergo military training in Angola and the Soviet Union. The ANC appointed her to a commission that investigated unhappiness within MK ranks in the 1980s.

She was a member of the ANC's political and military structures until 1988 when she served for the next two years as a representative of the ANC Women's Section in Angola. She returned to South Africa in 1990 to help the movement rebuild its structures, and was elected Women's League organiser in 1991.

Elected to Parliament in 1994, she was soon appointed chairperson of its joint standing committee on intelligence. When chief whip Tony Yengeni was forced to resign his post pending investigations into bribery allegations in connection with the arms deal, she replaced him as chief whip. She was appointed deputy chairperson of the ANC parliamentary political committee in 2001.

She is married to Safety and Security Minister Charles Nqakula.
Date of birth: 13 November 1956

Marshoff, Beatrice
Free State Premier

Frances Beatrice Marshoff is the third woman premier in the Free State. She succeeds Winkie Direko and Ivy Matsepe-Casaburri.

Her appointment by President Thabo Mbeki in May 2004 was a total surprise as her name had not even been on the initial top 30 list drafted by Free State African National Congress branches. It was later included by ANC leadership – but still no one bargained on Marshoff being named premier.

Marshoff is not a senior member of the ANC in the Free State, and will need the cooperation of its leadership in implementing provincial programmes.

Her ten-person team includes five new faces. She has also appointed just two women as MECs. She apparently ignored most of the names recommended to her by the provincial ANC leadership, including those of deputy chairperson Casca Mokitlane and deputy secretary Charlotte Lobe.

Of the ten people in her cabinet, only three serve on the ANC provincial executive. But she has made provincial chairperson Elias "Ace" Magashule her MEC for agriculture, a key portfolio in the province.

Publicly, the provincial ANC and Magashule, in particular, have pledged to support her. But privately ANC members are worried that Marshoff is determined to ignore them completely and sees herself accountable only to Mbeki, who appointed her. Even the opposition Democratic Alliance says whether or not the Free State government functions will depend on whether Magashule and Marshoff can hammer out a professional relationship.

Marshoff, who was born and educated in the Free State, became an MP in 1994 and served in the health, finance and public accounts committee. In 1998 she chaired both the RDP portfolio committee and the sub-committee on health financing.

She also served on ad hoc committees looking at the surrogate motherhood, termination of pregnancy and equality Bills.

When then premier Direko made a provincial executive reshuffle in 2001, she brought Marshoff back to the Free State and appointed her provincial minister for social development.

Marshoff's challenges are many, including the fact that she does not speak Sesotho in a province where the majority of the population is Sesotho-speaking.

She has made job creation a priority. Immediately after taking over, she declared that dramatic measures were needed to deal with the fact that 35% of the Free State population was unemployed and 48% live in abject poverty.

She started off by reviewing the provincial action plan, called the Free State Development Plan, with the aim of bringing fresh ideas to tackle the poverty and joblessness.

The Expanded Public Works Programme has been placed at the centre of the job creation strategy. Although mining is the biggest employer and agriculture is crucial to the provincial economy, tourism is seen as a main driver of economic growth under the public works programme.

Marshoff, who trained as a nurse, is a founder member of the National Education, Health and Allied Workers Union (Nehawu) in the Free State. She served as a member of the Health Workers Association and the Free State Health and Welfare Transitional Facilitating Committee.

Date of birth: 17 September 1957

Matsepe-Casaburri, Ivy

Minister of Communications

It has been a difficult and controversial five years for the communications minister. The track record of the erstwhile Free State premier and the performance of her department have been underwhelming.

Policy zigzags, vaguely drafted legislation and costly delays have become the hallmark of Matsepe-Casaburri's ministry, which has, during her tenure, served to foster investor uncertainty, both domestically and abroad.

It's unclear whether Matsepe-Casaburri has been kept on as minister for another term because the president thinks she is doing a good job, or whether her renewal in the post is due to the highly technical nature of her portfolio and the need for continuity. Continuity is particularly important because of the loss of the department's very senior director-general, Andile Ngcaba, but also because the 2004 national elections took place in the middle of the rollout of the mission-critical second national operator (SNO). The appointment of a new minister would inevitably result in more delays to an already delayed process. The president has now appointed a deputy minister, Radhakrishna "Ray" Padayachee, to the portfolio.

Matsepe-Casaburri's portfolio is a trail-blazing and difficult one by its very nature. The minister has to ensure the country and government keep up with the rapidly changing world of technology. She needs to ensure technology is used to transform the life of the poor and ensure it does not remain the traditional domain of the elite. Although Matsepe-Casaburri is known as a hard-working individual who doggedly pursues her aims, it's questionable, given her track record, whether she has carried out her portfolio with the broad vision needed for success.

The minister's reign has been marked by the need to control and attempts at increasing power. In 2002 she drew heavy fire for the Draft Broadcasting Amendment Bill, which proposed that SABC journalists and the SABC board be subject to "minister-approved policy on reporting". The Bill never made it to law.

Matsepe-Casaburri was also criticised locally and internationally for sidelining the Independent Communications Authority of South Africa (Icasa) during the SNO bid process and damaging South Africa's reputation in the eyes of the international community over the whole affair. Matsepe-Casaburri drew criticism when she and Icasa butted heads after she bypassed the regulator for the appointment of a 51% stake in the SNO to "fast-track" the process. But the SNO process, which Matsepe-Casaburri presided over, has suffered delay after delay and uncertainty.

However, there have been some successes. There was Matsepe-Casaburri's promotion of universal access to information and communication technologies. There has been an impressive rollout in poor and rural areas, not least through the extension of phone services and the launch of multipurpose community centres.

Before her tenure as minister, Matsepe-Casaburri was also South Africa's first female premier, although her tenure of the Free State was generally described as "unremarkable". Before her premiership, she was the first woman and first black person to chair the SABC. It wasn't a very happy posting: the old guard at the SABC was hostile towards her, and she struggled for resources and to inform herself about her new field, but she stayed the course and by the end of her term had learned a prodigious amount and managed a large and extremely disparate board.

Known as one of the more favoured exiles in the corridors of power, Matsepe-Casaburri returned to South Africa in 1990. She was born in 1937 in the Free State, in Kroonstad. Her father was a principal, musician and sportsman, and her mother a teacher and social and community worker. She earned a degree at the University of Fort Hare, taught in KwaZulu for two years, and moved on to Swaziland. In the 25 years that she was in exile, she obtained a PhD in sociology at Rutgers University in the United States, and worked for the United Nations Institute for Namibia in Lusaka, where much of the current leadership was taught or worked in exile.

On her return she was appointed executive director of the Education Development Trust, working with the National Education Crisis Committee and becoming involved in the internal politics of education and youth development. She coordinated the National Education Policy Initiative process, mapping out goals for education for a new South Africa, and was expected to continue playing a prominent role in education policy when she was later deployed to the SABC board. That she persevered at the SABC says a great deal about her intelligence, strength and determination. Her leadership style has been described by observers as unemotional, almost distant and cerebral.

Date of birth: 19 September 1937

Mbeki, Thabo

President

South African President Thabo Mbeki has repeatedly faced the criticism, during his time in office as president of both the African National Congress and South Africa, that he has no popular support in his organisation or the country.

His critics have often maintained that he owed his position to his skills as a shrewd politician, able to intimidate and sideline his opponents and build power-blocs based on personal loyalties and patronage. This view was supported by Mbeki's apparent preference for the international stage, and tackling the problems of Africa and the developing world. His public persona was that of a worldly intellectual for whom the challenges of South Africa had become too small.

The overwhelming victory which the ANC scored in the last election, in a campaign led by Mbeki as a "man of the people", has effectively disproved that view. Mbeki has led the ANC to its greatest majority in an election yet, and his credibility as a popular leader of South Africa has been firmly established. Not even under Nelson Mandela was the ANC able to win effective control of all nine of South Africa's provinces.

The image of Mbeki as a distant, ruthless politician is partly the result of him having vigorously to drive the ANC's and South Africa's political and economic transformation; and partly because of his personal style.

For example, Mbeki has been seen as stamping out all dissent in the ranks of the ANC in an attempt to impose "uniform think" on the organisation while it made the transition from a radical, mass-based liberation movement to a social democratic government with a free-market bias. Leaders of the Congress of South African Trade Unions and the South African Communist Party – who vociferously objected to government's relatively conservative economic policies and claimed to represent the masses – were seen particularly to be in the firing line.

His forcing the pace of black economic empowerment and his more overtly Africanist approach to the transformation of South Africa has also made the country's minorities uncomfortable.

Ironically, for somebody who very successfully headed the ANC's Department of Information and Publicity while the organisation was in exile, Mbeki has been very reluctant to engage in the public relations exercises which would have blunted many of the criticisms directed at him.

In the wake of the ANC's election victory, his political power in the organisation and the country is arguably at its greatest. He has responded by making his Cabinet more inclusive of political views in the ANC, including representatives of the organisation's independent left who have been cool towards his transformation of the ANC and his government's social and economic policies.

And, with widespread local support for the ANC, and South Africa's continued political stability accepted by the international community, Mbeki has taken the opportunity to make the present Cabinet the most strongly ANC and African yet. This is most probably the clearest signal that he believes South Africa's political transition − at least − is over.

Firmly in power and facing his last term in office, Mbeki is likely to adopt a more statesman-like role. Rather than overtly fight a corner, he is likely to spend more time trying to constructively manage conflicts in the organisation and country.

For example, his controversial questioning of the link between HIV and Aids and the effectiveness of anti-retrovirals − drugs which reduce the spread and effects of the disease − has badly damaged his government's and his personal standing among key local interest groups and in the international community. Despite holding on to his own views, he has now given the go-ahead for South Africa to roll out what will be the world's largest HIV and Aids treatment programme, and appointed a Deputy Minister of Health, Nozizwe Madlala-Routledge, who is an ardent campaigner against the disease. He has left his chosen Health Minister, Manto Tshabalala-Msimang, who is broadly disregarded by HIV and Aids campaigners, in place.

When Mbeki's legacy is written, his Achilles heels in office will come to haunt him. Undoubtedly these have been the president's dalliance with Aids denialists and the failure of the government to take a sterner line on the systemic rights abuses in Zimbabwe, South Africa's neighbour.

Between 1999 and 2004, Mbeki stalled an effective response to the prevention and treatment of HIV/Aids by questioning the link between the virus and the disease. By consorting with global denial science, Mbeki lost his stature at home and among key global players, for the science had long been proven and the denialists ostracised. He gave them a political lifeline (albeit short) by including them on the Aids advisory panel. Pressure from the Treatment Action Campaign, global players and from within the party forced him to back-track, effectively disbanding the panel and adopting a conventional model of treatment. Mbeki still does not speak out on Aids.

Since the political crisis began in Zimbabwe in 2000 with an illegal land reform programme, South Africa has maintained a policy of quiet diplomacy – government claimed to be making great progress behind closed doors instead of using the political megaphone of sanctions and censure. It has come to nought with President Robert Mugabe tightening the political screws as his Zanu-PF tries to hang onto power.

Mbeki has perhaps been over-analysed by too many people under-qualified for the job. The roots of much of his political and personal style can be found in the traditions of the ANC – many of which have become idealised over the past years. The ANC during its many years fighting apartheid was a political roughhouse, where factions fought hard to stay on top and determine the course of the organisation. It was in this arena that Mbeki learned the political skills which he has used to become president of the ANC and South Africa, and which he will use to attempt to clear the way for his successor and secure his legacy.

He is married to Zanele Mbeki (nee Dlamini), a founder and director of the Women's Development Bank.

Date of birth: 18 June 1942

Mbete, Baleka
Speaker, National Assembly

With her penchant for elegant African-inspired dress, Mbete presides over MPs in the National Assembly with a bold, no-nonsense approach. She seldom raises her voice to enforce order when parliamentarians get a bit too rowdy in their heckling.

The new speaker wants to jack up the level of debates, and make them "more natural" instead of consisting of speeches prepared in advance and read, as has become the norm.

Having served as deputy speaker for almost two terms, Mbete has an intimate knowledge of Parliament. She was closely involved in its day-to-day running, chairing, among other committees, the joint internal arrangements and management committees.

Mbete is one of eight siblings. After completing school in Durban, she obtained a teaching qualification from Loveday Teachers' College in 1973 and went on to teach at KwaMashu. She went into exile in May

1976 and, after an initial stint as teacher, worked in various positions in the African National Congress women's and information sections. Her 15 years in exile took her to Swaziland, Tanzania, Kenya, Botswana, Zimbabwe and Zambia.

Mbete returned to South African in 1990 to join the ANC's interim leadership. She was key to re-establishing the ANC Women's League in the country, and served as its secretary-general from 1991 to 1993. She remains a league heavyweight, currently serving on the national executive committee. In addition, she has been a member of the ANC's NEC since 1991.

At the heart of the ANC in the early 1990s she took part in the multi-party talks at the Convention for a Democratic South Africa, where she worked closely with chief negotiator Cyril Ramaphosa. After the 1994 elections, as ANC MP, Mbete became a key player in the Constitutional Assembly which, under the direction of Ramaphosa and then National Party's Roelf Meyer, drafted the 1996 Constitution.

In 1995 she was appointed chairperson of the ANC parliamentary caucus, and in May 1996 deputy speaker.

Mbete was said to have lobbied strongly for the speaker's position in 1999 but, as she was regarded as being outside President Thabo Mbeki's inner circle, the job again went to Frene Ginwala. But as relations between the ANC and Ginwala hit a rocky road, the party frequently turned to Mbete.

One blot on her track record remains the allegation that she obtained her driver's licence via long distance without taking a driving test; it was a favour from officials in Mpumalanga, who agreed that she was "too busy to queue". This sparked a government investigation into corruption at the provincial licensing department. No charges were brought against her; and when the story came out, she apologised.

Mbete describes herself as a music person with a love of jazz, classical, choral and spiritual music, in a 2000 interview with the newsletter of the European Parliamentary Support Programme, where it was also noted that she writes poetry.

But her love of music is not just in the listening. Mbete, alongside Archbishop Desmond Tutu and several ANC officials, is featured on the CD "South African Freedom Songs".

A key mover in making Parliament more woman-friendly, Mbete regards as key challenges the strengthening of Parliament's oversight role and steps to ensure ordinary people are able to make inputs into the legislative process.

Date of birth: 24 September 1949

Mboweni, Tito

Governor, South African Reserve Bank

The appointment of Tito Mboweni as governor of the Reserve Bank was probably one of the government's most inspired decisions since it took power in 1994, ranking alongside that of Trevor Manuel as Finance Minister.

Born in Tzaneen, Limpopo in 1959, Mboweni has made his intellectual and political mark in the economics arena. He joined the African National Congress in 1980 while exiled in Lesotho, having left the country the previous year, which was also his first year as a BCom student at the then University of the North. In 1985, he completed an honours equivalent of a BA in economics and political science at the National University of Lesotho, Roma. This was followed by a Masters in development economics from the University of East Anglia in England, which prepared Mboweni for work in the economic policy arena after the unbanning of liberation movements and subsequent ascent to power of the ANC.

In the early 1990s, as a member of both the ANC's national working committee and its national executive committee, Mboweni was deputy head of the ANC's economic policy unit (he was promoted to head in 1997) and chairperson of the NEC's economic transformation committee.

Between May 1994 and July 1998 he was minister of labour, laying much of the groundwork for the current labour legislative framework.

His appointment to the Reserve Bank in July 1998 was, like Manuel's appointment two years earlier, greeted with scepticism. In Manuel's case, concern centred on competence; in Mboweni's it was partly about race, and partly about whether he would be able to exercise independence in this crucial position. Mboweni's position was strengthened by the fact that, having resigned all elected and appointed positions in the ANC, he served a year as adviser to former Reserve Bank governor Chris Stals before assuming the governorship in August 1999. In that position he is a custodian of price stability in the interests of growth and development, by protecting the internal and external value of the rand, or the exchange rate, among a range of duties.

Mboweni is a powerful figure in South Africa's social and economic life, and he revels in it. While in charge, he has undergone what many see as a complete metamorphosis. Along with Gauteng premier Mbhazima Shilowa, he is the epitome of the former comrade who has joined the upper-middle-class world of pricey suits and cigars. He has added a dimension of flash and ego to his historically grey Reserve Bank job, which appears to have endeared him to, rather than alienated him from, the broader public. He is now a firmly entrenched member of the coterie of guests invited to the country's most exclusive functions; has found time to speak at the launch of a jazz club in middle-class Johannesburg; insists on being called "governor"; and has been deemed cool enough to be interviewed on the Phat Joe Show.

In 2000, government decided to lower inflation, excluding mortgage rates, to between 3% and 6%. Mboweni has been single-minded in his determination to achieve this.

His first test came in 2002, in the wake of the rand's 37% depreciation against the dollar during the previous December. This caused runaway imported inflation which threatened to overshoot the target. Many observers assumed that the Bank would simply use an escape clause that allowed it to miss the target if factors that caused inflation were exogenous, or outside of its control. However, Mboweni stuck to his guns and raised the interest rates four times in the dogged pursuit of his target. He went on to tell a parliamentary committee that the escape clause was "a mistake" that should never have been inserted.

Manuel's proposal for the formation of a "super-regulator" that would supervise commercial banks, currently the task of the Reserve Bank, set him in conflict with Mboweni, who argued that banking supervision requires swift action and specialised knowledge that a super-regulator might not possess. These clashes came to be viewed largely as ego-driven, and the two men insisted relations between their offices were cordial.

Mboweni's pet hatred is the corps of financial journalists, for whom he displays ill-disguised contempt. He once famously clashed with Lukanyo Mnyanda, then Business Day economics editor, after Mnyanda had argued it was incorrect for Mboweni to drop hints on what he thought should happen to interest rates, known as Open Mouth Operations, because such talk moves markets. Mboweni insisted on his right to use OMO as a way of talking down inflationary expectations. In retrospect, Mboweni has clearly succeeded in selling the importance of consistently low inflation, except perhaps to organised labour.

He also expresses indignation at journalists who quiz him on speculative information, and shows displeasure at criticism from leading economists like Iraj Abedian, a key contributor to much of the economic policy framework Mboweni operates in.

Mboweni is regarded as globally conservative; even conservative commentators say interest rates are too high and that Mboweni's target should be growth, leading to jobs.

His ultra-defensive position that inflation targeting is his only and ultimate goal has distracted from the fact that it does serve growth and development. In late July his contract was renewed for another term.

Date of birth: 16 March 1959

Mdladlana, Membathisi Shepherd

Minister of Labour

The appointment in 1998 of a trade union leader to replace Tito Mboweni as labour minister was a wise move – especially as the trade unionist in question was Membathisi Mdladlana, a man known for listening to all sides and for stepping in when issues became too heated.

Policy had been set by Mboweni, while implementation was Mdladlana's job. That meant balancing the interests of organised labour with those of business, whose leaders were unhappy with aspects of new labour legislation.

One of the issues he had to deal with soon after he took office was controversy over the Labour Relations Act and the Basic Conditions of Employment Act, which had led to accusations and counter-accusations between the labour movement and business, with both sides claiming the laws would lead to job losses.

Business, on one hand, was saying the country's labour market was over-regulated and that government has gone too far in protecting workers' rights, instead of keeping a balance with employers' rights.

Organised labour, on the other hand, complained about a provision of the LRA, requiring employers to consult employees, with a facilitator present, when embarking on retrenchments; the Congress of South African Trade Unions argued that the section should have been amended to force companies to negotiate retrenchment rather than merely consult on it.

Mdladlana was able to defuse the tension by introducing amendments to both Acts.

Although the minister has not gone in for initiating new laws, he has introduced amendments to most of the labour laws drawn up during his predecessor's tenure. Among those amended are the Employment Equity Act, the Unemployment Insurance Fund Act, the Skills Development Act, the Labour Relations Act and the Basic Conditions of Employment Act. All these initiatives have been characterised by Mdladlana's desire to establish labour standards and support workers' rights.

Mdladlana's passion for supporting labour rights became apparent in 2002 when he introduced new sectoral determinations – controlling the terms and conditions of employment – in terms of the Basic Conditions of Employment Act, aimed at prescribing minimum wages and employment conditions for vulnerable workers who were not covered by bargaining councils.

He introduced minimum wages and basic conditions of employment in the wholesale, retail, domestic and farming sectors – a move met with resistance from some employers, with many threatening retrenchments. But for workers – especially those in the farming community, many of whom still worked on a casual or seasonal basis for low wages – the sectoral determinations came as a triumph.

Mdladlana's grasp of labour issues, coupled with what many have described as natural leadership skills, have won him respect, and during his first term he was considered one of the most competent ministers in the Cabinet. The fact that the President kept him in the post backs up that opinion.

Born and reared in Qoboqobo, a small village in the Eastern Cape, Mdladlana relocated to Cape Town in 1972 to take up a teaching job at Vukukhanye Primary School in Gugulethu. At the time he only had matric; he obtained his primary teacher's diploma at Goodhope College in Cape Town in 1993.

However, his leadership skills were evident from the start, and after seven years of teaching he was named deputy principal at Vukukhanye. In 1982 he became principal of Andile Primary School at New Crossroads, a post he held until 1994.

At the same time, he became involved in politics and trade union activities. He was provincial chairperson of the South African Democratic Teachers Union in the Western Cape from 1985 to 1990, the year he assumed Sadtu's national presidency. He also served as vice-chairperson of the African National Congress branch in Gugulethu between 1990 and 1992. In 1990 he joined the South African Communist Party.

In 1994 he went to Parliament, where he served as chairperson of a theme committee in the Constitutional Assembly, and deputy chairperson of the portfolio committee on education.

Those who have worked with him say Mdladlana is a tough but a very principled man, easily irritated when tasks are not performed properly.

He is also an extremely religious man, an elder and session clerk of the Gugulethu Presbyterian Church. A snappy dresser, he arrives at union congresses in a cowboy hat instead of the usual union cap.

The only major controversy surrounding Mdladlana comes from those who believe he interferes unnecessarily in union matters.

In August 2003, for example, he tried to break an impasse in wage negotiations between mining companies and the National Union of Mineworkers. The union had threatened a countrywide strike if the mining companies did not meet its demands. The strike would have been the biggest in the mining industry in 16 years.

It was not the first time Mdladlana had become involved in a strike. In 2002, he intervened in a wage dispute between the South African Municipal Workers' Union and the South African Local Government Association. He personally directed the Commission for Conciliation, Mediation and Arbitration to bring the parties together to reach a settlement.

Senior staff in Mdladlana's office say that although he clearly assumes the leadership position during discussions, he accommodates other people's views on issues. And – perhaps unusually for politicians – he prefers his own staff, not outside consultants, to advise him on policies.

When he took the post, Mdladlana said he'd only serve one term before retiring to farm in the Eastern Cape. The farm looks set to do without him for the foreseeable future, as he begins his second term.

Date of birth: 12 May 1952

Mlambo-Ngcuka, Phumzile
Minister of Minerals and Energy

A reflection of Minerals and Energy Minister Phumzile Mlambo-Ngcuka's diligence and commitment can be seen, perhaps appropriately, from her reaction to her reappointment to serve a second term in charge of mining, gas, electricity and petroleum industries. Said to have greeted her retention with humility and relief, Mlambo-Ngcuka set to work, not only to finish what she has started during the past five years, but to set the agenda for the next five. Her spokesperson Khanyo Gqulu tells of how she convened an executive meeting, enquiring not only about broad policy detail, but the nuts and bolts of implementation.

Mlambo-Ngcuka's enduring legacy has been to make charters the most viable tool to benchmark transformation. On the first day of her second term, she is said to have overseen the dispatch to mining houses of application forms for the conversion of mineral rights from old order rights, which are owned by the mines, to new order mining rights, owned by the state, issued on a 30-year lease and reviewed subject to compliance with empowerment requirements.

Mlambo-Ngcuka took her first degree, a BA in social sciences and education, at the National University of Lesotho, Roma. This was followed by a three-year teaching stint in KwaZulu-Natal. Between 1984 and 1987 she worked for the Young Women's Christian Association in Geneva, where she founded the Young Women's International Programme. In the late 1980s she was a director of Team, a Cape Town-based development NGO, and up until 1992 she was a director of a funding agency called World University Services.

She established a management consultancy company, Phumelela Services, in 1993 but her entrepreneurial career was cut short with a call-up to South Africa's first democratically assembled Parliament, where she enjoyed a rapid rise to power. Chairperson of the portfolio committee of public service, she was elevated to deputy trade and industry minister in 1996. After the second democratic elections in 1999, she quietly slipped into her portfolio of Minerals and Energy, succeeding minister Penuell Maduna, and eventually totally eclipsing him in that role.

She soon set about making charters fashionable as an instrument of measuring progress in economic transformation. She quietly negotiated a charter in the liquid fuels industry, put in place in November 2000. But that did not prepare her for the acrimony she was to encounter in trying to bed down a similar, industry-wide, consensus-driven document for mining: a century-old industry built on slave wages, the migrant labour system and exploitation of communities.

The process came to a head in June 2002, when a draft version of the charter was leaked to the markets. Its most contentious proposal was to transfer 26% of ownership to blacks within a decade. The result wiped off R50-billion in value of mining shares on the JSE Securities Exchange in one afternoon. Mlambo-Ngcuka seemed unfazed by this and went on to fashion the charter that set trends for other industries to follow.

Her strength is her grace, which she uses to conceal toughness to clash with vested, monolithic capital interests. She not only imbues industry functions with elegance, but also displays a refined detailed grasp of challenge in all her spheres of influence. Be it the launch of the annual results of the National Electricity Regulator or a launch of an empowerment mining deal, Mlambo-Ngcuka, like Finance Minister Trevor Manuel, is an uplifting presence. Of the many industry awards she has received for her role in transformation, the most richly deserved is the Isithwalandwe/Seaparankoe, awarded by the Congress of South African Trade Unions for her role in advancing workers' rights.

The nadir in her tenure, sadly, had very little – in fact, nothing – to do with her competency or area of operation. It came in late 2003 when her husband, then-National Prosecutions Director Bulelani Ngcuka, faced an accusation that he had been an apartheid spy. The allegations turned out to be baseless innuendo, but throughout the Hefer Commission of Inquiry in Bloemfontein they appeared to exert their strain on a quietly confident couple. The minister, especially, appeared forlorn but brave, deeply hurt but resilient.

Yet that did not distract her from her broader mission of transforming and optimising the country's use of its minerals and energy resources. Now she is readying herself to restructure the gas and electricity supply and distribution industries. She will need all the grace and humility, and toughness, she can muster.

Date of birth: 3 November 1955

Mokgoro, Yvonne

Justice, Constitutional Court

Feminist, activist, academic-turned-judge, Yvonne Mokgoro is committed to the transformation of the judiciary and the establishment of its legitimacy among the people of South Africa by making people feel they "own" the system. She believes firmly that the judiciary must contribute to a rights-oriented culture in a society cognisant of both the rights aspect of human rights and of the duties she sees as an inextricable part of those rights.

She also believes that "there is no way that the legal system itself generally can be divorced from the politics of its jurisdiction".

Born in Galeshewe, Kimberley, where her mother worked as a washerwoman for a white family, she obtained a scholarship that enabled her to matriculate from St Boniface High School in 1970. Her first job was as a nursing assistant, and she later became a salesperson before being appointed as a clerk in the Department of Justice of the former Bophuthatswana.

She graduated from the then University of Bophuthatswana (now the University of the North-West) with a BJuris degree followed by an LLB, after which she became a maintenance officer and public prosecutor in the Mmabatho magistrate's court.

In 1984 Judge Mokgoro became a lecturer in the Department of Jurisprudence of the University of Bophuthatswana, where she rose through the ranks to associate professor. From 1992 to 1993 she served as associate professor at the University of the Western Cape, from where she moved to the Centre for Constitutional Analysis at the Human Sciences Research Council, serving as specialist researcher (human rights).

Throughout her legal career she has written extensively, and presented papers to and participated in many national and international conferences in South Africa and abroad. Her field of interest is sociological jurisprudence, particularly human rights, customary law and the impact of law on society generally and on women and children in particular. She has served extensively as a resource person in this regard for non-governmental and community-based organisations and initiatives.

A founder member of the Lawyers for Human Rights committee in Mafikeng in 1990 at a time when political repression was still the order of the day, she was also involved in the Mafikeng Anti-Repression Forum which took up cases of repression, referring them to LHR or to individual attorneys. A member of the African National Congress until the time of her appointment to the Constitutional Court, she served on its regional executive council, on the regional executive of the Northern Cape, the ANC Women's League in the Northern Cape, and Justice for Women, which she headed.

Date of birth: 19 October 1950

Moleketi, Jabu

Deputy Minister of Finance

Jabu Moleketi, a former member of the South African Communist Party and MK cadre, knew more about guerrilla tactics than economics when appointed as Gauteng MEC for finance in 1994.

His first preference was a posting in the security portfolio, but then Gauteng premier Tokyo Sexwale had other plans for him.

So Moleketi rolled up his sleeves and, with the encouragement of then trade and industry minister Alec Erwin, went back to school. In 2001 he earned a master's degree in financial economics from the University of London, and later completed an advanced management programme at Harvard Business School.

He disported himself admirably in his role as finance MEC, introducing spending controls and accountability within the province's various departments. Under Moleketi's watch Gauteng managed an annual economic growth rate of 3,3% between 1995 and 2002, versus national growth of 2,7%. He won praise from his Democratic Alliance colleagues – a rarity in these days of political enmity – and enjoys strong support within the African National Congress.

His ability to run a tight treasury and his support for President Thabo Mbeki's efforts to isolate the "ultra-left" within the ruling alliance won him promotion to the national Cabinet as Deputy Finance Minister in 2004. Moleketi is being groomed to succeed Finance Minister Trevor Manuel, who is probably serving out his last term in this post.

Manuel will be a hard act to follow. He brought order to the nation's finance, slashed the budget deficit, rammed home unpleasant spending controls, and finessed the art of global finance-speak – for which he deservedly commands huge respect among local and overseas businessmen.

Moleketi must slip into these ample shoes and earn the same degree of respect. Journalists and fund managers will dissect his every utterance for hints of policy shifts and changing priorities, so the first lesson he will learn in Cabinet is to say as little as possible.

He managed a R30-billion budget in Gauteng, but now shares responsibility for a much larger national budget of R381-billion. But Moleketi is not shy of grand visions, as demonstrated during his previous tenure in Gauteng.

Among the milestones he achieved as Gauteng MEC for finance were the formation of Blue IQ, a visionary project to accelerate Gauteng's economic growth and transform it into a "smart" province, and the launch of the Gauteng Economic Development Agency, which attracted R1,5-billion in new investment to the province in 2003. These were by no means solo efforts, but Moleketi was instrumental in getting them off the ground. Another milestone was the launch of a trade and industrial strategy to introduce more hi-tech industries to the province, and so move it up the value chain. All this is driven by a vision to create winning industries and sustained, higher-paid jobs for the province.

His priorities as Deputy Finance Minister will be to raise the country's investment as a percentage of gross domestic product to 25% from the current 16%, halve the unemployment rate by 2014, reduce poverty by creating work opportunities, improve the returns on education spending, build a more robust social security system, and improve national competitiveness.

Moleketi was born in Pimville, Soweto, and attended Musi High School where amenities were sparse and Afrikaans the language of education. This was the tinderbox that ignited the 1976 Soweto uprising. Moleketi slipped across the border to Swaziland soon afterwards and was sent for military training to the Soviet Union and Angola, where he met his wife Geraldine Fraser, the current Minister of Public Service and Administration, in the early 1980s. Some years later he returned to South Africa as an undercover MK operative – and has the scars to prove it.

He's a keen marathon runner, having completed Two Oceans races, and says one of his next targets is to compete in the Comrades. He is known as a determined and diligent minister, capable of assembling competent teams around him.

Moleketi has served alongside Manuel on the national budget council for many years. His appointment to this key ministerial post is an endorsement of his leadership and administrative skills. Perhaps the greatest qualities recognised in him by Mbeki are his loyalty and his unshakeable commitment to transparent and accountable government.

Date of birth: 15 June 1957

Molewa, Ednah

Premier, North West

When President Thabo Mbeki announced her name as the new premier of North West province, the general reaction was cold. Ednah Who? But Ednah Molewa has, in fact, served on North West's provincial legislature for eight years.

As if she had been patiently waiting for the position, Molewa quickly identified the challenges facing the province. "As government we have heard what our people have said and it is our intention to continue finding appropriate responses to their needs, key among which are poverty and unemployment," she said after her appointment.

While she is determined to be loyal to the former premier, Popo Molefe, and says she will carry forward his legacy, "the proud legacy" that she refers to left the people of North West feeling a bit poorer than they were before 1994.

During Molefe's second term, the economy of the capital city, Mafikeng, fell to pieces, although Rustenburg – site of Sun City – realised an economic boom. This has raised speculation that Rustenburg might become the new capital. Research done by the Human Sciences Research Council on unemployment and poverty in North West highlighted the fact that Rustenburg is the most developed district in the province.

While the government of North West claims to be resuscitating Mafikeng, Molewa knows that five years will be too short to revive "the city of goodwill", as it is affectionately known. Roads are in an unacceptable state, and approximately R2-billion is needed to fix them over the next three years, according to the Department of Roads and Public Works.

Even though she is new in the job, Molewa has a back-up of experienced MECs – like Phenye Frans Vilakazi, who is in the provincial executive council for the third time. Vilakazi was the MEC for Transport, Roads and Public Works in Molefe's executive council. He witnessed the closure and the re-opening of Mafikeng Airport, and his experience will be valuable in the province's attempts to sustain the air route. It was re-opened in December and is being subsidised by the provincial government with an investment of R5,8-million over three years. The North West government also undertook to buy 16 seats per aircraft every day.

Molewa might have succeeded in her previous position as MEC for agriculture, conservation and environment, but economic challenges are wider than drought relief. She was voted the best performing MEC of

Agriculture for 2003 by the National Emergent Red Meat Producers' Organisation. Molewa's Department of Agriculture also won the platinum award for best performing department in North West for 2003. Mandlekosi Mayisela, spokesperson for the African National Congress in the province and also the new MEC for Health, says Molewa deserves the premiership position. "She has distinguished herself in all the leadership roles that she was assigned."

He says Molewa's ability to survive infighting while provincial chairperson of the ANC Women's League is an indication she will be a successful premier. He describes her as assertive and forceful, and well able to operate within a collective. This could be due to her trade union background. A teacher for five years, she moved into the trade union movement in an entirely different field, becoming deputy president of the South African Commercial, Catering and Allied Workers Union, and was a regional executive committee member of the Congress of South African Trade Unions in the former Northern Transvaal for two years.

The province is dominated by rural areas of the former Bophuthatswana, with a high – 30,7% – unemployment rate. Less than 20% of the houses have piped water.

In a bid to attract local and foreign investors, Invest North West, the provincial investment and trade promotions agency, aims to promote the image of the province as a preferred destination for investment. At an international investors' conference it hosted at Sun City in Rustenburg in March 2004, business deals worth more than R1-billion were signed and the people of North West are waiting anxiously for the projects to get off the ground and create an estimated 19 000 jobs. Invest North West says it will take three to four years before people can be employed in the new projects, which will include jewellery design, food processing and cement manufacturing. The province has long relied for jobs on the mining, agricultural and tourism sectors built around gambling.

With her former membership of the executive council for economic development and tourism, Molewa has an idea of what the province needs. Attracting Botswana's lively currency, the pula, is also one of Molewa's big tasks. Batswana used to shop in Mafikeng, but the city lost customers after a decline in its economy. Batswana now choose Gauteng cities over their neighbour.

Date of birth: 23 March 1957

Moloto, Sello
Premier, Limpopo

Limpopo's new premier has been overshadowed on the national stage by his predecessor and mentor, Ngoako Ramatlhodi, but his strengths are recognised locally, where he is admired for his consultative leadership, accessibility to ordinary citizens, and genuine passion for rural development.

A soft-spoken 40-year-old former pharmacist, Sello Moloto cut his political teeth at the University of the North in 1985, where he won admission despite starting primary school later than most and hailing from an extremely poor rural family.

Heated late-night philosophical debates with Marxist lecturers awakened a social consciousness that, combined with a pragmatic leadership style and unassuming "common touch", led to his presidency of the local South African National Students Congress in 1989 simultaneously with an active role in local South African Communist Party cells.

He continued playing a key role in building the SACP's Limpopo structures in the early 1990s while working as a pharmacist at the rural Groothoek and Mokopane hospitals, and soon also took up leadership in African National Congress structures in his rural Waterberg constituency.

Moloto's rural activism was rewarded in 1994, when he was sent to Parliament.

In 1996 he was redeployed as CEO of Limpopo's conservative Bushveld District Council, where he is credited with radically transforming the predominately white administration without promoting a racist backlash.

His consensual leadership and growing managerial skills saw him promoted to the provincial cabinet as MEC for health and welfare in 1999, elected chairman of the provincial SACP in 2001, and deputy secretary general of the provincial ANC in 2002.

The challenges as a first-time MEC were huge: Limpopo spends only 16% of its budget on health in contrast to the national average of 22%. Even worse, the province only spent R637 per capita on health in 2003, almost 30% below the national average, and about one third of Gauteng's R1 668.

Undaunted, Moloto tackled backlogs by streamlining administrative support and improving service standards, as well as championing exchange programmes with Cuba to recruit additional rural doctors to redress imbalances that see each Limpopo public sector doctor serve an astounding 8 544 patients.

Although the province continues to lag behind national benchmarks, Moloto is credited with narrowing the gap and aggressively targeting the rollout of social welfare pensions, primary health services, and HIV/Aids treatment.

Moloto has opted for continuity, retaining eight of Ramatlhodi's ten-person cabinet and pledging to remain faithful to his predecessor's agro-processing and mining development-focused policies that resulted in South Africa's highest average real-economic-growth rate of 3,8% between 1995 and 2001.

But the impressive growth rates mean little to most of Limpopo's 5,2-million residents, 46% of whom are unemployed and 65% of whom live in dire poverty.

The province remains one of South Africa's poorest, representing 10,2% of the country's total land mass but contributing just 6,5% of the national GDP. Illiteracy remains high, as does malnutrition, child mortality, and deprivation of basic amenities such as water, electricity, and telephones.

Limpopo's people were, however, not always poor. The province is home to the remnants of some of the sub-continent's mightiest pre-colonial kingdoms centred on the ancient stone-walled citadels of Mapungubwe, Dzata and Thulamela.

Mapungubwe was, archaeologists believe, the precursor civilisation for the famed Great Zimbabwe empire, and has produced some of the region's most celebrated gold artefacts. Mapungubwe, Dzata and Thulamela all traded with counterparts as far away as China and India long before white colonialists arrived, and finally appear to have succumbed to environmental degradation – a powerful message for a province still gripped by drought and floods.

But Limpopo's rich culture is not all "dead" history. The province remains home to southern Africa's only female monarch, the legendary Rain Queen Modjadji, and southern Africa's largest grassroots religious movement, the Zion Christian Church, based at the holy city of Moria. It can also boast southern Africa's lost tribe of black Jews, the Lemba, who began moving down the continent from Yemen some 2 500 years ago.

Although a communist, Limpopo's youthful leader is himself a devout Christian with an abiding passion for philosophy.

Date of birth: 27 August 1964

Morobe, Murphy

Deputy Director-General in the Presidency

When many of his African National Congress colleagues entered Parliament to usher in democracy, engaging in the cut-and-thrust of party politics, Murphy Morobe took a different route, accepting a post as chairman and CEO of the Financial and Fiscal Commission. The FFC was set up in terms of the Constitution to make recommendations as to how revenue is disbursed among the three tiers of government, and to advise Parliament to that effect. Morobe has served two terms, and his tenure was extended for a further two years in January 2003.

He is also chairman of South African National Parks, and in August 2003 he was appointed chair of the Johannesburg Housing Company, a Section 21 not-for-profit company dedicated to inner city regeneration.

However, politics seems to continue to attract Morobe, for in mid-May 2004 he suddenly took up a post as deputy director-general of communications in the Presidency, returning to the political life he seemed to have left behind.

He has for some time been a player in the financial services sector, as director of Old Mutual SA and non-executive chairman of Ernst & Young.

Morobe signalled his intention to pursue a career in economics in 1990 when he enrolled for a course in economics and management at Princeton University and followed it up with a diploma in project management at Damelin. He'd had some experience in the latter; he spent two years as head of administration at the Convention for a Democratic South Africa. In 1994, he served briefly as secretary of the Gauteng provincial legislature before taking up his position at the FFC.

It's possible that finance, however high-flown, lacks a certain excitement after a role played in liberation politics from the early 1970s. When the Soweto Students' Representative Council, which initiated protest campaigns, was formed in August 1976, Morobe was elected deputy chairman. In December 1976 he was arrested, charged with conspiracy to commit sedition, and sent to Robben Island for six years, emerging to join the newly formed Congress of South African Students and the executive of the Soweto Youth Congress (Soyco) while serving as an organiser for the General and Allied Workers Union.

He was publicity secretary of the United Democratic Front in 1985, but soon had to go on the run, and after eluding the police for more than a year, he and then UDF activist, later environmental minister, Valli Moosa were arrested. They later staged a dramatic escape: they feigned illness, were hospitalised and, with the help of a sympathetic doctor, fled to the US consulate, where they stayed for 37 days before securing passports and flying out of the country to meet ANC leaders in exile.

Date of birth: 2 October 1956

Moseneke, Dikgang Ernest

Justice, Constitutional Court

Judge Moseneke is widely tipped as a possible successor to Arthur Chaskalson as the next chief justice. Lured back to law from a successful and lucrative corporate career (from 1995-2001) as chief executive of New Africa Investments Ltd (Nail) and chairman of, among others, Telkom South Africa, African Merchant Bank, Metropolitan Life and African Bank Investments, he returned to the Bench in the High Court in Pretoria before being appointed to the Constitutional Court in November 2002, replacing retiring Judge Johann Kriegler.

Moseneke is more equipped than most of his fellow judges to empathise with South Africa's prison population, having spent ten years on Robben Island, starting at the age of 15. Born in 1947 in Pretoria, he completed primary and secondary schooling before being arrested, detained and convicted for participating in political activities as a member of the Pan Africanist Congress. While on Robben Island he matriculated and obtained a BA (English and Political Science) and a BJuris through Unisa. He subsequently completed an LLB, also through Unisa.

In 1978 he was admitted and practised as an attorney. In 1983 he was called to the Bar, where he practised as an advocate in Johannesburg and Pretoria – the first black advocate to be admitted (reluctantly) to the Pretoria Bar. He took silk in 1993. In the same year he served on the technical committee which drafted the 1993 interim Constitution. In 1994 he was appointed deputy chairman of the Independent Electoral Commission, which conducted the first democratic elections. In September 1994 he was appointed to the Supreme Court as an acting judge.

He is a founder member of the Black Lawyers Association and of the National Association of Democratic Lawyers of South Africa, and has served several community-based and non-governmental organisations in a variety of positions including that of chairman of Project Literacy for more than ten years, trustee of Sowetan Nation Building, and deputy chairman of the Nelson Mandela Children's Fund. He is the first chancellor of Pretoria Technikon.

Immediately after the election in April 2004, President Thabo Mbeki appointed him chairperson of the independent commission for the remuneration of political office-bearers, succeeding retired Constitutional Court Judge Richard Goldstone.

Date of birth: 20 December 1947

Mpahlwa, Mandisi

Minister of Trade and Industry

Trade and Industry has to drive the government's black economic empowerment and job-creation initiatives. The new minister, Mandisi Mpahlwa, has a passion for BEE, and insiders say the promotion of small business during his term will be high on his agenda.

Senior National Treasury and African National Congress sources said that as an MP and then as Trevor Manuel's deputy he made a good impression, and they were not surprised that he was promoted. But possibly his exile struggle background and political history were equally important factors in the promotion.

An electrical engineer – he holds diplomas from the Umtata and Mangosuthu technikons – he worked for the Umtata municipality in the early 1980s. Like many political activists of his time, in 1985 Mpahlwa went into exile.

He continued his work for the ANC inside the country after the organisation was unbanned, and was employed by the ANC as a regional elections coordinator for Transkei, being elected to Parliament in 1994.

He also continued his education, but switched fields, completing a post-graduate diploma in economic principles at the University of London in 1996, and studying towards an MSc in financial economics at the University of London.

His five-year stint as deputy finance minister can be of benefit in Trade and Industry issues such as incentives, export insurance and desperately needed development finance for small, medium and micro enterprises. His history at Treasury might also strengthen ties between that department and Trade and Industry.

Former minister Alec Erwin won praise from some sectors on his achievements on positioning South Africa on the world trade stage, and Mpahlwa will have to make sure none of that hard-won ground is lost.

The former minister describes his replacement as "a fine economist and thinker on the economy. He is very familiar with the work area of the DTI."

Mpahlwa's position will be strengthened by the fact that his deputy, Lindiwe Hendricks, is well experienced in this field, having served in that position for the past five years.

Date of birth: 21 August 1960

Mufamadi, Sydney Fholisani

Minister of Provincial and Local Government

Sydney Mufamadi has spent the past five years encouraging all sections of his constituency to work with one another.

It has been an ongoing challenge for the minister, despite his widely acknowledged diplomatic and organisational skills, to promote the concept of cooperation among national, provincial and local governments and to get individual government departments and councils to deal with local communities. Now he wants new intergovernmental legislation as a priority to lay down the law. Mufamadi's record as minister of safety and security was not too shining; the boys in blue did not respond to a quietly-spoken minister.

Matters, however, have picked up in his current portfolio. With a strong deputy minister and director-general, he has steadily worked his way through a plethora of local and provincial government problems. Perhaps it's a case of putting his MSc in state, society and development from the University of London into practice.

That's not to say there aren't many problems left: councils are owed some R26-billion, but there are steps under way to make state departments, at least, pay their 6% share of the debt. And even though the laws are there to turn councils into the coalface for development, implementation drags; so instead of consulting communities directly about their needs, many councils hire consultants instead.

As the changes at local government level continue the minister may face legal action by unhappy ratepayers' associations fearing vast rates increases under new property rates legislation, which annuls 131 different laws to standardise what councils can demand.

But it would not be the first time the minister would have to deal with powerful interests. The amakhosi who demanded a constitutional amendment to enshrine their powers were eventually persuaded to accept what government touts as a democratic role in the new South Africa. After years of consultation Mufamadi finally steered through Parliament the Traditional Leadership and Governance Framework Act.

Perhaps that's why since 1999 Mufamadi has been touted as a potential foreign affairs minister. His forte in diplomatic matters came to the fore as early as 1998 when he represented South Africa in the Southern African Development Community's peace-brokering efforts before and after South Africa's invasion of the Lesotho mountain kingdom.

In late 2002 Mufamadi was co-facilitating the Democratic Republic of Congo peace talks in Pretoria, and clinched the all-important settlement. In March 2004 he hosted a joint DRC-South Africa ministerial meeting to finalise a host of bilateral agreements, including investments, avoidance of double taxation and diplomatic consultations.

Born in Alexandra township near Johannesburg, Mufamadi grew up in Venda where he completed school while looking after his grandfather's cattle. His mother was arrested for selling home-brewed beer; the money had gone to pay his school fees.

According to African National Congress lore, Mufamadi was "conscientised" during the 1960s terrorism trial of his distant cousin, Samson Ndou, a trade unionist and ANC member.

Active in student politics at high school, Mufamadi started his "official political career" when he joined the ANC in 1977. But a year later he also became a founder member of the Azanian People's Organisation. By 1981, then a trade unionist for the General and Allied Workers' Union, he had also joined the South African Communist Party.

Wearing too many hats would describe Mufamadi's roles quite easily. From 1983 he was the publicity secretary of the United Democratic Front in the then Transvaal. He is also credited as being a key mover towards the formation of the Congress of South African Trade Unions.

He was arrested at least seven times, and served 14 days' house arrest in 1988.

Mufamadi participated in the talks at the Convention for a Democratic South Africa, and as a member of the National Peace Committee helped draft the National Peace Accord in September 1991.

It was in that year that he was given a two-year suspended sentence for kidnapping and assaulting a police officer who had been caught snooping around Cosatu offices. This conviction led to a few hassles around getting a US visa some years ago, but the US government in 2003 ordered a ten-year waiver – perhaps testimony to Mufamadi's diplomatic skills.

Date of birth: 28 February 1959

Mushwana, Mabedle Lawrence
Public Protector

Mabedle Lawrence Mushwana has had to deal with a flurry of politically-tinged complaints: a property deal involving the First Lady; the fundraising efforts of a former Western Cape premier whose donors included a property developer awaiting approval; the deputy president's complaint against the national director of public prosecutions for abuse of office in an investigation involving the deputy president. Mushwana's findings in the last case – that National Prosecutions Authority director Bulelani Ngcuka had treated the deputy president in an "unfair and improper" manner – and his complaint that Ngcuka had refused to cooperate with his investigation set off a war of words between Ngcuka and Mushwana.

The Democratic Alliance's Sheila Camerer has pointed out that politicians facing allegations of wrongdoing charges by the Scorpions tend to hot-foot it to the Public Protector's door, thus setting up a fight between the two institutions. The very public row that erupted in June 2004 between Ngcuka and Mushwana is the fall-out.

Mushwana had already cleared Deputy President Jacob Zuma of financial improprieties stemming from a failure to declare "interests and receipts" under the executive ethics code. The "interests and receipts" in question related to R1,2-million Zuma had received allegedly from his financial adviser Schabir Shaik, indicted for fraud and corruption. The truth could only be determined at Shaik's trial, Mushwana found, and the matter was sub judice.

In October 2003 Mushwana found that Zuma had declared all his financial interests related to companies and loans in the confidential section of the register. Parliament's ethics committee subsequently also ruled that Zuma had not contravened the members' register rules, accepting his explanation that funds he had received were interest-bearing loans excluded from compulsory declaration.

The Public Protector is a key anti-corruption institution which can "investigate any conduct in state affairs ... that is alleged or suspected to be improper or to result in any impropriety or prejudice", according to the Constitution. The Public Protector, appointed for a seven-year term, is one of several independent watchdog institutions established in Chapter 9 of the Constitution to "strengthen democracy".

The Public Protector can probe and make recommendations to government departments on any conduct which has prejudiced a citizen, including improper, dishonest acts, abuse of power and maladministration.

Although the office is most associated with the incumbent, there are over a hundred people working in all nine provinces. But resources are scarce, and backlogs have built up.

The Democratic Alliance has made much use of the Public Protector, even though it voted against Mushwana's appointment in late 2002 because of his links with the African National Congress.

But Mushwana, who was serving as deputy chairperson of the National Council of Provinces at the time – he replaced Bulelani Ngcuka, who had been appointed national director of public prosecutions – dismissed these objections. "Throughout my career, I occupied positions of partiality and impartiality, and in each of them I've excelled.

"Perceptions will depend on the product," he told the parliamentary interviewing panel. "If the results will suggest that I am biased, then people will have the right to think that I'm biased."

Born in 1948 in rural Limpopo, Mushwana started his legal career in 1972 as an interpreter in the Mhlala magistrate's court at Bushbuckridge – he now speaks ten of South Africa's 11 official languages. Three years later he was a public prosecutor there, and in 1977 he became a magistrate. He completed a BJuris degree at the University of South Africa, and an LLB at the University of Zululand, and was admitted to the Bar.

He was twice detained under state of emergency regulations. In 1992 he established his own firm of attorneys in Pretoria and Bushbuckridge.

From 1994 he served as an ANC MP in the Constitutional Assembly. He also served on the Audit Commission and the Judicial Service Commission. A member of the ANC's national executive committee, as recently as 2001 he was sent as part of a team to his home province to help resolve ANC grassroots problems.

As co-chairman of Parliament's ethics committee, Mushwana was involved in early 2002 in kick-starting the probe into Madikizela-Mandela's failure to declare an additional R50 000 monthly income in early 2002. In her bail application at her trial for fraud, she had declared this additional income. She was eventually found guilty of contravening the code of members' interests; she was reprimanded before her peers in the National Assembly and suffered a loss of salary for a month.

Thus being in prickly situations is nothing new for the Public Protector. In the property deal involving Zanele Mbeki, he found there had been no impropriety related to the 2001 purchase and resale of a Public Works-owned Port Elizabeth home by the First Lady. Her father-in-law, Govan Mbeki, had lived there under a lease from the state before his death.

Date of birth: 31 March 1948

Napier, Cardinal Wilfrid Fox

Catholic Archbishop of Durban

Cardinal Wilfrid Fox Napier OFM, Archbishop of Durban, not only brings African culture to the Vatican but is also known for his strong stands on issues affecting the marginalised, especially in the third world, and his promotion of social justice and peace.

Declared a cardinal by Pope John Paul II in February 2001, Napier is South Africa's first black cardinal and only the second South African to be elevated to this position.

Born in Matatiele and growing up on the family farm with his seven brothers and sisters in Swartberg, Eastern Cape (then Transkei), he experienced the injustices brought about by the apartheid regime. On completing his high school studies he followed his brother Peter to Ireland and was encouraged by the Franciscans who ministered in the area to pursue a vocation in the Irish province's novitiate in Killarney. He entered the novice house in Killarney in September 1960 and, defying custom, declined to take a new religious name.

He studied for a BA degree in Galway, Ireland, majoring in Latin and English, and was then sent to Belgium's Catholic University of Louvain, where he studied philosophy and theology, earning an MA.

In 1970 he returned to South Africa, was ordained as a priest, studied isiXhosa at the Lumko Institute, and was sent as parish priest to the rural areas of Lusikisiki and Tabankulu near Kokstad. He was appointed apostolic administrator of Kokstad in 1978, ordained bishop of that diocese in 1981, and appointed archbishop of Durban in May 1992.

During the political changes and unrest of the early 1990s, Napier became involved, along with other national and provincial church leaders, in mediation and negotiation work. He was present at the signing of the Peace Accord in September 1991.

He served as president of the Southern African Catholic Bishops' Conference from 1987-1994 and again in 1999. As president of the SACBC, he is known for condemning all forms of abuse, especially the abuse of power and sexual abuse. He calls on government to be serious about moral renewal; takes a pro-life, anti-abortion stance that puts him in the firing line during abortion debates, and describes South Africa's crime wave as a "low-intensity war against ordinary people".

He was involved in the preparation of the Special Assembly of the Synod in Africa, and serves as a member of the Special Council for Africa of the General Secretariat of the Synod of Bishops. He is also a consultant to the Pontifical Commission for the Cultural Heritage of the Church.

Date of birth: 8 March 1941

Ndebele, Joel Sibusiso
Premier, KwaZulu-Natal

For S'bu Ndebele, the premiership of KwaZulu-Natal has come five years later than expected. He made a bid for it after the 1999 general elections. Unfortunately for Ndebele, in that year his party, the African National Congress, only managed 39,7% of the vote, while the Inkatha Freedom Party secured 40,45%.

According to a story often recounted by both ANC and IFP leaders, Ndebele suggested to President Thabo Mbeki that he offer IFP leader Mangosuthu Buthelezi the position of deputy president in exchange for the premiership of KwaZulu-Natal, and Buthelezi turned the offer down.

Ndebele returned to the Transport portfolio he had been managing since 1994, and by all accounts continued doing a first-rate job of it, brokering piece between the warring taxi associations in the province. Following the death of his young son in a car crash during his first term as MEC, he began the first Arrive Alive campaign, followed – in his second term – by the province's policy of zero tolerance for motorists breaking the speed limit.

A product of KwaZulu-Natal schools – he studied library science at the University of Zululand in the early 1970s – he studied international and African politics through Unisa while serving ten years on Robben Island in connection with his ANC activities.

When apartheid ended and ANC exiles returned, he was overshadowed by other luminaries from the province: leaders like Harry Gwala, Jacob Zuma and Jeff Radebe. Zuma, particularly, brokered peace with Inkatha in a province ravaged by political violence right through the 1980s to the early 1990s. Retaining him as ANC chair in the province was crucial.

Ndebele was named regional secretary of the ANC's Southern Natal office in 1990, and was considered one of the emerging young leaders of the province. So when Zuma took up the Economic Affairs and Tourism portfolio, his protégé, Zweli Mkhize, took up Health, and Ndebele was given the Transport portfolio.

When Zuma moved onto the national stage in 1998, Ndebele beat Mkhize for the chair of the ANC's provincial structures, putting himself in position to lead the province if the ANC won KwaZulu-Natal in 1999. However the ANC lost, by less than one percentage point.

Ndebele clearly never gave up on his dream to take over the province. When floor-crossing legislation came into effect towards the end of 2002, Ndebele managed to coax several members of the opposition, including the chief whip of the Democratic Party, over to the ANC. After the 2004 elections, with the IFP's fortunes in a steady decline and ANC on its way up, he was sworn into office.

He has plenty to deal with as premier. Besides working with the IFP, key challenges he will be grappling with immediately are attracting investment and making sure anti-retrovirals get to those who need them.

A cooperative arrangement with the IFP will ensure that departments under the ANC's control will be able to access Inkatha strongholds which mostly lie in the predominantly rural northern KwaZulu.

The closing of several factories including textile plants, meat processing units and leather plants in the Midlands and in coastal Durban has left several hundred people unemployed. Ndebele will have to compete with neighbouring Gauteng to offer attractive packages to encourage entrepreneurs to invest in KwaZulu-Natal.

With the highest HIV/Aids infection rate in the country – an estimated three in ten adults – the province is in great need of anti-retrovirals. According to estimates, three babies die of Aids each day in the province, which is expected to be home to at least half a million Aids orphans in another five years. So the need is for more than anti-retrovirals; the provincial government will have to be sure there is a strong social support system in place to take care of the orphans and households who have lost their income earners to the disease.

Date of birth: 17 October 1948

Ndungane, Njongonkulu Winston Hugh
Anglican Archbishop of Cape Town

Njongonkulu Ndungane has followed the outspoken tradition of his predecessor, Desmond Tutu, taking the government and his co-religionists to task on a range of issues and making it clear that his sympathies lie with the poor.

His tendency to criticise where he believes it is most needed has sometimes alienated him from his former comrades and friends, but he sees his position as a way to make a difference. He may well be right; his comments are taken seriously.

Ndungane found himself in hot water early on during the pension crisis in the Eastern Cape, when the provincial government failed to pay pensions and the government had not yet stepped in.

He also criticised the government for its poor handling of the HIV/Aids pandemic. He was especially critical of the government's refusal to provide anti-retroviral drugs to pregnant women. In an astonishing demonstration for a cleric, he went for a public Aids test to show that there should be no stigma attached to the disease.

The archbishop got involved in the Zimbabwe crisis last year when President Robert Mugabe asked him to mediate between Zimbabwe and ex-colonial power Britain. However, the mediation did not get off the ground.

Ndungane has not shied away from the debate on homosexuality in the church, and has called for a deeper understanding of the sexuality of clergymen. He has encouraged dialogue to generate mutual understanding and bring people out of their "corners of conviction". The issue, he says, is threatening the unity of the Anglican Communion and is causing deep pain on both sides of the debate.

Ndungane firmly believes that poverty is one of the biggest enemies facing humanity today, and has consistently campaigned for the cancellation of unpayable debts owed by developing countries.

He was born in Kokstad, and matriculated at Lovedale High School in Alice. In 1960, while a student at the University of Cape Town, he was involved in anti-pass law demonstrations. His political activism did not go unnoticed and he was imprisoned for three years on Robben Island. It is here that he discovered his calling to the priesthood.

He was ordained a deacon in the Diocese of Cape Town, and was posted to his home town of Alice as an associate of the Federal Theological Seminary. He became an Anglican priest in 1974, was appointed bishop of Kimberley and Kuruman, and went on to study further at King's College in London, where he was made a Fellow in 1997, a year after his appointment as archbishop.

Date of birth: 2 April 1941

Netshitenzhe, Joel
CEO, GCIS

Joel Netshitenzhe is the chief executive officer of the Government Communication and Information System – in other words, the state's chief spin doctor.

It's a role he's been groomed for since 1987 when he became deputy head of the African National Congress's Department of Information and Publicity. Netshitenzhe was also the head of communication in former president Nelson Mandela's office between 1994 and 1998. He now runs the entire government communications machinery, and has smartened it up.

Even critics agree that information flows a lot more smoothly between state and public. He is the architect of a weekly Cabinet statement and biannual ministers' press briefings, and he tries (not always successfully) to make government departments more accountable and available for comment.

As a renowned technophile, Netshitenzhe has made sure that the Internet is used to communicate – not only with the media, but with communities, by starting over one hundred public information terminals. While GCIS does have its own branded news service, Netshitenzhe has shown no desire to start state newspapers.

An ANC brain often touted as presidential material, Netshitenzhe also holds down a key job in the Presidency. Since 2001 he has been the head of Policy Coordination and Advisory Services in President Thabo Mbeki's office. The job may sound ungainly but it is quite crucial, for it involves coordinating all policies and managing the Cabinet.

Cabinet now functions through a system of clusters, as opposed to individual ministries and departments, to create a system of "joined-up government".

The plan was originally hatched by United Kingdom Prime Minister Tony Blair's new labour strategists, and was imported by Mbeki, who is a great admirer of greater managerialism in government.

The jury's still out on the plan; ultimately its success can only be measured by delivery, and South Africa is still far from attaining world-class levels of development for a country of its composition and size. But there is far more synchronicity in Cabinet than there was in the first term.

Mild-mannered and open (not common qualities across Mbeki's administration), Netshitenzhe is a popular political figure. He left the country for exile in 1976, abandoning his studies at the University of Natal's medical school.

He trained in Angola, worked on Radio Freedom, and edited Mayibuye, an ANC journal. He was also known as Peter Mayibuye in exile.

Netshitenzhe has always held strategically important posts in the ANC. He was a member of its politico-military council and a member of the negotiating team and the Convention for a Democratic South Africa. To a media that is forever watching for presidential candidates, Netshitenzhe always has one answer when asked whether he will ever run for president: "It's not in my career path."

Date of birth: 21 December 1956

Ngcobo, Sandile
Justice, Constitutional Court

Sandile Ngcobo, described by legal observers as "very competent, thorough and careful, sober, solid, and sound", was appointed to the Constitutional Court after the death of Judge John Didcott; his closest rival for the post was Judge Edwin Cameron.

Son of a schoolteacher and a driver, Ngcobo, who grew up in Natal, had personal experience of the effects of apartheid's social engineering when his family was forced by group areas legislation to move home twice.

Soon after his graduation from the University of Zululand, Ngcobo was detained for a year. On his release he began to practise as an attorney. His experience in the following 15 years was richly varied: he worked for the Legal Resources Centre in Durban; received an LLM from Harvard; and worked as a clerk for the eminent African-American judge, Leon Higgenbotham, at the US Circuit Court of Appeals in Philadelphia. He then worked for a private law firm in Philadelphia, interrupting his practice for a year to direct a legal aid clinic at the University of Natal.

On his return to South Africa, he practised as an advocate in Durban. From early 1996 he served variously as a judge of the Cape High Court, a judge of the Labour Court, and Acting Judge President of the Labour Appeal Court. During 1994 he presided at a tribunal of the Independent Electoral Commission, and later served on the Amnesty Committee of the Truth and Reconciliation Commission.

Date of birth: 1 March 1953

Ngcuka, Bulelani Thandabantu

National Director of Public Prosecutions

"Asoze ndijike (I will not turn back)" promised Bulelani Thandabantu Ngcuka after months in the spotlight, bathed in the fallout from his investigation of the financial affairs of Deputy President Jacob Zuma.

Ngcuka's team was looking at Zuma's possibly improper links to a French company contracted to the controversial multi-billion-rand arms deal, as well as his relationship with his adviser, Schabir Shaik, who faces a fraud and corruption trial this year.

Ngcuka, however, is not likely to be part of the prosecution team; he tendered his resignation months before the trial was due to begin.

Until late 2003 Ngcuka, who was enormously popular with the public and the President, could do no wrong. But in August he dropped the investigation into Zuma, along with a bombshell: he said he had a prima facie case against the deputy president but not enough to succeed in court.

Understandably, Zuma complained to the Public Protector, alleging Ngcuka had abused his office, and an investigation was begun.

Ngcuka had already made enemies when he called in editors for behind-the-scenes briefings on other cases his staff had investigated but could not prosecute. Rumours were put round that Ngcuka had been an apartheid spy — and President Thabo Mbeki appointed Judge Joos Hefer to look into it.

The claims were not proved to the satisfaction of the judge, who wound up his commission by stating that Ngcuka "probably never" had been a spy.

Said the country's top prosecutor, bruised, but not defeated, "No-one is above the law, no matter how wealthy or powerful they might be. This is a sacred constitutional principle. It is precisely because the National Prosecuting Authority has upheld this principle that it has come under very serious and sustained attack ... I am here because I lead the organisation."

The suave, well-dressed prosecutions head is no stranger to hard times in the public eye, or ruffling political feathers: as witness successful prosecution of African National Congress heavyweights Winnie Madikizela-Mandela and Tony Yengeni for fraud, corruption and theft in 2003.

Ironically there had been many grumblings that Ngcuka was in too deep with the ruling party when he was appointed to head the newly formed National Prosecuting Authority in mid-1998.

He had strong, public ties with the ANC. His struggle credentials included detentions, exile and, when practising law inside the country, the defence of anti-apartheid activists. He represented the ANC at the Convention for a Democratic South Africa and in Parliament, as chief whip and later as deputy chairperson of the National Council of Provinces.

Described as "a talented parliamentarian" he played a key role in laying the groundwork to implement the new Constitution and some of its key watchdog bodies, the Public Protector and the Human Rights Commission.

Critics believed they had been proven right in December 1998 when Ngcuka told his staff to stop opposing bail for three ANC members who were appealing against a murder conviction. But a leader of the Pan Africanist Congress's armed wing, the Azanian People's Liberation Army, had admitted the killings. The "Eikenhof Three" case was Ngcuka's first test.

There have been many since, including the (non)-prosecution of Inkatha Freedom Party warlord Phillip Powell for gunrunning after he pointed out some arms caches. Ngcuka indicated his wish to prosecute, but Powell claimed the KwaZulu-Natal prosecution authorities had promised immunity; he later left the country.

Ngcuka's work in radically refocusing the NPA – prosecution policy is now laid down by the national office – cut the independence enjoyed by apartheid attorneys-general, and linked prosecutions to investigations and the collection of intelligence.

Ngcuka is hard-working. Convictions have increased, as have court hours. Conviction rates in the specially created commercial courts in Pretoria and Johannesburg stood at 96,2% and 93,54% respectively in the 2002/3 financial years. Even in ordinary courts, the rates of conviction have improved: in 2002 the average rate in the high courts stood at 82%, up from 77% the previous year, while regional courts' conviction rates increased from 66% to 74%, and those in district courts by one percent to 83% in the same period.

Persuasive, with a reputation of being able to mediate consensus amid disputes, he holds an important and powerful post. "[S]ubject to the Constitution and this Act, no organ of state and no member or employee of an organ of state nor any other person shall improperly interfere with, hinder or obstruct the prosecuting authority" states the NPA Act.

The NPA includes the Scorpions – branded for using "Hollywood-style tactics" when tempers flared in the Zuma affair – which have taken out several crime syndicates, high-profile fraudsters and the like.

The Human Rights Investigative Unit, which probes potential criminal prosecutions against those who refused to apply for amnesty or failed in their applications before the truth commission, in February 2004 made its first arrest: ex-security policman Gideon Nieuwoudt, who was refused amnesty for the murders of three Port Elizabeth activists in 1985 – the "Pebco Three".

The Asset Forfeiture Unit has fallen under the NPA umbrella since 2001. It has been repeatedly challenged – often successfully – in court; its explanation for these setbacks is that it has been pursuing "test cases".

It had however deposited R18-million in the Criminal Asset Recovery Fund by the 2002/3 financial year, ready for use by the criminal justice system, and says its focus now is increasing volumes. And this it has done: in the 2002/3 financial year there were 147 seizures, up from 86 the previous year. But the pressure has led to mistakes: in February 2004 it lost a R1,1-million case by failing to lodge court papers in time.

Hitting the headlines less often is the NPA's Sexual Offences and Community Affairs Unit, which aims to fast-track the prosecution of crimes against women and children, and is involved in training on domestic violence legislation and establishing "user-friendly" structures for survivors of rape and violence. It has helped establish four such Thuthuzela Care Centres countrywide, with plans for another two under way. And maintenance-defaulting dads are increasingly being brought to book with the appointment of 69 maintenance prosecutors and additional support staff.

The prosecuting authority which Ngcuka heads is based at the Griffiths and Victoria Mxenge Building in Pretoria – another part of Ngcuka's past staying with his present.

Between 1978 and 1981 he worked at Griffiths Mxenge's Durban law firm. A year after Mxenge's assassination by apartheid agents, Ngcuka was jailed for three years because he refused to give evidence against a fellow activist during the trial of Patrick Maqubela. Ngcuka left the country, working at the human rights section of the International Labour Organisation between 1985 and 1987, then returned to Cape Town.

In the heat of the Hefer controversy he said he'd considered calling it quits before his term expires in 2008, but he changed his mind and decided to get on with the job "without fear or favour". In June 2004, however, Public Protector Lawrence Mushwana found that Ngcuka had treated Zuma in an "unfair and improper" manner, and again it was thought he might resign. Instead, the combative Ngcuka responded somewhat intemperately, and insults flew between him and Mushwana as Parliament scheduled an inquiry into Mushwana's report. Finally, in late July, he submitted his resignation.

He is married to Phumzile Mlambo-Ngcuka, Minister of Minerals and Energy.

Date of birth: 2 May 1954

Ngwane, Trevor
Secretary, Anti-Privatisation Forum

Trevor Ngwane was a councillor representing Pimville in Soweto when the Johannesburg Metro came up with a plan, called Igoli 2002, which involved the privatisation (or "corporatisation") of a range of city services, from rubbish collection and parks to the provision of water. He wrote a piece opposing it, and was promptly suspended from the African National Congress.

In retrospect, it was probably not one of the ANC's wiser moves. Ngwane, who refused to recant in order to shorten his suspension, served out his term on the council as an independent and, with a few like-minded compatriots, largely radical left-wing trade unionists and ex-South African Communist Party and ANC members, founded the Anti-Privatisation Forum.

The forum acts as an umbrella for 16 smaller organisations, including the Soweto Electricity Crisis Committee, which Ngwane leads, the Katlehong Concerned Residents' Forum, and the Working Class Coordinating Committee. It has links with the Education Rights Project and the Centre for Applied Legal Studies at Wits University. It is a political rather than a non-governmental organisation, serving as a socialist alternative to the ANC, and like the SECC it is confrontational.

Ngwane grew up in KwaZulu-Natal where both his parents were medical nurses. He was expelled from his Catholic high school for taking part in a school strike in 1976 – one of the repercussions of the June 16 Soweto uprising – although he claimed he was not particularly political.

He studied psychology and sociology at the University of Fort Hare from 1979-82 but was expelled for political activities, so moved to Soweto and finished his degree via Unisa, then earned an MA at the University of the Witwatersrand and began lecturing in the sociology department. One course which he designed was called "Class and Nationalism" – the history of the ANC, the Pan Africanist Congress, the South African Communist Party, and Afrikaner nationalism. He was a Marxist, he says, but "our orientation was towards the ANC: we supported the workers who wanted to fashion it as a weapon of struggle, and always argued against the two-stage theory. 'We unban the ANC!' was one of our slogans."

He joined the ANC in 1990. In 2004, the Forum and several other social movements chose not to contest the elections. Rather, at a meeting of the Social Movements Indaba, it was decided to join in a longer-term struggle to build an alternative to the ANC.

Date of birth: 16 August 1960

Nqakula, Charles

Minister of Safety and Security

There has been quite a lot of restructuring going on since Charles Nqakula took over the post in May 2002. In 2003 he closed down all 288 specialised police units and redeployed the detectives to police stations. Unfortunately this had little impact, and within months new specialised units sprang up. These include 27 for serious and violent crime, 24 for organised crime, 17 for commercial crime, one for serious economic offences, and 46 focusing on family violence, child protection and sexual offences.

Nqakula is less abrasive than his predecessor, Steve Tshwete, but he doesn't bring the same charisma to the ministry. He is unassuming, quiet and considered and, like his predecessor, has not yet broken the back of South Africa's criminal underworld – drug and firearm trafficking, car theft and hijacking, commercial crime and public service corruption – although the situation is apparently improving.

He leaves important political debates to national Police Commissioner Jackie Selebi. For example, during the parliamentary debate to amend Section 49 of the Criminal Procedure Act that effectively forbids police officers to use deadly force, it was Selebi who defended the right of policemen to use force while pursuing dangerous criminals.

Nqakula has also declined to comment on allegations of maladministration in the police Secretariat, the independent civilian office that is supposed to monitor the South African Police Service's abuses of power, among other things.

He is known to be very close to President Thabo Mbeki, and so his position in the national Cabinet may be less about performance and more about pedigree.

The heavy load on the SAPS has however been lifted with new technology for firearms control and border monitoring of stolen goods and illegal immigrants. These include an automated fingerprint identification system, an extensive criminal database, and an integrated database with the Department of Transport to stem car theft and hijackings.

Nqakula has prioritised restructuring and expansion, and in his second term plans to increase the police service by 31% to over 156 000 members by March 2007.

A recent survey by the Institute for Security Studies shows that major crimes, including hijacking, have stabilised or declined over the past two years. The ISS credits the SAPS but also the entry into the market of private tracking companies like Netstar and Business Against Crime, which works in partnership with the government to develop strategies and implementation.

Born in the Eastern Cape, Nqakula matriculated at Lovedale in Cradock and began his career working for the weekly Midland News. He had been working for the Daily Dispatch in East London for two years when he was banned because of his political reporting. The ban was revoked because he lived in a village in then Ciskei, but he was declared an illegal immigrant instead and forbidden to enter South Africa.

By the time in 1983 that he was elected publicity secretary for the United Democratic Front he had become an underground operative for the ANC, specialising in propaganda.

The following year he went into exile in Angola where he underwent military training for the ANC's armed wing Umkhonto we Sizwe. He received further training in the Soviet Union and East Germany, and in 1988 he was infiltrated back into South Africa as one of the commanders of Operation Vula, with a mission to build underground and military structures.

In 1991 he was elected as the deputy general secretary of the South African Communist Party, and then general secretary after the death of Chris Hani. Today he is the party's national chairperson.

In 1994 he was elected to the national executive committee of the ANC, and served as the deputy minister of home affairs until he was appointed to his current portfolio.

He is married to Nosiviwe Mapisa-Nqakula, current Minister of Home Affairs.

Date of birth: 13 September 1942

Ntopile, Kganyago

Deputy Minister, Public Works

This post was originally earmarked for the Inkatha Freedom Party's Musa Zondi, but when the IFP ordered Zondi to delay, President Thabo Mbeki said he would give it instead to someone "willing to work".

The IFP's loss is the United Democratic Movement's gain. Kganyago Ntopile is a UDM stalwart; and bringing UDM president Bantu Holomisa's party into government is perhaps the next best thing to bringing Holomisa back to the African National Congress fold.

Ntopile is, by all accounts, an industrious man — a skill he will need to employ if he is to survive his time alongside Public Works Minister Stella Sigcau.

Growing up in a rural area of Polokwane called Moletji, he was forced to leave school at 17 because his family couldn't afford to pay his fees. Undaunted, he decided to work for a year and save money to study; by day he worked as a gardener, and at night he washed dishes.

It worked. He completed the equivalent of grades nine and ten simultaneously while studying carpentry; he bartered his woodworking skills for a year back in school to complete his matric. After matriculating he did a teaching course, and obtained a BA from Unisa and a BEd degree from the University of the North.

While working for the Department of Education as the head of psychological services for Limpopo province in 1977, he was granted a scholarship to study at the University of Delaware in the US. Two years later he returned with an MA in psychology.

A founder member of the United Democratic Movement, he had a brief three-month stint this year in the Limpopo legislature as leader of the official opposition before he was appointed Deputy Minister of Public Works.

Asked how he feels about working in the ANC-led government, Kganyago replies, "I definitely have a different approach in dealing with issues. [But] ultimately [government is] working for the nation and our aim should be to deliver." The good news is that Ntopile has a secret weapon should he encounter any problems — he is a member of the South African Society for Clinical Hypnosis.

Date of birth: 10 December 1940

Nyanda, Siphiwe

Chief, South African National Defence Force

General Siphiwe Nyanda became the first black leader of the South African National Defence Force in 1998. A former liberation army leader, Nyanda took over from General Georg Meiring, who resigned over his links with a discredited report alleging a coup plot against former President Nelson Mandela.

The promotion of Nyanda, who was a lieutenant-general at the time, was seen as a major step towards integrating senior black officers into the ranks of the country's armed forces.

Nyanda took over at a time when the army, inherited from the old regime and still dominated by whites in the upper ranks, was under political pressure to reflect the democratic order in South Africa. He oversaw the integration into the South African army of almost 30 000 soldiers who fought in the armed struggle against apartheid – and this transformation has not been without controversy.

In 2003, an organisation called the Former Black South African Defence Force Members' Forum, which represents black soldiers who joined the defence force before 1994 and who served alongside whites during the apartheid era, claimed that their white colleagues have apparently been forgiven for their role in oppression, while the black foot soldiers of the apartheid regime are still seen as "collaborators".

Nyanda's tenure has been a relatively smooth one, but he has also encountered some obstacles along the way. In 2003, Nyanda angrily objected to a proposal to restructure the Department of Defence.

The plan was for Defence Minister Mosiuoa Lekota to strip Nyanda of some of his powers in favour of Director-General January Masilela, who heads the Secretariat, the civilian section of the defence department.

Masilela made the proposals in July 2003 and Lekota endorsed them in the same month – despite Nyanda's protest that the proposals were "untenable and unlawful". Among elements of the plan is the transfer of a number of key defence force divisions from Nyanda's command to the Secretariat. These include human resource management, military logistics, command and management information, and military legal services.

The move was the first major step by Masilela, formerly Mpumalanga minister for agriculture, since his appointment in 1999, to ensure tighter civilian control of the military, which Nyanda heads.

Nyanda served as chief of staff of the African National Congress's military wing, Umkhonto we Sizwe, from 1992. After the election of the ANC to government he became chief of staff of the SANDF in 1994, and deputy chief of the SANDF in 1997.

Schooled in Soweto and expelled from the University of Zululand for his political activities, Nyanda became active in the ANC underground in the 1970s.

He rose through the ranks of Umkhonto we Sizwe during the 1970s and 1980s, receiving military training in the former East Germany and Soviet Union, and was active in Operation Vula, the ANC's plan to beef up structures inside the country in the late 1980s and early 1990s.

Date of birth: 22 May 1950

Oosthuizen, Gert

Deputy Minister, Sport and Recreation

The new position of Deputy Minister of Sport and Recreation (previously the minister had no deputy) has already given the government some headaches. The president's first choice, Vincent Ngema of the Inkatha Freedom Party, did not take up the post as the IFP was holding an urgent caucus on ministerial appointments at the time of the swearing-in.

His replacement is Gert Oosthuizen, a former National Party MP for Pretoria who quit the New National Party in 2000 when it linked up with the Democratic Alliance. He joined the African National Congress in 2001.

Oosthuizen was born in the Afrikanerweerstandsbeweging stronghold of Ventersdorp, and played prop for Western Transvaal in the Craven Week schools rugby tournament. He holds a BA and BA Honours from Rand Afrikaans University, and was a captain in the South African Air Force in the early 1980s. According to a report in Beeld in May 2004, he is "very proud to be an Afrikaner in the ANC".

Date of birth: 10 May 1957

O'Regan, Catherine (Kate)

Justice, Constitutional Court

A former academic lawyer with a wide range of interests, Kate O'Regan, a member of the original Constitutional Court, is at once its youngest (she was 37 at the time of her appointment) and one of its most imaginative and innovative judges.

O'Regan grew up in Cape Town where she obtained an LLB degree cum laude from the University of Cape Town in 1980. She went on to study at the University of Sydney where she earned an LLM degree with first class honours in 1981. In 1988 she received her PhD from the London School of Economics with a thesis on interdicts restraining strike action.

From 1982 to 1985 she worked for a firm of attorneys in Johannesburg specialising in labour law and land rights. During this time she did extensive work for the emerging trade union movement, bringing cases of unfair labour practice before the Industrial Court. Through her involvement in Actstop (an organisation opposing the Group Areas Act), the Transvaal Rural Action Committee (which opposed forced removals) and the Black Sash she also did a considerable amount of work for both rural and urban communities that were either under threat of forced removal or faced eviction.

In mid-1988 she returned to UCT as a senior researcher in the Labour Unit. In 1992 she was promoted to associate professor. During her years at UCT she taught a wide range of courses including civil procedure, evidence and labour law. She also introduced courses on gender and the law and race and gender and the law. She was a founder member of the Institute of Development Law and the Law, Race and Gender Research Project, edited the Arbitration Digest, and mediated labour disputes.

From 1991 to 1995 she was a trustee of the Legal Resources Centre, a non-profit public interest law centre. She was one of the authors of *A Charter for Social Justice: A contribution to the South African Bill of Rights Debate*, which was published in December 1992.

O'Regan says she believes the function of judges of the Constitutional Court is to help bring to fruition the values that underlie the Constitution rather than to be a body that should be seen as being in conflict with the legislature. Conscious of the need for judges to be sensitive to the concerns and anxieties that cause people to bring matters before the Constitutional Court, she believes the members of the court require "a particular humanity" to deal with these concerns.

Date of birth: 17 September 1957

Padayachee, Radhakrishna

Deputy Minister of Communications

Radhakrishna "Ray" Padayachee is the first Deputy Minister of Communications, appointed after the 2004 elections Cabinet reshuffle.

Like his minister, Padayachee has a background in the education sector, serving as the development director of the Community Education Development Trust and as a consultant in the Ministry of Education under Sibusiso Bengu in the mid-1990s. He has also worked as a research chemist for a major multi-national oil company, and has been a microbiologist. He holds a BSc from the University of Durban-

Westville in chemistry and microbiology, and an MSc in agricultural economics from the University of London.

Before being appointed to the position of deputy minister, Padayachee undertook consultancy work as a "development specialist" and economic and business development consultant and advisor to small and medium micro enterprises.

Date of birth: 1 May 1950

Pahad, Aziz

Deputy Minister, Foreign Affairs

The "permanent deputy" is how the Sunday Times characterised Aziz Pahad, the Deputy Minister of Foreign Affairs, early in 2004, when he was appointed to the same position for a third term.

Pahad seems quite happy as deputy – he exhibits no ambition for the top job. It's probably realistic of him: for the foreseeable future, South Africa will have a black African foreign minister. His comfort in office also comes from the fact that he is close to power. While many speculate about who is in President Thabo Mbeki's inner circle, there is no doubt that Aziz and brother Essop occupy the innermost sanctum.

Both studied with Mbeki at Sussex University in the United Kingdom. Pahad went into exile after successive banning orders slapped on him in the late 1950s. He worked with the African National Congress in exile, spending most of his political energy building the anti-apartheid movement. He returned to South Africa in 1990 and was made head of the international affairs 'department, a post which paved his way into Foreign Affairs. He was also part of the Transitional Executive Council's foreign affairs negotiating team.

Pahad is a strategic brain at Foreign Affairs and he plays a wide-ranging role, most notably in the Middle East. He is usually deployed to the tough crises: he's been involved in negotiations in Zimbabwe; on Palestine; and on efforts to prevent a war in Iraq in 2003, among many others.

With a charm deficit in the high ministry office, Pahad does a more than adequate make-up as he is both personable and easy to debate with. He is popular with the staff of the Department of Foreign Affairs. When he is not doing the diplomatic shuttle-work, he does a mean shuffle on the dance floor. Pahad cites music, watching sport and reading as his favourite hobbies.

Date of birth: 25 December 1940

Pahad, Essop

Minister in the Office of the Presidency

When Pahad was first appointed to his current post there were worried murmurs that he was effectively a prime minister because of his status as presidential confidant.

Pahad has been a close friend and political ally of President Thabo Mbeki at least since the two were in exile. Pahad also served as a deputy minister in Mbeki's office when Mbeki was deputy president in South Africa's first post-apartheid government. First appointed as Minister in the Presidency in 1999, Pahad has been re-appointed to his post.

But rather than emerging as a prime minister, Pahad has seemingly been fighting the president's ideological battles in the African National Congress; with the organisation's allies, the Congress of South African Trade Unions and the South African Communist Party; and wider afield. For example, when the United Nations Development Programme issued a report calling on the government to review its economic policies because they were failing the poor, Pahad led government's defence of its development programmes, mainly by attacking some of the UNDP's researchers as "doctrinaire". He also fronted for the government when Cosatu and the SACP vociferously opposed its relatively conservative economic and social development policies.

Although Pahad had grounds for many of his remarks, often his lack of tact meant his comments were characterised as those of a henchman, when in fact he has a sharp intellect and a good mind for strategy and tactics. It is these talents which make it wrong to assume that Pahad's influence in the ANC derives solely from his relationship with the president. He was formerly a member of the SACP central executive committee, the ANC's political and military council, and its national executive committee.

As Minister in the Office of the Presidency, Pahad is responsible for the Office of the Rights of Children, Office on the Status of Disabled People, Office on the Status of Women, the National Youth Commission, and the Government Communication and Information System. He has received mixed reviews from interested groups on the performance of these offices.

Date of birth: 21 June 1939

Pandor, Naledi

Minister of Education

Naledi Pandor brings with her a struggle pedigree and education credentials that make her a welcome incumbent as the new Minister of Education. Indeed, given that she was rumoured to be in the running for the post back in 1999, it would seem her appointment is somewhat overdue.

Pandor is the granddaughter of the famed ZK Matthews, the first African to register at, and gain a degree from, a university in South Africa. Her father, Joe Matthews, was also a struggle stalwart (both he and his father were among the 156 on trial for treason in 1956), and a life of exile from 1961 until 1984 resulted in a decidedly international flavour to her education. Spending her formative years in Lesotho and England, she matriculated from Gaborone Secondary School in Botswana in 1972.

Similarly, her higher education credentials include a certificate in education from the University of Botswana and Swaziland in 1977, and a diploma in education and an MA degree from the University of London in 1978. She concluded her formal education with a masters in general linguistics from Stellenbosch University in 1997, while she was still serving as a member of Parliament (to which she was elected in 1994).

Pandor's involvement in education spans a full two decades, beginning with her work in the former homeland of Bophuthatswana in 1984 where she lectured in English and education at the Taung College of Education, as well as teaching English at Ipelegeng night school. At tertiary level, she has lectured at the University of Botswana and the University of Cape Town, and was appointed as the second chancellor of Cape Technikon in 2000.

Outside education, Pandor has amassed impressive experience in positions of authority, including deputy chief whip of the ANC in the National Assembly from 1995 to 1998. During this time she served on several portfolio committees, most notably as the convenor of the sub-committee on higher education.

Pandor went on to become deputy chairperson of the National Council of Provinces in 1998. She moves to her new portfolio from her most recent position as chairperson of the NCOP, which she has held since June 1999.

Known as a leader who is both level-headed and authoritative, Pandor must now give direction to a vital sector of society that is not exactly in crisis, but neither is it thriving. Her appointment coincided with major student protests over financial aid at the University of the Witwatersrand and the newly formed University of the North West, and she has set about putting out this particular fire with some high-level interventions and promises to review the efficacy of the current National Student Financial Aid Scheme (formerly known as the Tertiary Education Fund of South Africa, of which she was formerly chairperson).

Other education issues Pandor has identified as pressing include that of school fees, which urgently needs to be addressed to ensure access to education for all; the arena of teacher development and recruiting new teachers; and forging a meaningful partnership with the Department of Labour to ensure that education amounts to more than a place in the unemployment lines after leaving school.

Pandor describes all issues to do with education across the nation as her problem, indicating that she will not shy away from giving provincial education authorities some additional push if they are not performing.

Date of birth: 7 December 1953

Peters, Elizabeth Dipuo

Premier, Northern Cape

Dipuo Peters, former MEC for health in the Northern Cape, was one of the president's surprises when he announced his new slate of premiers. She is a senior player in African National Congress circles, and this probably won her the premiership over her main rival, Tina Joemat-Pettersson, the successful education MEC.

Peters has close ties to Mbeki and has shown loyalty to the president. She was also the only provincial minister in the province on the ANC's national executive committee.

Peters is reputed to be a hardliner who endorsed the government's policy of refusing to provide anti-retroviral drugs in public hospitals and clinics. In 2002 she lambasted health officials at Kimberley Hospital for giving the anti-retroviral AZT to a raped baby. She allegedly phoned the CEO of the hospital in question, Deon Madyo, and demanded to know why the drug had been provided, and whether provision of anti-retrovirals had been widespread.

The hospital subsequently released a circular reminding doctors that they were barred from administering anti-retrovirals to rape victims.

She later explained her actions by saying that her intervention was "in accordance with the national policy".

But overall, and aside from her hostility to the provision of anti-retroviral treatment to people with HIV, she has a good record of service delivery under trying circumstances, and her compliance with government policy has not hurt her stature inside the ANC.

Peters comes from a social worker's background and has a long history of advocacy of women's rights. She was an MP from 1994 to 1997, handling the ANC's Northern Cape and ANC membership register. From 1997 to 1999 she was the ANC chief whip in the Northern Cape provincial legislature.

Her political consciousness began to grow after she joined a branch of Young Christian Students and began to participate in other youth formations in the church and community. She was also a member of the Galeshewe Youth Congress, an affiliate of the United Democratic Front.

She attended the University of the North and obtained her BA in social work in 1987. In 1987 she worked as a volunteer regional organiser for the South African Domestic Workers Union; among her tasks was recruiting, organising, educating and counselling domestic workers in the Northern Cape.

Between 1987 and 1990 she was head of the women's department at the South African Youth Congress. In 1990 she joined the African National Congress Youth League, as the national secretary for women's affairs.

Peters was not the choice of the ANC in the Northern Cape as a candidate to replace Manne Dipico; John Block was their pick. Up to the end of last year, Peters was a distant second to the popular MEC, who seemed a natural choice for the premiership. Block then headed the ANC's candidates list for next year's elections. But he disgraced himself when he used government resources to fund his personal travels. He has since resigned from all public posts.

The Block corruption scandal and the resulting Auditor-General's report revealed shocking irregularities in the granting of tenders. Thus tackling widespread allegations of corruption in the provincial government and facing down a possible rebellion by factions in the provincial ANC will be among the biggest immediate challenges facing the new premier.

The corruption allegations are perhaps unexpected, since the province has long had a reputation as being one of the best run in the country.

The ability of Peters to tackle the allegations of corruption in the provincial government may be hindered by local political considerations.

Before his resignation Block had great support, especially around Upington. Peters, as the new premier, now has to find a way to maintain unity in the ANC, which is threatening to split into a number of race- and personality-based factions.

Date of birth: 13 May 1960

Radebe, Jeff
Minister of Transport

The new Minister of Transport is known among the residents of informal settlements as "Mr Privatisation" because of his drive during his term as minister of public enterprises to privatise state assets. Once regarded as a champion of the poor, he was later lambasted as a sell-out by leftists in the tripartite alliance when, in 2000, he announced his intention to restructure South Africa's major state-owned assets – the electricity utility Eskom, Transnet (which operates the railways, ports and South African Airways), and telecommunications provider Telkom.

Most recently, Radebe has become the arch-enemy of the South African Transport and Allied Workers Union (Satawu) over the concessioning of Durban's port to alleviate problems with traffic in the harbour. The port concessioning has been put on hold because of union-government clashes; by mid-2004 a committee to sort out the problems had not met since late 2003. Telkom has been partially listed, and the privatisation of Transnet and Eskom is also set to go ahead this year.

Radebe is regarded as an astute strategist. On Robben Island during the 1980s he was head of the African National Congress's political education department. He grew up in KwaMashu in Durban, and his first foray into politics was within the black consciousness movement. He cut his teeth helping to form youth organisations before going into exile, where he served the ANC in several areas, including the movement's information and international departments.

The South African press declared him dead after the South African Defence Force's raids into Matola in Mozambique between 1980 and 1981. In fact he was in East Germany at the time, studying for an MA in international law from Leipzig University to add to the BJuris with which he had graduated from the University of Zululand. After he returned to South Africa in the early 1980s he was an active leader in the National Association of Democratic Lawyers.

Radebe was arrested in 1986 and sentenced to ten years for terrorism and other offences. The sentence was reduced to six on appeal. He was released in June 1990. After his release he was elected ANC Southern Natal deputy chairman, and later chairman. He also played a crucial role in the KwaZulu-Natal peace talks in 1994.

Despite his talent for pulling together interests from across the political spectrum, in 2002 Radebe's commitment to privatisation led to his being voted off the central committee of the South African Communist Party (along with Minister in the Presidency Essop Pahad).

Some see his appointment as Minister of Transport as a demotion, though it should probably be viewed as a promotion – this ministry faces some major restructuring challenges in the next few years. For this reason Mbeki's decision to appoint him is a smart strategic move to use Radebe's technocratic dexterity to put this house in order.

Radebe will have to work closely with new public enterprises minister Alec Erwin because the transport and public enterprises ministries have to evolve a coordinated strategy for rail, air, marine and road-based transport systems. Radebe's major challenge will be to implement the much-discussed reduction in the number of heavy-haul loads on the national roads. If these trucks disappear, rail networks will have to move goods around South Africa, but this can happen only if Spoornet improves its efficiency levels. The endlessly delayed taxi recapitalisation plan and the toughening of sentences for negligent drivers are some of the other crucial challenges facing Radebe in the next five years.

In 1997 Radebe married former beauty queen, now businesswomen and mining magnate, Bridgette Motsepe, making him and businessman Cyril Ramaphosa brothers-in-law – Ramaphosa is married to Motsepe's sister.
Date of birth: 6 August 1953

Rasool, Ebrahim
Premier, Western Cape
The newly installed African National Congress premier in the Western Cape, Ebrahim Rasool, has promised the province the best five years ever. A tough job awaits him.

Housing is the Western Cape's Achilles heel, with a backlog of 350 000 homes. Unemployment, while the lowest in the country, is increasing. About 500 000 of the province's 4,5-million residents are jobless.

Also topping the agenda is a need to forge unity among residents, still sharply divided by race and economic class. The Western Cape is a region of shacks and multi-million-rand seaside homes, overcrowded township classrooms and quality schools, ill-paid restaurant workers and diners-out with large disposable incomes.

Keenly aware of these challenges, Rasool has pledged to make the province "a home for all". His sincerity cannot be disputed.

With luck he may not only be the first ANC premier in the province, but the first to serve a full five-year term. The first post-1994 premier, the then National Party's ex-apartheid police minister Hernus Kriel, resigned well before the June 1999 election, while his successor, Gerald Morkel, fell on his sword during the political machinations around the break-up of the Democratic Alliance towards the end of 2001. Under the ANC-New National Party cooperation pact, Morkel became Cape Town mayor, effectively swapping posts with Peter Marais, who took the premier's job.

Six months later, Marais resigned under a cloud, to be replaced by NNP national leader Marthinus van Schalkwyk, who has now gone into the national Cabinet.

Rasool has promised stable government, but to succeed he must bring his often-fractious party into line. So far he has managed to do so, withstanding several leadership challenges.

The son of a District Six vegetable hawker, Rasool taught for six months at a Cape Flats high school before his political activism led education authorities to ban him. Moving on to Call of Islam and then to the United Democratic Front, he was detained in the 1980s. He also rose steadily up the ranks of the provincial ANC, becoming treasurer and then chairperson.

He has been waiting in the wings for a long time. In the 1999 elections, the ANC scored more votes in the Western Cape than any other party (42%) but was kept from power by an NNP-Democratic Party opposition coalition, the forerunner of the Democratic Alliance.

Although it still fell short of an absolute majority in the April 2004 election, the 45,25% polled by the ANC in April 2004 leaves it by far the largest party in the province.

Rasool is not a charismatic politician but is known to stubbornly grind away at obstacles. He has a sharp analytical mind and a taste for debate and persuasion rather than strong-arm tactics.

Finance MEC for 30 months, he put in place the foundations of key policy initiatives like iKapa Elihlumayo — the "growing Cape" — which acknowledge not only the economic potential of the province but also its divisions and inequalities.

Under this strategy, R77-million has been allocated by the province for support to learners to stem the 50% drop-out rate between grades eight and ten, and for the establishment of small, medium and micro enterprises to fight joblessness. Increased spending on infrastructure in the province's 2004 budget is to be tied to a public works programme to drive job creation.

While Health MEC between 1994 and 1998, Rasool's hands-on approach helped reduce the Western Cape's extraordinarily high tuberculosis infection rates. For this, he received the Nelson Mandela Award for Health and Human Rights in 1998.

Described as decent and self-effacing, he is a devout Muslim. In a corner of his office hangs a salaah thobe (prayer robe) for Friday's compulsory communal noon prayers. In the heady activist days of the 1980s, the robe was adorned with beads in ANC colours.

In line with Islam's ban on alcohol, the wine-cellars at Leeuwenhof, his 300-year-old official residence, are to be emptied.

Date of birth: 15 July 1962

Sachs, Albert Louis (Albie)
Justice, Constitutional Court

Writer, activist, lawyer, academic and cultural fundi, Albie Sachs is the most flamboyant member of an otherwise fairly sober Constitutional Court, of which he is one of the original members. His judgements (often in dissent from the view of the majority of his colleagues, sometimes in what he calls "con-dissent" — a concurring view but with a different emphasis) are characterised by references to literature, history and sociology. Midwife to the court's new home on the site of the Johannesburg Fort, he helped adjudicate the competition for the design of the building, selected the art collection, and organised many of the events around the grand opening on Human Rights Day in 2004.

Johannesburg-born Sachs matriculated at the South African College School in Cape Town in 1950, and graduated from the University of Cape Town with a BA LLB. He was arrested for the first time at the age of 17 during the African National Congress's Defiance Campaign. He started his practice as an advocate in Cape Town in 1957, a time he dubbed the "golden age of the Cape Bar", working mainly in the field of civil rights. Twice detained without trial, he went into exile in England in 1966. He completed a PhD at the University of Sussex in 1971, and taught in the Law Faculty of the University of Southampton from 1970 to 1977. He was the first Nuffield fellow of socio-legal studies at Bedford College, London and Wolfson College, Cambridge.

In 1977 he became professor of law at the Eduardo Mondlane University in Maputo, Mozambique, holding the position through times he has described as "turbulent". In 1983 he was appointed director of research in the Mozambican Ministry of Justice where he worked on developing a new family law system. An apartheid-era car bomb attack in 1988 left him near death and minus one arm and one eye. After the attack he returned to England.

In 1978 Sachs became the founding director of the South Africa Constitution Studies Centre, based at the Institute of Commonwealth Studies at the University of London. In 1992 the Centre moved to the University of the Western Cape where he was made professor extraordinary. He was also appointed honorary professor at the University of Cape Town law faculty.

Sachs worked with Oliver Tambo in the legal department of the ANC and, later, describing himself as a "convert to constitutionalism", took an active part in the negotiations for a new Constitution as a member of the ANC's constitutional committee and the national executive committee.

Sachs sees his long involvement with the ANC as an advantage, believing that "if you are going to have somebody who is going to act as a brake on Parliament, a brake on the executive, it is better to have people, at least some of them judges, who know the mechanisms and the working and the thought processes to be able to be most effective in that respect". The test, he avers, is not "whether or not you are being politically active and involved; [it] is do you have the independence and the credibility as a thinker and as a person to work well".

He has written voluminously – books, papers and articles – and his published books include three autobiographical works: The Jail Diary of Albie Sachs, Stephanie On Trial and The Soft Vengeance of a Freedom Fighter.

Date of birth: 30 January 1935

Selebi, Jackie

National Commissioner of Police

When Jackie Selebi, South Africa's ambassador at the United Nations, was appointed as the first black national police commissioner, the question that came to the minds of many was: "What does a diplomat know about police work?"

His diplomatic skills were not in evidence the day before he started his official duties, when he was accused of having called a female police officer who hadn't recognised him a chimpanzee.

Selebi's version was that he went to a police station to see for himself how police treated members of the public. Instead of getting service he was sent from one officer to the next, so he asked why he was being "shunted around like a chimpanzee".

The experience was to form the basis of his managing the police service.

For those who held to Selebi's version, it made sense for the former chairperson of the United Nations Human Rights Commission – the first South African to be elected to the post.

For those who rather thought the policewoman's version closer to the truth, the memory of a younger Selebi – who had been a boxer – convinced them that here was a man never afraid to slug it out. After all, he has noted that "I have always had to prove myself everywhere I go".

By "everywhere", Selebi includes his tenure as South Africa's representative to the UNHRC in Geneva.

In 1998 Selebi, as the chairperson of a UN conference on the banning of anti-personnel land mines, managed to get diplomats to agree in three weeks about the shape of the eventual treaty – a record of sorts.

During his tenure at the UN, Selebi proposed setting up an ad hoc Committee on Nuclear Disarmament "to deliberate upon practical steps for systematic and progressive efforts to eliminate nuclear weapons as well as to identify if and when one or more such steps should be the subject of negotiations in the Conference."

He argued that "the time has come for the states trapped between [the] two extremes to mobilise their strength and to set an agenda for 1998 which would allow nuclear disarmament to be substantively considered while avoiding the security concerns which are so closely associated with nuclear disarmament issues."

A former schoolteacher in Soweto and at the Solomon Mahlangu Freedom College (Somafco) in Tanzania, in 1981 he said that the common theme running through the offices he has held – in the diplomatic corps, as the foreign affairs director-general (from 1998-2000) and leader of the ANC youth section (before the Youth League was relaunched after the unbanning of political organisations in 1990) has been about building organisations.

Selebi is credited with having reduced the number of police units from 503 to three to increase coordination. Existing units now handle commercial crime, organised crime and serious and violent crime.

According to the Institute for Security Studies, crime is decreasing as police salaries improve; strategic thinking has entered the police service; and conviction rates are on the increase.

Selebi speaks often of the "burden of command". In 2002 he was elected vice-president of Interpol, the international police network.

Date of birth: 7 March 1950

Shilowa, Mbhazima

Premier, Gauteng

The humble beginnings of Gauteng premier Mbhazima "Sam" Shilowa cast a special light on his steady political ascent. A former security guard and shop steward, he is the only premier to be appointed by President Thabo Mbeki in 2004 for a second term in office, and of the nation's wealthiest province at that. He has done well at the helm of the golden province, credited for its sound financial management and for creative initiatives like Blue IQ, which is successfully stimulating private sector investment in key growth areas like manufacturing and tourism.

Shilowa, the youngest of seven children, was born in 1958 in Olifantshoek, Limpopo. After matriculating at Akani High School he came to Johannesburg in 1979 in search of a job. He started off as a security guard, working in Germiston and Roodepoort and ending up at PSG Services in Johannesburg. He became a shop steward after joining the union movement in 1981.

His popularity with ordinary workers and astuteness as a negotiator contributed to his steady rise up the ranks of the Congress of South African Trade Unions. He began as deputy chairperson of Cosatu in Gauteng, and also held the positions of vice-president and then president of the Transport and General Workers Union. Shilowa was elected deputy general secretary of Cosatu in 1991, and general secretary in 1993. He held this position until 1999, when he was appointed Gauteng premier. He was elected to the African National Congress's national executive committee in 1997, and has been a member of the South African Communist Party's central committee since 1991.

Though he has been criticised for his extravagant tastes and love of cigars and fine wine – he is said to take his recreation activities seriously – he is undoubtedly blessed with "the common touch". He can talk to "paupers and princes alike", says one insider. He is well-liked both in business circles, in which he mixes with ease (his wife is leading multi-millionaire businesswoman Wendy Luhabe), and at grassroots level. His successes as premier have vindicated him against those opponents who called for his head in 1999 after news of bad-debt judgements against him hit the press. His extensive experience, as Cosatu secretary general, with the National Economic Development and Labour Council has given him a keen understanding of how business and government can cooperate in developing the country.

Shilowa is described as a strong leader with a clear sense of purpose. He governs with vision and has a solid grasp of the big picture. He is good at identifying strategic priorities for the province and gives his MECs lots of support, say insiders. He is also not afraid to surround himself with strong people, according to one source, and is a political steward rather than a micromanager. Shilowa is said to be passionate about promoting gender equity, and Gauteng has made impressive strides, with half his MECs women and with a bigger gender budget than any other province. He is said to make maximum use of provincial-level powers without stepping too heavily on the toes of either the local authorities or national government.

He did ruffle feathers at the top, however, when – prompted by pressure from the populace – he jumped ahead of national government's time frame for its anti-retroviral rollout. By drawing on Gauteng's own financial reserves and cooperating with Aids lobby groups, he expanded the province's mother-to-child prevention programmes and kickstarted its ARV treatment services for those in need. Now, like the Western Cape, Gauteng has forged ahead, sidestepping the delays experienced by national government in procuring ARVs.

Shilowa's responsiveness to the mood on the ground doesn't always endear him to everyone. He has been criticised for his handling of an unruly taxi industry, for example. Although the province embarked on careful, step-by-step measures to regulate the industry by introducing registration and licensing and limiting rank use for taxi drivers, Shilowa did a U-turn before elections and bowed to the industry's demands to operate freely. This is seen as a blot on an otherwise consistently good track record.

Despite a decline in the annual GDP growth, from 3,6% in 2002 to 1,9% in 2003 – due to the effect of bad weather on the agricultural sector and the stronger rand on the manufacturing sector – there is plenty to boast about. In the past few years the province has jacked up its public service delivery with good policies, sound strategies and more effective administration. Strides have been made in the areas of health care, schooling, social housing and social service delivery. Shilowa has echoed Mbeki's pledge to put poverty alleviation at the top of the political agenda for his second term in office.

Blue IQ, aimed at promoting business investment in key areas of the provincial economy, has enjoyed unprecedented success, particularly with regard to its urban regeneration and tourism projects. Since it was launched in 2000 Blue IQ has invested more than R350-million in Newtown and over R420-million in Constitution Hill. These investments are starting to pay off, with inner city property prices and rentals on the up.

Another ambitious Blue IQ project is the Gautrain Rapid Rail Link, dubbed the "Shilowa Express" because of Shilowa's enthusiastic backing for the hi-tech rail service between Johannesburg and Pretoria via Johannesburg International Airport. Expected to start in 2005, the project was delayed by the objections of residents – some 650 houses will be expropriated. The train is expected to alleviate traffic congestion, stem air pollution, save commuters time, and create jobs for 18 000 people over the next 20 years.

That said, the challenges ahead – poverty, joblessness, homelessness, HIV, unacceptable crime levels – are immense. Although Gauteng is by far the smallest province in the country – comprising only 1,4% of the land – it has the second-largest population (8,8-million) after KwaZulu-Natal (9,4-million). Gauteng is also home to the highest percentage of non-South African residents – around 2,4% of its entire population. The latest census figures showed an increase of 20% in Gauteng's population between 1996 and 2001.

So the stresses on provincial services are great and growing. People are streaming into the province in search of jobs and health care. The demand for Aids-related care threatens to swamp a system that is already overloaded, partly owing to high levels of trauma patients who are victims of car accidents and violence.

Although crime appears to be levelling off, showing little change over the past few years, violent crime is still frighteningly high and Gauteng is still regarded as a hijacker's paradise. Surveys show that crime levels are stabilising but the public perception is that crime is on the increase, particularly among Gauteng residents. According to an Institute for Security Studies survey, Gauteng residents have the lowest amount of confidence, compared with the rest of the population, in the police force.

Date of birth: 30 April 1958

Sigcau, Stella

Minister of Public Works

The Cabinet reshuffle after the 2004 elections left Sigcau in place, still occupying the top seat in Public Works. Popular opinion has it that her ten-year stint in the Cabinet – she was formerly minister of public enterprises – stems from the Pondo princess's royal lineage and her strong links to the former homeland of Transkei, where she was prime minister briefly in the 1980s.

Her performance as Minister of Public Works could be described as mediocre but for the competent management team the hands-off minister has put in place. As a result she has a new gem in her crown: the planned Expanded Public Works Programme. The EPWP has been hailed as the government's largest poverty alleviation and job-creation drive ever. The programme is expected to provide skills training opportunities for the unemployed and create more than a million jobs over five years, at a cost of R15-billion. The department initiated a repair and maintenance programme in 1999 to tackle its other function – the management of state property. To date it has spent R5,9-billion on 490 repair and maintenance projects. Sigcau's department has also gained R67-million through the sale of 203 state properties.

Sigcau's political past has been the subject of much speculation. Then General Bantu Holomisa led a bloodless coup in the 1980s to unseat Transkei chief minister Kaizer Matanzima and install Sigcau as prime minister, but accused her of corruption and unseated her, in turn, three months later. In 1997, he accused Sigcau of approaching South Africa's then foreign minister Pik Botha in 1989 to ask for help in deposing her successor. In 1990, the South African government was involved in a failed coup attempt against Holomisa.

Holomisa testified before the Truth and Reconciliation Commission that Sigcau had accepted a R50 000 bribe while Transkei prime minister. His allegations led to a series of fights between Holomisa and the ANC leadership, in which the general – then deputy minister of environmental affairs – lost his job. Sigcau emerged unscathed and later said that she had taken a R50 000 loan to pay school fees.

Sigcau's father was paramount chief Botha Sigcau, who became the first president of Transkei when it was declared "independent" in 1974. She received a teaching diploma from Lovedale Institute and a BA degree from the University of Fort Hare. After eight years as a teacher, Sigcau won the Lusikisiki seat in the 1968 elections. Over the next six years her portfolios included Posts and Telecommunications, Public Works, Education and the Interior.

Date of birth: 4 January 1937

Sisulu, Lindiwe Nonceba
Minister of Housing

The new Housing Minister has her work cut out for her. The former intelligence minister has been redeployed to a discipline in which she has no experience and where her director-general reportedly holds a great deal of power. Despite earlier successes, the provision of housing seems to have stalled; and it will be up to Sisulu to sort out the problems and get it moving again.

Housing is one of the most important ministries, but is considered by observers less politically influential than Intelligence, whose minister can influence policy in other departments and works closely with the president.

Some observers feel that it is not only housing that has hit a snag, but Sisulu's career as well. A member of what is arguably South Africa's best-loved family, the daughter of struggle icons Albertina and the late Walter Sisulu, Lindiwe Sisulu seemed set for stardom when she returned from exile. Detained in the 1970s under the Terrorism Act, she left the country in 1977, joined Umkhonto we Sizwe and worked underground for a decade while lecturing in history at the University of

Swaziland. She also earned an MA and then an MPhil from the University of York.

On her return to South Africa in 1990, she worked in the African National Congress's intelligence department and represented the ANC on the Transitional Executive Council's intelligence committee. It seemed a logical move, when she went to Parliament, to deploy her as chair of the parliamentary joint standing committee on intelligence.

She was named deputy minister of home affairs two years later – a job, it was generally agreed, that consisted largely of keeping an eye on the minister, Mangosuthu Buthelezi. In 2001 she returned to the area she knew best when she was named minister of intelligence. In that post, she tried to extend her influence over all of the country's intelligence apparatus, which exacerbated the traditional competition between the police and the intelligence community.

Intelligence came in for a hammering during the Zuma Affair in 2003. The Director of Public Prosecutions, Bulelani Ngcuka, conducted a bribery investigation against the deputy president, announced he had a prima facie case but couldn't win it in court, and soon afterwards was accused – by former transport minister Mac Maharaj and former ANC spook Mo Shaik – of having been an apartheid spy. Although Sisulu kept a strictly neutral stance throughout the hearings that followed, some among the security people were believed close to the Deputy President; and some of that mud might have splashed onto her.

It is possible, however, that the move from Intelligence to Housing is not a demotion but merely a manifestation of the presidential strategy to put people in unexpected positions where, often, they do very well; or to shift ministers around, moving them from "hard" portfolios to "soft" ones, then back to "hard" ministries.

In any case, Intelligence's loss should be Housing's gain. Certainly Housing needs a strong minister. Sisulu can be quite tough, say those who have worked with her, and makes good use of her charm and considerable intelligence.

Date of birth: 10 May 1954

Skweyiya, Thembile Lewis

Justice, Constitutional Court

One of the two new judges on Constitution Hill, Skweyiya began his term in February 2004, with Judge Johann van der Westhuizen, replacing the retired judges Laurence Ackermann and Richard Goldstone.

Born in Worcester in the Western Cape, Skweyiya matriculated from Healdtown Institution in the Eastern Cape and went on to receive a Bachelor of Social Science degree and an LLB from the University of Natal, where he was a member of the students representative council, after which he served his articles in an attorney's office and then went to the Bar.

A member of the Society of Advocates in Natal, he was later also admitted as an advocate of the High Court of Lesotho and as a senior counsel by the High Court of Namibia.

He conducted a varied practice both in Durban and in other divisions of the Supreme Court, with the bulk of his work between 1981 and 1989 involving cases associated with civil liberties and human rights. After he took silk in 1989 he was involved almost exclusively in commercial and civil work.

Skweyiya has been active in numerous civil society organisations including the Committee for Clemency for all political prisoners and banned and house arrested persons, and as legal adviser and member of the panel of advisers of the South African Students Organisation. He has been chairman of the Institute for Black Research, of which he is also a trustee, a member of the Free Mandela Committee, chairman of the Association for Rural Development, a trustee of the Black Lawyers Association Legal Education Centre, and a member of the editorial board of the South African Journal on Human Rights.

He has acted as a judge of the High Court of South Africa in the Natal and Eastern Cape Divisions of the Supreme Court, and took up a permanent appointment in 2001; he also served as an acting Constitutional Court justice.

Date of birth: 17 June 1939

Skweyiya, Zola

Minister of Social Development

Zola Skweyiya came in for a great deal of criticism as minister of public service and administration because some of his plans to rid the public service of the old – white – guard backfired badly when experienced staff took packages, while much of the dead wood clung on, blocking transformation.

But he has performed his new job with great aplomb, showing humanity sorely needed in the portfolio. A man who travels the length and breadth of the country speaking to ordinary people and assessing their needs, Skweyiya occupies a key position in fighting poverty.

The African National Congress had announced after its 2002 national congress that a comprehensive social welfare scheme was needed to deal with the endemic poverty in South Africa. By 2004, eight million South Africans were receiving some form of government grant. Skweyiya was the right minister in the right place.

Having seen the devastation, misery and poverty caused by the Aids pandemic, Skweyiya is said to have been one of the ministers within the Cabinet who pushed hard for a comprehensive anti-retroviral treatment plan. This was finally approved in 2003 and implemented in 2004 after initial resistance from government.

Skweyiya has had running battles with some of the non-governmental organisations that often accuse social development officials at local level of incompetence and a failure to care enough for people who seek help. The minister has often intervened in cases brought straight to him, but has also criticised some NGOs he describes as elitist.

After initial speculation that Skweyiya might be moved to the Ministry of Justice and Constitutional Development after the 2004 elections, President Thabo Mbeki decided to keep him in the same portfolio, but with added powers.

Skweyiya has been given the responsibility to set up a nationally run agency to administer grant payments. The National Social Security Agency will assume what has been a provincial responsibility, on a budget of R60-billion per annum. The government decided on the agency after its research showed that some provinces were battling to pay grants effectively to beneficiaries. This will allow provinces to focus on poverty alleviation programmes. The agency is set to take off in 2005, and will report to Skweyiya.

Skweyiya was born in Simonstown in a poverty-stricken community, and grew up in Port Elizabeth and Alice, where he went to Lovedale College. He participated in school boycotts against the introduction of Bantu education, and joined the ANC in 1956.

At Fort Hare University he met Govan Mbeki and mobilised fellow students to join Umkhonto we Sizwe. Now wanted by the police, Skweyiya left the country for Tanzania to work for the ANC. He later went to study at the University of Leipzig in the German Democratic Republic where he obtained a doctoral degree in law – an LLD – in 1978.

He worked for the ANC in different capacities, including as head of its legal and constitutional department, until 1990, when he returned home. Skweyiya worked for the ANC's Department of Legal and Constitutional Affairs before his appointment to the Ministry of Public Service in 1994.
Date of birth: 14 April 1942

Sonjica, Buyelwa Patience
Minister of Water Affairs and Forestry

The new Minister of Water Affairs and Forestry, appointed after the April 1994 elections, has a varied background that includes education, arts and culture, science and technology, and economics. An MP from 1994 to 1997, she has more recently been deputy minister of arts, culture, science and technology.

Born in the Eastern Cape, Buyelwa Patience Sonjica attended school in Port Elizabeth. She worked as a student nurse for a while in 1971/72 but presumably didn't take to it, because she moved on to train as a teacher. She obtained a BA from Vista University, majoring in English and isiXhosa, and went on to gain a BA Honours in isiXhosa from Rhodes University in Grahamstown.

Inspired by the Black Consciousness Movement, Sonjica became involved in student politics in 1976 and 1977 (the year Steve Biko was murdered by security police in the Eastern Cape), particularly in the Mass Democratic Movement, and the United Democratic Front. She joined the South African Democratic Teachers Union and was also active in the African National Congress and the ANC Women's League. She headed the department of arts of the ANC in the old Eastern Cape region, and was involved in both transformation of the arts and the development of ANC policy under Wally Serote, who then was national coordinator.

She was elected to Parliament in 1994 and served on the first parliamentary portfolio committee of arts and culture (1994 to 1997), and then on a variety of other portfolio committees, including finance, trade and industry, and in her new discipline, water affairs and forestry. She was ANC whip from 1994 to 1999 and appointed deputy minister in the then Department of Arts, Culture, Science and Technology in 2003. She held that post into the elections in April 2004.

As deputy minister in a portfolio ranging from street theatre to space technology, Sonjica was active in all spheres. She swung from meeting musicians in Newtown to formulating policies on the standardising of contracts, to discussing southern Africa's bid to host the massive Square Kilometre Array project.

Her first speech after being sworn in as deputy minister called on the South African Reference Group on women in science and technology to "project a bold vision of a world where valuable resources are no longer squandered on the instruments of death and destruction, but are creatively harnessed for economic development and opportunity... Let's dare to dream of creating a community where poverty and underdevelopment will not go unchallenged, where we will all be proactive in addressing the needs of our communities and our world."

She made it clear that science should serve humanity and be made accessible to ordinary citizens. The theme in almost all her speeches was upliftment.

She will be well suited, then, to her new role as Minister of Water Affairs and Forestry, as it is the portfolio where underdevelopment at a basic level is being addressed, by way of hands-on relief to poor and rural communities who lack water and sanitation. Rural women, especially, who have traditionally needed water most, and have been the managers of it, will benefit from the provision of clean, accessible water.

Date of birth: 23 March 1950

Stofile, Makhenkesi Arnold

Minister of Sport and Recreation

Makhenkesi Stofile's elevation to the Cabinet is proof that competence is not necessarily a prerequisite for higher honour – but popularity at grassroots level counts for a lot.

Under Stofile's stewardship the Eastern Cape – of which he was premier from January 1997 to April 2004 – lurched from administrative crisis to crisis. Mismanagement and corruption were rife in almost all areas within his provincial government. The African National Congress itself sent in a task team to sort out the mess in late 2002.

But Stofile is enormously popular among the rank and file in the ANC. So although it is clear he is not premier material, he has been given another chance – this time in a post where the problems might actually lend themselves to solution, unlike the apparently intractable mess in the Eastern Cape.

And on the plus side, the reverend – who has a master's in theology from the University of Fort Hare – has long experience as a sports administrator in rugby, cricket and netball from local to national level. Stofile was also a rugby coach at junior and club level for 20 years, so he might have some useful ideas on how to make the Springboks world-beaters again.

The Presbyterian cleric earned his political spurs while lecturing in theology at Fort Hare. He was general secretary of the United Democratic Front's Border region when he was sentenced to 11 years in prison for promoting the aims of the ANC, and a further year for possession of arms.

He was released in 1990 along with many other political prisoners, and resumed university lecturing until elected to Parliament in 1994. He was the ANC's chief whip and the party's treasurer-general until appointed to the premiership of the Eastern Cape.

In a sports-mad country such as South Africa, the position of sports minister is not quite the quiet sinecure it might be – few other countries even bother to have a specific ministry to deal with sport. A history of apartheid-era sports boycotts and post-apartheid wrangles over racism and quotas have made the job quite testing, as both Steve Tshwete and Ngconde Balfour found out.

Probably the biggest task Stofile will face as Sports Minister is coordinating the hosting of the 2010 Soccer World Cup. The tournament is the second-largest sporting event in the world after the Olympic Games, and attracts a huge amount of media attention.

To prevent a raft of unwelcome publicity, Stofile would be wise to turn his attention first to cleaning up soccer.

"Mr Buffet" Balfour steered clear of the problem. Tshwete made a stab at cleaning out those Augean stables when he appointed the Pickard commission in 1996. As a result of Judge Pickard's report, former South African Football Association boss Solomon "Stix" Morewa was forced out of the game, but little has been done to implement the judge's other recommendations. Meanwhile each season there are tales of match-fixing, incompetent match officials and other forms of corruption. These may go unreported by the local media, but international reporters will not shy away from exposing wrong-doings.

Stofile's record in the Eastern Cape does not augur well for much change on this front, however.

What will be different is the style of the Sports Minister, as Stofile is a no-nonsense politician. A blunderbuss has been replaced by a rapier, and with Balfour's experienced assistant, Graham Abrahams, to guide him, Stofile might yet surprise us all.

Date of birth: 27 December 1944

Surty, Enver

Deputy Minister of Education

Besides his many years as a student, Enver Surty may not have engaged much with the education system so far in his career, but his legal background and the role he played in the National Council of Provinces should stand him in good stead as the new Deputy Minister of Education.

Having matriculated from Lenasia High School in 1970, Surty went on to get his BA (Honours) in philosophy from University of Durban-Westville (1974); his BProc degree from Unisa in 1977; and finally his LLM degree in constitutional litigation from the University of the Western Cape in 1995.

Surty is an experienced legal practitioner, having practised as a human rights lawyer in his home town of Rustenburg in the North West Province from 1977 to 1994. During this time he acted on behalf of the Congress of South African Trade Unions' affiliates – especially the National Union of Mineworkers – against the apartheid regime, and also for the African National Congress after its unbanning.

Surty was also a key negotiator in the ANC team that helped draw up the 1996 Constitution and was influential in shaping the Bill of Rights.

Another plus he brings with him to the portfolio is the long working relationship he has with his new boss, newly appointed Minister of Education Naledi Pandor. Having joined the National Assembly in 1994, Surty was redeployed to the NCOP as the ANC's chief whip in 1999 until his most recent appointment as deputy minister, while Pandor was the NCOP's chairperson during the same period.

Surty does have one high-profile contribution in school management to his credit: he was a member of the progressive parent-teacher body at Zinniaville Secondary School in Rustenburg that defied apartheid policy from the 1980s onwards by admitting African learners.

His legal background and involvement in such school-based structures may see him take responsibility in his new portfolio for matters such as the functioning and powers of school governing bodies, a parent–teacher–learner structure that is supposed to lead schools in matters ranging from drawing up a school code of conduct to managing the budget. The role of school governing bodies in the new dispensation has suffered from various contradictory interpretations, with the government emphasising their autonomy in certain matters (such as making the school as financially self-sufficient as possible), but then undermining this autonomy when it comes to other issues (such as appointing teachers, and admissions criteria). Pandor has already noted that the current status and functioning of school governing bodies represents something of a misinterpretation of government policies and provisions, and it is likely that Surty's legal mind will be turned to ironing out these issues.

While Surty's obvious strength is legal matters, it remains to be seen how much influence he will exert towards improving conditions at schools. He himself has been on the "intolerable" side of rotten government facilities: while working in the parliamentary buildings in Cape Town in 2002, he and Pandor made much fuss about toilets not working for five months. Whether this extends to an empathetic drive to relieve the thousands of schools that don't even have toilets to complain about will be interesting to see.

Date of birth: 15 August 1953

Shabangu, Susan

Deputy Minister, Safety and Security

In her former post, as deputy minister of minerals and energy, Susan Shabangu is credited with a wide range of successes: encouraging mining companies to come up with a comprehensive Aids policy; promoting small-scale mining; devising nuclear energy strategies.

Nothing in her background would seem to have prepared her for the job: her life, before 1994, was centred on women's and trade union issues. She was assistant secretary for the Federation of South African Women in then Transvaal in 1980, and involved in the formation of the Release Mandela Campaign. In the mid-1980s, she became involved in the labour field as organiser and administrator for the Amalgamated Black Workers' Project. She was national women's issues coordinator for the Transport and General Workers Union, and a member of the national women's sub-committee for the Congress of South African Trade Unions. It was via

Cosatu that she went to Parliament in 1994, and two years later was made deputy minister.

Nothing in her official background would seem to prepare her for her new posting, either. However, based on her performance in her former post, one can expect her to take on the new job with enthusiasm – and to offer some innovative ways to deal with crime in South Africa.

Date of birth: 28 February 1956

Tshabalala-Msimang, Mantombazana
Minister of Health

Drugs have been at the centre of Tshabalala-Msimang's time in office: her implacable hostility to the provision of anti-retrovirals to people with HIV or Aids, even to curtail the transmission of the virus from mother to child; and her successful battle to lower the price of other drugs for the South African consumer.

The minister's reluctance to provide anti-Aids drugs in the public health sector, and her repeated statements that the drugs are toxic, have earned her many detractors. In a country where an estimated five million people are living with HIV, her promotion of "alternative therapies" to anti-AIDS drugs has been severely criticised; her "anti-Aids diet" of lemon, garlic and the African potato to boost the immune system has been repeatedly mocked.

Tshabalala-Msimang is still best remembered for her highly publicised spats with lobby groups like the Treatment Action Campaign, and her insistence that the country was "not ready" to provide ARVs. Her refusals to provide anti-Aids drugs in the public health sector dragged the government into a messy court battle with the TAC in 2002, where she lost a Constitutional Court case which forced the health sector to provide ARVs to HIV-positive pregnant women. And even though the government's policy on provision of ARVs in state hospitals for all who need them changed in late 2003, it was a change apparently forced through by Cabinet.

Yet ironically, some of the minister's more positive contributions to public health also revolve around drugs. Tshabalala-Msimang clashed with the Pharmaceutical Manufacturing Association in 2001 which challenged a proposed law allowing South Africa to import medicines from the cheapest source – perhaps India or Brazil – and so widen access. The drug firms withdrew from the case.

She has been a vocal supporter of initiatives to promote awareness amongst health professionals and the public on the use of generic drugs, in a bid to cut treatment costs. A transparent pricing system for medicines came into effect in mid-2004.

She was educated at Inanda Seminary in Durban and earned a BA degree at the University of Fort Hare before leaving the country. She earned a medical degree at the First Leningrad Medical Institute in the Soviet Union, a master's in public health from the University of Antwerp in Belgium, and a diploma in obstetrics and gynaecology at the University of Dar es Salaam before returning to South Africa when the African National Congress was unbanned.

In 1996, an African National Congress MP and chair of the parliamentary portfolio committee on health – with a good reputation among activists for her stance on Aids, women's health and primary health care – she was promoted to deputy minister of justice, and was named Health Minister in the 1999 Cabinet.

The minister has continued the legacy of her predecessor, the equally controversial Nkosazana Dlamini-Zuma, on several fronts. She has eased the entry of foreign medical professionals to work in public health facilities here, in a bid to improve service delivery, especially in rural areas. To encourage health practitioners to stay in South Africa, she entered into an agreement with the United Kingdom in October that would allow doctors and nurses to earn pounds and then return home.

But she has clashed with doctors on new legislation which requires doctors to apply for a "certificate of need" before opening practices. And she has enforced her predecessor's policy of requiring two years of community service for graduates in a range of medical fields.

She has also enforced controversial legislation banning smoking in public places.

As chair of the World Health Organisation's Regional Committee for Africa, she has advanced the country's position on continental health matters, for example malaria and childhood immunisation. And last year Tshabalala-Msimang introduced free health services for the disabled in South Africa.

She is married to ANC treasurer-general Mendi Msimang.

Date of birth: 9 October 1940

Tutu, Desmond Mpilo

The diminutive archbishop in his clerical garb, flashing his wicked, toothy grin, is almost as iconic a South African figure as his fellow Nobel Peace laureate, Nelson Mandela, who has said of him, "Sometimes strident, often tender and seldom without humour, Desmond Tutu will always be the voice of the voiceless."

Tutu has had a long history of being that voice. He cites as his most formative childhood experience the sight of Father Trevor Huddleston, the white, English-born clergyman whose name is synonymous with the Sophiatown in which he lived and worked, doffing his hat to Tutu's mother, a black domestic worker – an act that was unheard of during the depths of apartheid. The gesture sowed the seeds of compassion and humanity in the young Tutu.

Desmond Tutu was born in Klerksdorp in the former Transvaal in 1931. He initially followed in his father's footsteps by becoming a schoolteacher, but later attended St Peter's Theological College in Rosettenville, and was ordained as a priest in 1961.

He spent four years in the United Kingdom, from 1962 to 1966, to further his theological studies, and obtained a master's degree. On his return to South Africa Tutu taught theology at St Peter's Seminary in the Eastern Cape, and later in Lesotho at the University of Botswana, Lesotho and Swaziland. In 1972 he returned to England to work for the World Council of Churches. In 1975 he became the first black person to be appointed Anglican Dean of Johannesburg; he was also the first black person to become general secretary of the South African Council of Churches and, later, Anglican Archbishop of Cape Town.

Tutu's role in the struggle against apartheid and his reputation as a man of peace won him worldwide recognition, and in 1984 he was awarded the Nobel Peace Prize, an honour he shares with the late Chief Albert Luthuli and former presidents Nelson Mandela and FW de Klerk.

In his lecture on receiving the award, Tutu said: "Perhaps oppression dehumanises the oppressor as much as, if not more than, the oppressed. They need each other to become truly free, to become human. We can be human only in fellowship, in community, in koinonia, in peace."

His commitment to peace made him the natural head of the Truth and Reconciliation Commission, established after South Africa's transition to democracy. Ten years on he continues to work for world peace and is characteristically outspoken on issues ranging from South Africa's stance in relation to human rights abuses in Zimbabwe: "If we are seemingly indifferent to human rights violations happening in a neighbouring country, what is to stop us one day being indifferent to our own?"; to Israel's treatment of Palestinians, which he has described as a form of apartheid; and to the United States's "immoral war" with Iraq.

Unshakeable as he is in his moral convictions, he is a humane and tolerant man. Commenting on the Episcopal Church's ordination of a gay bishop he said he didn't know what "all the fuss" was about. "For us [the Anglican Church in South Africa] that doesn't make any difference, the sexual orientation."

His impeccable human rights record aside, Tutu has gained popularity for his warmth and his generous wit. His impish sense of humour and ability to laugh at himself were probably best displayed when he wore a T-shirt emblazoned with "Just call me Arch" at a garden party in Cape Town in the Eighties. Speaking after South Africa had won the right to host the 2010 World Cup, "The Arch", a member of the bid team, quipped, "To those members of FIFA, I hereby undertake to give you an air ticket to heaven. But don't use it immediately." And added, "I am very good at soccer ... from the safety of my couch."

Date of birth: 7 October 1931

Van der Merwe, Sue

Deputy Minister of Foreign Affairs

Her love of running will suit Sue van der Merwe's position as Deputy Foreign Affairs Minister very well.

Appointed in April 2004, Van der Merwe deputises with Aziz Pahad at a ministry becoming busier by the year. While her final job description was still being written at the time of publication, it is likely that she will bring a management hand to the department.

It sorely needs one, though the appointment of director-general Ayanda Ntsaluba last year has seen key posts filled after lengthy delays. Van der Merwe was an African National Congress MP and parliamentary counsellor to the President between 2000 and 2004.

Parliamentary counsellors serve as eyes and ears on matters in the legislature which need to be brought to the president's attention.

Van der Merwe became an MP in 1996; was a whip between 1999 and 2000; and served on several committees including finance, intelligence, environment and tourism.

She cut her political teeth in the Black Sash, where she worked as a coordinator between 1988 and 1991; she also worked at the Open Society Foundation and was a participant in the Mont Fleur scenario planning exercise between 1991 and 1993.

Date of birth: 29 May 1954

Van der Westhuizen, Johann Vincent

Justice, Constitutional Court

A new justice on the Hill, Johann van der Westhuizen has been a member of the Constitutional Court since February 2004, having been shortlisted on two previous occasions. Born in Windhoek, he went to school there and in Pretoria and graduated from the University of Pretoria after a glittering academic career, achieving his BA (law) and LLB (cum laude) with distinctions in all the prescribed courses. He went on to receive his LLD from UP, where he taught in the Department of Roman Law and Jurisprudence and was then appointed professor in the Department of Legal History, Comparative Law and Legal Philosophy in 1980, the youngest-ever professor and head of department at the university. He was responsible for the foundation and development of the university's Centre for Human Rights, which has gained wide national and international recognition and played a leading role in historical developments in South Africa and Africa. In 1999 he was appointed a judge of the High Court.

Van der Westhuizen contributed in a variety of ways to debate on the Bill of Rights, including organising a conference, co-editing a book that influenced the human rights and constitutional debate in the country, and participating in discussions on legal and constitutional issues with the then banned liberation movements.

As a member of the Independent Panel of Recognised Constitutional Experts advising the Constitutional Assembly and of the technical refinement team, he was intimately involved in drafting the Constitution; convened task groups at the Multi-Party Negotiating Process and the Transitional Executive Council; and coordinated the Equality Legislation Drafting Project of the Ministry of Justice and South African Human Rights Commission. He was also involved in human rights litigation, argued numerous censorship appeals, and acted as consultant and in-house advocate for the Legal Resources Centre and Lawyers for Human Rights.

Date of birth: 26 May 1952

Van Schalkwyk, Marthinus

Minister of Environmental Affairs and Tourism

The announcement that the leader of the New National Party would replace the energetic Valli Moosa as Minister of Environmental Affairs and Tourism in the new Cabinet was greeted with outrage and despondency from environmentalists. The appointment was regarded as a slap in the face, particularly at a time when progressive authorities in the field were advising that buy-in from a broader segment of society is essential for sustainable tourism growth and development.

Van Schalkwyk, disparagingly referred to in the media as "Kortbroek" (short pants), does not have the image to encourage broad-based public buy-in. Media caricatures of him in his new post feature an ageing white male in khaki shorts bashing through the bush with a rifle slung over his shoulder. Because of his ties to apartheid, his appointment appears to indicate that tourism and environment will remain the preserve of conservative, mainly white interests.

Turning 45 this year, Van Schalkwyk has represented the National Party and later the New National Party since he was a youngster. He was an MP for Randburg from 1990 to 1994, and leader of the NNP from September 1997 until he was appointed minister. It is widely accepted that his appointment was quid pro quo for his helping the African National Congress gain the Western Cape premiership. In the process, he succeeded in wiping the NNP off the political map – the party only won about 2% of the national vote in the elections.

Environmentalists are worried he is capable of selling off the country's precious natural resources. His track record in this respect is not good: evidence has arisen of various dubious land deals during his time as NNP premier of Western Cape. These include the scandal over a R400 000 bribe paid to the NNP by the developer of the Roodefontein golf course near Plettenberg Bay.

Official organisations such as South African Tourism and South African National Parks have put a brave face on his appointment. An optimistic interpretation was that he would encourage transformation among the mainly white, relatively conservative tourism operators, who had resisted overtures during Moosa's tenure.

Date of birth: 10 November 1959

Xingwana, Lulama

Deputy Minister, Minerals and Energy

An MP since 1994, the new deputy minister appears to have concentrated on rural development and the status of women. In 1985, the year she graduated from the University of the Witwatersrand, she went to work for Learn and Teach as a tutor, running classes for domestic workers – not only in the northern suburbs of Johannesburg but also in rural areas. She moved on two years later to the South African Council of Churches where she directed women's development programmes. Her background is shared between these two interests, and occasionally they have intersected: for example, when she chaired the Malibongwe Rural Development Project for women.

Her political involvement appears to have come via the Federation of South African Women, first, then the United Democratic Front and the African National Congress Women's League, and she has held a number of committee posts in Parliament, including the chair of the joint monitoring committee on the improvement of the quality of life and status of women. She has chaired the Southern African Development Community regional women's caucus since 2002.

Xingwana has also found time for post-graduate studies: diplomas in development and leadership and in rural development from the University of Zimbabwe, and a post-graduate diploma in economic principles from the University of London, where she's currently enrolled in an MSc programme in development finance.

Date of birth: 23 September 1955

Yacoob, Zakeria (Zak) Mohammed

Justice, Constitutional Court

Zak Yacoob is widely admired for his astuteness, his humanity and his formidable ability to absorb the details of documents that are read to him. As a result of his work as one of the architects of the Constitution, he is an acknowledged expert on some of its more technical aspects.

Yacoob was born in 1948 and became blind at the age of 16 months as a result of meningitis. He attended the Arthur Blaxall School for the Blind in Durban from 1956 to 1966, and studied for a BA degree at the University of Durban-Westville between 1967 and 1972.

He practised as an advocate in Durban for 25 years, representing and advising many victims of repressive security legislation. He was a member of the defence team that appeared in the lengthy Delmas Treason Trial of members of the United Democratic Front, and he represented the accused in the Operation Vula trial that involved high-ranking members of the African National Congress.

A political activist, Yacoob was a member of the underground structures of the ANC. He was also chairperson in 1980 of the Durban Committee of Ten, which aimed to alleviate the plight of pupils at schools, and a member of the executive of the Durban Detainees Support Committee; and he participated in the establishment of the UDF, serving as its interim publicity secretary and on its Natal executive. He was chairperson and a member of the executive of the Democratic Lawyers Association in Durban, a precursor of the National Association of Democratic Lawyers.

Yacoob played a material role in several structures that contributed to establishing systems for a democratic South Africa. During the multiparty negotiating process he was a member of the technical committee on fundamental rights. He was a member of the panel of independent experts of the Constitutional Assembly, and of a technical committee convened by the Department of Finance to advise on the legislation necessary to give effect to and implementation of the chapter of the Constitution concerned with finance. He served as a member of the Independent Electoral Commission that organised the country's first democratic elections, and advised local government bodies and assisted them in conceptualising, forming and constituting the South African Local Government Association.

He has also been an active member of the Natal Indian Blind and Deaf Society, and a member of the South African National Council for the Blind, of which he has been chairman since October 2001; and served two terms as a member of the Council of his alma mater (now the University of KwaZulu-Natal) of which he was chancellor from May 2001 to December 2003.

Date of birth: 3 March 1948

Zuma, Jacob

Deputy President

Allegations that South African Deputy President Jacob Zuma was involved in corruption in the country's multi-billion rand arms deal did little to detract from his popular support in the country or the African National Congress during the elections. Just as well, given that the Deputy President is a patron of South Africa's Moral Regeneration Movement.

Not only has Zuma shrugged off the allegations – made by the National Director of Public Prosecutions, Bulelani Ngcuka – he has also dodged the fall-out from a bungled attempt by his supporters to discredit Ngcuka, by alleging the national prosecutor was an apartheid spy. Despite South African President Thabo Mbeki making it clear he did not approve of the "apartheid spy" allegations that emanated from the Zuma camp, he re-appointed the Deputy President for a second term.

The re-appointment says much about Zuma's popularity, especially in KwaZulu-Natal, where the ANC has had to fight hard to narrowly secure the province from the Inkatha Freedom Party and its allies, and the strength of his support in the ANC. In any event, Zuma is not facing any formal charges and is unlikely to do so for the foreseeable future. No matter the conventional wisdom, the ANC and Mbeki are under no immediate political or popular pressure to deal with the allegations around Zuma. His continuation in the post of deputy president says nothing about his chances of succeeding Mbeki as president of the ANC and South Africa.

He has been a member of the ANC since the age of 16, and much of Zuma's support in the organisation comes from his time in its armed wing, Umkhonto we Sizwe, and as chief of its intelligence department. However, since his return to the country he has also courted key ANC allies, like the Congress of South African Trade Unions.

At the height of government's fight with Cosatu over the government's relatively conservative economic policies, and with the Aids lobby – because of Mbeki's controversial questioning of the link between HIV and the disease – Zuma was sent in to placate the ANC's allies. He brokered talks between the ANC, Cosatu and the South African Communist Party which patched up the Tripartite Alliance for a while, and as chairperson of the South African National Aids Council he attempted to protect the government from increasingly sharp criticism from Aids activists.

He had done this sort of trouble-shooting before. After the unbanning of the ANC in 1990, he returned to South Africa and was sent to KwaZulu-Natal, where the ANC and its allies were involved in a bitter turf war with the IFP which threatened South Africa's political transition. Zuma, a traditionalist in many respects, succeeded in splitting the IFP from the Zulu monarchy and many of the traditional leaders who were the backbone of the party.

While weakening the IFP's support-base, he simultaneously managed to establish good personal relations with many of its leaders, leaving them convinced that he was an ANC man with whom they could work. As a result, Zuma was able to negotiate peace pacts between the warring parties, which held to varying degrees of success. Over the past years, Zuma has regularly been deployed by the ANC to build its support in KwaZulu-Natal and patch up its relations with the IFP, when necessary.

In the 2004 election, the ANC and its allies finally won control of the province which had narrowly eluded it for the past two elections. Zuma received much of the credit because of his work in the province.

Although Zuma tends to come across as slightly nervous at formal occasions, like sittings of Parliament, he is an affable character with a common touch that he can use well for political ends. However, as those who ran into him during the controversy about his involvement in corruption in the arms deal can testify, he is also a skilled and ruthless political fighter. For now, his position in the ANC is secure.

Date of birth: 12 April 1942

2

Departments

Department of Agriculture

The department's agenda is the empowerment of black farmers and the establishment of a black commercial farmers' class. So far, it has financed more than a hundred programmes aimed at empowering a new class of black farmers – and its programmes have created over eight thousand permanent jobs.

It is faced with the enormous challenge of addressing poverty, landlessness and a general skewed participation of black people, youth and women in the sector, and has set up a strategic plan to implement its vision for the sector. The vision includes addressing the historical baggage that resulted in skewed access and representation, and it implies sustained and profitable participation by all stakeholders in the South African agricultural economy. But it also recognises the need to maintain and increase commercial production and to build international competitiveness.

There are three core strategies in the department's strategic plan.

The first concentrates on deracialising land and ownership and unlocking entrepreneurial potential.

Another is promoting global competitiveness in all aspects of agriculture – production, processing, even agritourism.

For example, the department has closely monitored negotiations between the European Union and South Africa which resulted in the signing of a wine and spirits agreement, and was involved in the negotiations at Cancun in 2003 in an effort to protect third world farmers who are often priced out of the international market because they do not receive the subsidies granted to their first world counterparts.

The third core strategy aims to enhance farmers' capacity to use natural resources in a sustainable manner.

Natural resource conservation management is one of the trickier local issues the department has to manage. Conservation officers and farmers are constantly at each other's throats over acceptable good soil or water conservation policies on farms, for what is good for mielies is not necessarily good for indigenous wild plants of the area.

The department's land care programme increases production in poor soils by methods such as the addition of lime to the ground to change its consistency. The object is for communities and individuals to adopt an ecologically sustainable approach to the management of the country's environment and natural resources, while improving their quality of life.

This means that people must use the soil, water and vegetation resources in a responsible manner to ensure that future generations will also be able to use them. It also implies that cultivation, livestock grazing and harvesting of natural resources should be managed in such a manner that no further degradation (such as soil erosion, nutrient loss, loss of components of the vegetation, and increased run-off of water) occurs.

An agricultural census was initiated in April 2003, in conjuction with Statistics South Africa. The census, funded by the Department to the tune of R17-million, will be updated every five years.

The establishment of the Agricultural Geographic System, a Canadian-developed computer-based geographical system with maps of each municipal district showing agricultural information such as rainfall patterns and soil types, is one of the department's biggest successes.

Director-general Bongiwe Njobe, an Africanist and feminist with a strong personality, is reported to be President Thabo Mbeki's preferred policy adviser at administrative level in the department. Her influence has played an important role in the appointment of key figures inside the department, and beyond it; she is said to have played a major role in preventing Totsie Memela, the Land Bank's former acting managing director and a protégé of Helena Dolny, from being confirmed in the post.

Njobe's parents, both teachers, went into exile in the 1950s and taught in West Africa; Njobe spent most of her childhood in Zambia. She worked in farm management in Zambia and Tanzania when in exile, and later moved to Canada. Back in South Africa she lectured at the School of Agriculture and Rural Development at the University of Pretoria, and enrolled to study for a PhD on gender issues in agriculture.

She entered politics through the African National Congress Women's League. In 1995 she became involved in the development of the ANC's agricultural policy, and was appointed to her current post when Thoko Didiza became minister in 1999.

Her interest in promoting black women to executive positions has spilled over to the leadership of the Agricultural Research Council. The current president, Nthoana Ntau-Mzamane, took the reins after the successive replacement of three men – one white, one Coloured and one black.

The Council performs research on agricultural goods produced in South Africa with the aim of improving production for both commercial and subsistence farmers. It supports the national and provincial departments – and is currently one of the most troubled sections in the national department's stable.

Protests alleging mismanagement and a decline in agricultural research broke out in 2003, with staff at the famed veterinary establishment at Onderstepoort joining in for the first time ever.

Department of Arts and Culture

The establishment of the Department of Arts, Culture, Science and Technology in 1994 was greeted with a degree of ambivalence by the arts and culture community. On the one hand, a national department with "arts and culture" in its title signalled at least a recognition of the sector. On the other hand, that the department was assigned to the Inkatha Freedom Party as a junior political partner, and that arts and culture were linked to science and technology, hardly a synergetic partner, reinforced the marginal status of the sector.

Nevertheless, there was a great deal of optimism initially because the Arts and Culture Task Group process that led to the adoption of the White Paper on Arts, Culture and Heritage in 1996 was a broadly consultative policy-making process that affirmed all the right values of participatory democracy, transparency and partnership.

This optimism was short-lived, however, and by 2000 there were loud questions as to whether the department actually warranted its existence. Whereas arts and culture at 45% and science and technology at 49% shared the departmental budget almost equally in 1995/6, by 2000/1 arts and culture's share had declined to 31% against science and technology at 61%, while the overall departmental budget had increased by 88% in the five-year period. That year, the State Theatre in Pretoria was mothballed; the Market Theatre in Johannesburg retrenched half its staff; the Cape Town Philharmonic Orchestra was liquidated; the Windybrow Theatre in Hillbrow faced imminent closure; one of the country's longest-surviving community arts centres, the Community Arts Project in Cape Town, was struggling to survive; and heritage institutions received yet another paltry subsidy increase. All of these symbolised the decline or the stagnation in the institutional framework underpinning the sector.

While some notable achievements had been made in establishing the National Arts Council, the National Film and Video Foundation and the Pan South African Language Board, as well as launching various music, craft, film and publishing initiatives through the cultural industries growth strategy, the overall impression of the department was that it had become increasingly alienated from its constituency, and that it lacked the political will and expertise to provide the leadership necessary to realise the vision articulated in the task group report.

After a year characterised by controversies of poor governance, mismanagement and reactionary policy changes culminating in the sudden departure of the minister who was appointed ambassador to Japan, there is cautious optimism due to a more favourable set of post-election political conditions. The separate department has now grown up to have its own ministry. The new Minister of Arts and Culture, Pallo Jordan – an intellectual with artistic sensibilities – is of the governing party where he enjoys political stature. There are new MECs for arts and culture in all nine provinces. Against the background of the untimely death of music icon Brenda Fassie, the ANC's secretary general, Kgalema Motlanthe, has written profoundly of the need for South Africa to take greater care of its artists. The parliamentary "arts and culture opposition" has also been strengthened with the Democratic Alliance appointing the knowledgeable and passionate Dianne Kohler-Barnard as its official spokesperson on arts and culture, and the Independent Democrats' electoral campaign had a muscular arts and culture component.

These conditions and the marking of ten years of democracy present Jordan with a window of opportunity to reverse the decline in the sector and in relations between government and civil society.
In this regard, four key areas are crucial:
- the involvement of the cultural sector in reviewing the weaknesses and gains of the last decade, and in formulating and implementing a fresh vision, policies and strategies that will move the sector forward in the next five to ten years;
- to restore respect for and the practice of good governance within the sector by addressing its absence or undermining in key cultural institutions;

- to recognise capacity, administrative and leadership problems within his department, provincial departments and other government-aligned structures, and to take corrective action as appropriate in order to give effect to government's stated commitment to delivery; and
- to open up and defend the political spaces for artists to work and practise their right to freedom of creative expression without fear.

The election in 2009 and the Soccer World Cup in 2010 will provide initial targets for achieving deliverable and sustainable outcomes.

Department of Communications

The Department of Communications is one of the major drivers of the economy, watching over the country's key sectors: telecommunications and information technology. Local and overseas investor confidence and the government's revenue base are at stake.

It's been a busy ministry that has produced extensive legislation – some would say too much legislation. The laws produced by the department have generally been poor, vague and heavy-handed. And all this has led to delays, uncertainty and confusion in the sector, instead of desperately needed clarity and direction.

The three key areas that have been the focus of the department in the last few years are the rollout of the second national operator, the Electronic Communications and Transactions Act and, most recently, the Convergence Bill.

The mission–critical SNO process – which will spell a crucial end to Telkom's inefficient monopoly of landline telecommunications – has been dogged by uncertainty as a result of many delays. Fraught with allegations of corruption and insinuations that the government has been stalling the process to give the parastatal time to fatten its coffers, the department has been seen to be dithering, rather than firmly driving a process that is key to the government's information and communications development strategy.

It's arguably the most important event in the history of telecoms in this country, and the licensing process has been less than exemplary.

Like the SNO process, the granting of the third cellular licence also suffered delays and turned out to be a long, drawn–out affair.

Under Communications Minister Ivy Matsepe-Casaburri, Telkom has extended its monopoly instead of facing up to much–needed competition. The high cost of telecommunications continues to be the key obstacle to the development of information and communications technology in South Africa – and the minister has been seen as not doing enough to make them more affordable.

Telkom still sets telecommunications rates, which have to be approved by the Independent Communications Authority of South Africa.

The Electronic Communications and Transactions Act, which was designed to regulate e-commerce transactions, has also resulted in unnecessary over-regulation. Experts say it is another prime example of badly written law, which has stifled development in e-commerce rather than facilitated its improvement. The Act gives the minister the power to identify databases within the republic that could be deemed "critical" to the safety of the nation, among other things. There is concern in many quarters that it gives the Communications Minister the power to act like Big Brother.

The latest Bill to come from the Department of Communications, the Convergence Bill, also came under fire.

At heart it is an innovative Bill for which the department can take some kudos. It is a law designed to update the country's laws and create more competition in the telecoms environment. But experts and industry bodies have lambasted it for being vague and for its apparent intention to regulate content. The Bill also gives the minister increased control in a manner that could mean the department's actions would be open to less public scrutiny.

South Africa was one of the first countries to adopt e-commerce laws and explore convergence legislation, which, it could be argued, is better than chaos – an inaction that exists in the communications sectors of many other countries – and for this the department has been praised.

The loss of the department's powerful, knowledgeable and energetic director-general, Andile Ngcaba, at the end of 2003 to the business world has been a blow. Ngcaba, one of the longest-serving directors-general in government, has long been considered the strategic thinker and the power behind the minister – and his departure could impact badly on the future performance of the ministry. At the time of going to press, an acting director-general, Mpumelelo Zimande, had taken Ngcaba's place.

Correctional Services Department

The Jali Commission, set up in 2001 to probe allegations of corruption and maladministration in South African jails, was meant to last a year. That it has continued well into 2004 is testament to the mess the Correctional Services Department finds itself in.

Judge Thabani Jali told Parliament's correctional service committee in August 2002 that the investigations had been far more extensive and time-consuming than initially estimated, and it had become "patently clear that the investigation may take longer than initially anticipated.

"This being an independent judicial commission, time should, however, not necessarily be the primary concern, but rather that a thorough investigation be done to restore the image of the holding institutions in the country once and for all, not forgetting that five or six investigations into the department have already previously been undertaken."

The original R5,8-million budget for the commission's work had to be increased; it currently stands at R10,5-million.

The public perception of things going awry at a department responsible for the safekeeping and rehabilitation of those who have harmed society has been reinforced by former minister Ben Skosana, who said that half the prisoners in South African jails, once released, are likely to return to crime.

The department is therefore at the coalface of challenges facing society, among them a lack of skills, thereby leaving newly released convicts with little option but to return to a life of crime.

Be that as it may, the department has not moved far to confront its challenges. In its annual report, the department acknowledges that corruption is still widely prevalent – hence the marathon Jali Commission.

Corruption is still rife among those charged with keeping an eye on offenders. Almost six hundred employees have been charged with various types of wrong-doing, including falsifying their qualifications, fraud and abuse of state resources. According to the annual report, the number of personnel fired for corruption has more than doubled. An optimistic view would be that screws are being tightened against the bad apples. But pessimists would hold that there are increasing numbers of corrupt officials.

Fighting corruption is not the only challenge, by a long shot.

Jails are still hopelessly overcrowded, rendering a blow to prospects of rehabilitation and to staff morale. In 2003 there were 127 600 offenders and 58 100 awaiting-trial prisoners in South Africa's prisons, built to accommodate just over 111 200. The department is transferring some unsentenced juveniles to places of safety, and some sentences have been converted to correctional supervision. But there are still young offenders held with adults, and mother-and-child units have not yet spread to all provinces.

Stop and start processes such as the electronic monitoring model to supervise paroled prisoners, later suspended because a proper feasibility study had not been done, speak to an organisation that has no plan of action for dealing with prisoners, apart from locking them up.

The department is trying to upgrade some of the more dilapidated facilities among the 241 prisons countrywide. Construction started on four new prisons in 2004, but completion is two years down the line. Also planned are "new generation" prison facilities for medium- and low-risk inmates.

And the private sector is getting in on the act. The Correctional Services Act of 1998 authorises the department to form partnerships with private firms to design, construct, finance and operate any prison. So far there is only one, the Mangaung Maximum Security Prison near Bloemfontein. The Katuma Sinthumule Maximum Prison being built at Makhado, expected to be finished sometime in 2004, will be the largest in the world, with accommodation for 33 024 offenders.

Building new prisons, however, only addresses the superstructure. Inside the cell blocks, gangs, as a parallel authority, still keep prisons and prisoners in a stranglehold.

And an estimated 41% of all inmates are HIV-positive, according to an Institute for Security Studies report released in 2003. More than 90% of natural deaths in prison are believed to be Aids-related.

For now the department has adopted a unit management approach, dividing prisons into smaller, more manageable units, in the hope that this will encourage a shift in thinking: managing the offender rather than the prison.

Department of Defence

The Department of Defence spent the first five years of South Africa's democracy transforming the defence force and remoulding departmental structures. The former South African Defence Force, the former homeland armies and the liberation movement armies, Umkhonto we Sizwe and the Azanian People's Liberation Army, were integrated into the new South African National Defence Force.

At the same time, significant efforts were made to integrate senior black officers into the command structures of the SANDF. This led to the appointment of the first black chief of the defence force, General Siphiwe Nyanda, in 1998.

Today, the Defence Department is still actively pursuing transformation, especially at the lower levels of its officer corps. Although integration is complete, the army is still fraught with problems of racism. The situation has resulted in continuous reports of unhappiness from former members of the liberation armies. Racial tensions appeared to come to a head in 1999 at the Tempe military base in Bloemfontein, when a former MK guerrilla went on a shooting rampage, killing seven white colleagues and wounding five before himself being shot dead.

The staff composition of the SANDF now reflects South Africa's racial demographics, but whites still make up the majority of middle-ranking officers. These ranks will take many years to reflect South Africa's demographics, due to skills shortages.

New challenges facing the SANDF include ageing soldiers, budget constraints and new assignments, such as peacekeeping operations on the African continent.

Despite its novelty, SANDF peacekeeping operations have been relatively successful. The one major exception was the disastrous incursion into Lesotho in September 1998 under the auspices of the Southern African Development Community, which led to hardening of resistance in Lesotho and large-scale damage to property.

After the Lesotho debacle, the SANDF moved to repair its image, and in the past few years it has played an important and successful part in peacekeeping operations in Burundi and the Democratic Republic of Congo. The SANDF has also played a very important role in the security structures of the African Union.

Its African peacekeeping efforts have raised the SANDF's international profile and served to reinforce the government's commitment to the peaceful resolution of conflicts on the continent. The largest SANDF peacekeeping operation currently under way is the protection of politicians who have returned from exile in Burundi.

In the African Union, the SANDF has played a key role in drafting a plan to create an African stand-by force whose purpose would be to prevent genocide. The force would fall under the AU's newly constituted

Peace and Security Council which would be able to sanction intervention in African states without the consent of the country concerned.

The South African government regards security and defence cooperation in southern Africa as a priority, meaning that the peacekeeping and peacemaking demands on the SANDF are likely to increase in years to come.

Defence analysts say the SANDF remains over-stretched and under-resourced, despite the recent modest increase in the defence budget. South Africa's controversial multi-billion-rand arms procurement will also pose a challenge to it, because of a shortage of required skills and an increase in operating costs.

The burden on spending is likely to remain for some time, given the SANDF's peacekeeping operations and the Defence Department's plan to retrench ageing soldiers and to bring in significant numbers of younger people.

The recruitment plan, in which the SANDF will take in about 3 000 new recruits each year, is contained in the department's 2010 strategy. It followed a damning parliamentary report in 2002 which revealed that most of South Africa's personnel and equipment was unfit or too old to be operationally deployed. Only 3 000 out of the 77 000 soldiers, the report stated, could be deployed and only four tanks used in action.

The report also raised concerns that the army had too many generals. There is one general for every 293 men in the SANDF, compared with one to 2 000 in, for example, the United States military.

And the report raised the possibility that the incidence of HIV is much higher than realised by departmental officials. The SANDF has estimated the infection rate at between 17% and 23%, but the parliamentary report quoted an unnamed medical specialist at a military hospital as saying that six out of every ten soldiers admitted to hospital tested positive.

Department of Education

In one sense, the national Department of Education can be grateful for the incredible chaos bequeathed to it by apartheid: in comparison, absolutely anything is an improvement.

And as many an education official is quick to remind us, just restructuring the 16 apartheid education departments into nine provincial and one national department is, itself, approximately a miracle.

But having moved away from the miserable rock of apartheid education, the department still finds itself in a hard place. Not only are there a myriad of backlogs still to address – ranging from relatively simple things like infrastructure to more complex, elusive issues like racial and religious integration at schools – but there are the daunting set of ideals spelt out for it, not least the constitutional right for all to a free, quality education.

The Education Department is widely seen to be sadly lacking in both the "free" and the "quality" aspects of delivery. Very few can tell of being educated for free: while schools are supposed to waive fees for those who can't afford them, this doesn't always happen (not least because schools themselves are under pressure to sustain themselves). Add to this a range of "hidden costs" like school uniforms, stationery and transport, and the issue of access for the poorest continues to be a burning one.

Still, South Africa can boast a high level of school enrolment relative to many other countries. And former minister of education Kader Asmal responded to the issue of access for the poorest with a review of school funding norms, due to start being implemented this year.

As for quality, from the outset the department put all its eggs in the outcomes-based education basket. A radical break from previous rote-learning practices, OBE puts the child at the centre of the learning process, emphasises skills rather than content, and promotes capabilities like critical thinking and creativity. This – together with Curriculum 2005, which was introduced in grade 1 in 1998 and is being implemented incrementally through the higher grades – has formed the pillar of the new system.

But there are many question marks around the success of these approaches. Research in 2003 into the education levels of children after their first three years in the new system revealed appallingly low levels of literacy and numeracy – apparently because Curriculum 2005 did not explicitly state that educators must teach their wards to read, write and do numbers. Complaints are also plentiful from educators now inheriting learners in their first year of high school who are similarly derelict in such basic skills.

Thankfully, Asmal initiated a revision of Curriculum 2005 in 2001. The result was the revised national curriculum statement, free of the incomprehensible jargon with which the curriculum had previously been burdened, and introducing some key values and more explicit content.

However, the crucial issue of effective teacher-training in both OBE and the new curriculum continues to be a hit-and-miss affair – and until this process becomes more rigorous and comprehensive, the situation is unlikely to improve dramatically.

Meantime, the year-on-year improvement in the matric pass rate (47% in 1997 to 73% in 2003) is regarded by critics as more a matter of smoke-and-mirrors than a true reflection of the health of the education system. While director-general Thami Mseleku (among others) dismisses out of hand the idea that this reflects manipulated marks and slipping standards, the suspicion lingers that the matric results are more a major public-relations exercise for the department than an index of education excellence. This, at least, is the view of many in the tertiary sector and in business, both of which have experience of accommodating matriculants, and neither of which generally swear by the value of a matric certificate.

A bleak picture it may currently be – but there's reason to hold out some hope. Pockets of excellence continue to endure, and efforts to improve school environments and to inculcate a culture of learning and teaching are gradually paying off. Strike action by educators is rare and, on most days of the school year, the majority are making a genuine effort to do their best.

Efforts to make education more relevant to the needs of the economy have made some progress. Last year saw the launch of the country's 50 Further Education and Training colleges, meant to deliver scores of graduates with vocational skills into the hands of industry; and 25 Sector Education and Training Authorities were established by the Skills Development Act in 1998, replacing the old industrial training boards. Setas fall jointly under the Department of Labour and the Department of Education, and have the daunting task of promoting the skills development of employees in various economic sectors, a key part of the nation's human resource development strategy.

But both initiatives are currently on shaky ground – particularly among many of the Setas, which have been beset with accusations of financial mismanagement and a failure to effectively deliver on their mandate.

On the higher education front, the sector is also undergoing a massive overhaul. A process of mergers and incorporations will reduce the number of universities and technikons from 35 to 24 with the aim of promoting efficiency, equity and redress. While the process is well and truly under way – the first round of mergers takes place this year – it is predictably mired in politics and controversy, with critics arguing that the disruptive exercise will take years to have a positive outcome. And, of course, it's an expensive endeavour – the tertiary sector currently hogs the vast majority of the national department's budget (about 87% of 2004's budget of R11-billion). But, on balance, most agree that the massive shake-up is a necessary evil for the sector to begin to reflect the aims and values of South Africa's new dispensation.

In other areas, the bookends of the education system – early childhood development and adult basic education – continue to be treated like poor cousins and consequently hardly register progress. And while much is said about the importance of other initiatives, such as special needs and HIV/Aids education, delivery in these areas tends to be patchy at best.

One thing the department has certainly got a handle on is putting on feel-good functions – like when making awards to outstanding educators and most improved schools – and on such occasions the mutual back-slapping seems appropriate. Mseleku, who first occupied his post during education minister Sibusiso Bengu's tenure, is often to be seen wiping his mountainous brow at such functions as he fulfils his role as the truly hands-on manager of education, ushering winners towards the stage for their three minutes of fame.

Born in September 1961, Mseleku traces his involvement in education back to his first teaching post at Zibukezulu High in Pietermaritzburg from 1983-1986, which he took up after completing his senior secondary teacher's diploma at the University of Zululand the previous year. He went on to study at the University of Natal for a BA (Hons) degree, but following his detention for anti-apartheid and teacher union activities, Mseleku left the country to study for a master's degree in applied linguistics at the University of Durham in England, which he was awarded in 1989.

He became deeply involved in the South African Democratic Teachers Union after returning to South Africa, and was appointed as a member of its first national executive in 1989, and national vice-president from 1990 to 1993.

But there are few traces of Mseleku's long-standing involvement with teacher unions in his approach to education matters. In fact, when criticised for turning his back on his former union since joining the department, Mseleku retorted, "Sadtu is not a sweetheart union, and Comrade Thami is not a sweetheart bureaucrat".

Indeed, Mseleku has proved to be a hard-nosed bureaucrat, driving radical shake-ups that have been felt throughout the education system. But not all are viewed as being positive changes, and critics identify Mseleku as one of the culprits behind the department's stop-and-start performance in the past ten years. In particular, the process of teacher rationalisation from 1996 to 2000 led to an unholy haemorrhaging of professionals from the field – a factor partly responsible for the current teacher shortage. Mseleku's apparent unwillingness to take on the constructive criticism of independent education experts while formulating policies led to some costly backtracking – such as in the case of the 2002 revised curriculum statement, a move which compounded teachers' confusion and threatened to send an already beleaguered sector over the edge.

But for all the slipping the department has done on the steep learning curve it's climbing, it has ultimately done much in a relatively short time to tackle the incredible inequalities and lacks that apartheid actively enforced.

The Department of Environmental Affairs and Tourism

Though in the view of many people the Department of Environmental Affairs and Tourism carries the greatest responsibility – caring for the planet for future generations – it is often treated as a minor, marginal political entity. This is because environmental protection is often regarded as anti-progress and anti-prosperity.

In the past ten years the department has shifted its emphasis from conservation to sustainability, which it defines as "meeting people's needs while balancing our consumption of resources with our country's capacity to renew them".

Under the leadership of minister Valli Moosa and director-general Crispian ("Chippy") Olver in the past five years, this has translated into a wodge of legislation aimed at getting industries and individuals to clean up their act. Outdated legislation regulating pollution and waste has been revised, and regulations curtailing driving on beaches and the use of plastic bags have been introduced.

Other legislation introduced or amended in the past decade includes the Environment Conservation Act, the National Environmental Management Act, the Protected Areas Act; and the signing of various international biodiversity agreements. The department plays a lead role in facilitating and monitoring environmental impact assessments, which are required in terms of the Constitution before land-use change and development can go ahead.

South Africa hosting the World Summit on Sustainable Development in September 2002 was a highlight for progress in sustainable development, particularly in terms of raising local awareness of the issues involved. A challenge for the future will be keeping the momentum of the summit alive. The department is planning to host annual world summit-related events each September.

Another highlight was the World Parks Congress, hosted in Durban in September 2003. This resulted in the Durban Accord and Action Plan, which set out initiatives and recommendations for the future of protected areas. With the theme "Benefits beyond boundaries", the congress emphasised that people's needs are crucial to the future of conservation.

Conservation remains a focus of the department's programmes. The past five years have seen the transformation of South African National Parks, the statutory body in charge of the country's national parks. The number of parks has been increased to 20; in 2003 an extra 121 000ha of land was added to various parks around the country – marking the single largest proclamation of land for conservation since the 1930s – and creating transfrontier protected areas in partnership with neighbouring countries is an ongoing project.

The sustainable use of marine resources, regulated through its Marine and Coastal Management division, has been assisted by the launch of environmental courts, the "green Scorpions" policing division and new fisheries. Fishing licences and quotas are contentious, but many of the criticisms come from sore losers.

Other statutory bodies linked to the department are the South African Weather Bureau, which has been privatised; the National Botanical Institute, in the process of being restructured; and South African Tourism, headed by Cheryl Carolus.

Tourism is South Africa's fastest-growing industry, contributing to about 11% of GDP. Poverty-relief programmes linked to ecotourism over the past three years have created 1,1-million extra work days, 3 000 temporary workers, 100 permanent jobs and 100 000 training days.

After the appointment of Marthinus van Schalkwyk as the new Tourism and Environmental Affairs Minister in April 2004, it is clear that tourism growth will be the focus area. Van Schalkwyk was appointed after Moosa took his leave of politics; Olver's contract as director-general has been renewed.

Soon after his appointment, Van Schalkwyk said during his maiden public speech at Indaba 2004 – the annual gathering of South Africa's tourism operators – that increasing air access to the country would be one of his priorities. He also aimed to improve visa access and services for tourists. Domestic tourism and intra-African tourism presented some of the best growth opportunities, he said.

Getting local buy-in for tourism – in a country where the majority prefer to stay at home, or visit relatives or friends when they are on holiday – presents a major challenge for the future. Environmentalists say an even greater challenge will be to ensure tourism growth is sustainable, and not at the expense of the environment.

As Van Schalkwyk took over the reins, he inherited two heated controversies that illustrate the tension between delivery and sustainability. First, he has to decide on appeals launched against the department's decision in late 2003 to give the go-ahead for the construction of a toll road along the pristine Pondoland coastline in the Eastern Cape. Secondly, Moosa had barely stepped out of office when the lobbies in favour of beach driving and unrestricted plastic bag use were calling on the new minister to lift these restrictions.

Department of Foreign Affairs

For the past three years, the Foreign Affairs Department has usually made headlines because of its inaction (officially called "quiet diplomacy") towards Zimbabwe.

It also made news when it took in or supported deposed leaders like Haiti's Jean Bertrand Aristide who is staying in South Africa.

In the first months of 2004, its attitude towards a group of 78 mercenaries imprisoned in Zimbabwe and Equatorial Guinea defined the foreign policy agenda. While families, supporters and the Democratic Alliance pushed for the soldiers of fortune to be extended citizenship rights and for them to be extradited to South Africa, the Foreign Affairs Department refused.

All three themes reveal that which is at the core of South Africa's policy – Africa and the African diaspora is king, often even at the expense of domestic opinion and concern.

In her first term in office, Foreign Minister Nkosazana Dlamini-Zuma overhauled foreign policy, placing Africa at the apex. A number of missions outside Africa were closed to re-engineer the budget towards the central aim: for South Africa to have representation in every African country by 2007. It currently has 32 resident missions.

This diplomatic shuffle is an extension of President Thabo Mbeki's core policy agenda – to build the African Union and to make the New Partnership for Africa's Development a cornerstone of the continent's economic and social policy. Ultimately, it is about building Mbeki's influence and his legacy. Once he leaves office, he is likely to covet a job that has a continental footprint.

Yet in 2004 it became apparent that Nepad is not yet much beyond a paper concept. At the World Economic Forum's regional meeting in Maputo, Mozambique in May, it was revealed that the private sector had been lukewarm in signing up to Nepad infrastructure plans. And numerous critics lamented the slow progress in the system of peer review, the innovation by which African leaders are to assess good governance.

South Africa's budget and its political muscle have been crucial to establishing the AU and its attendant structures like the Peace and Security Council, the Pan-African Parliament and the Africa Standby Force. In addition, the country is pouring millions into bolstering African peace, notably in the Democratic Republic of Congo and Burundi.

For the next ten years, the Foreign Affairs Department has set itself the challenge of becoming a player in setting the global governance agenda – a difficult task in a time of US unilateralism. "Our challenge over the next ten years is to be a positive force in support of the entrenchment of multilateralism; the reshaping of the international trading and financial regimes to support development; and the advocacy of global peace."

South Africa is pushing with other countries of the South for the reconstitution of the United Nations Security Council – Mbeki covets an African seat.

Links with the developing South are growing. An India-Brazil-South Africa dialogue forum is being watched because the alliance brings together the giants of each – Asia, Latin America and Africa – to push for better terms of trade and to cooperate in trilateral agreements with one another.

And, finally, South Africa is also part of the plan to ensure that the set of Millennium Development Goals to halve world poverty by 2015 is effectively instituted. The programme is managed by the United Nations Development Programme.

Dlamini-Zuma and her team have done well to insert South Africa into the globe after its years of isolation. They have been less successful at making their work understandable and responsive at home. Take Zimbabwe. The neighbouring country is a skeletal version of the vibrant democracy it was until Zanu-PF signalled its intention to cling to power through its populist programme of land seizures. Since then, democracy has deteriorated as rights abuses have crept into every area of civil life, from press freedom to the freedom of association. The economy has flat-lined, making famine in Zimbabwe a very real and continual fear.

Instead of using its stature as a regional moral beacon and holding President Robert Mugabe to account (as peer review demands), South Africa has stuck doggedly to its method of quiet diplomacy – the belief that behind-the-scenes talks will right affairs and lead to fresh elections. The policy has failed, patently, but Foreign Affairs will not shift. Partly, this is because realpolitik means acknowledging that African leaders who try to meddle in one another's affairs get short continental shrift.

Department of Health

One of the greatest challenges facing the government has been the delivery of basic health care – a constitutional right. Not only did the department inherit a deeply inequitable system for rich and poor, but the HIV/Aids pandemic exploded, placing further strains on health care delivery.

The system inherited from the apartheid regime was fraught with shortages of clinics and staff and an inadequate budget allocation. The poor, largely living in rural black communities, suffered from high incidences of infectious diseases; low immunity, often caused by malnutrition; and few clinics to service their needs.

It is still common to see hundreds of sick people queuing for hours at state hospitals for their turn to consult a couple of overworked doctors. Clinics experience the same problems, and more – they are staffed by nurses who often lack adequate training to deal with patients suffering from HIV-related illnesses, malaria and tuberculosis.

But there are major differences between the early 1990s and 2004: at least now there are clinics; and hospitals are open to all.

Under the country's first post-apartheid health minister, Nkosasana Dlamini-Zuma, the department aimed to boost the health budget to build more clinics, and 700 have been built since 1994. Delivery also shifted to a district system; the country now has 180 health districts. But this meant cutbacks at tertiary hospitals. State hospitals have been forced to service more people on smaller budgets.

The per capita expenditure on primary health care has improved, from R58 in 1992/93 to R141 per person in the 2002/03 financial year. This is set to increase to R183 by 2005/06. The department has embarked on an expensive hospital revitalisation programme, intending to spend R8- to 10-billion to build and improve 27 hospitals which can deliver an acceptable level of health care.

But the failure to pass a national health Bill has meant that health delivery depends on effective management at provincial level, and not all provinces are equal. The South Africa Health Review 2002, compiled by the Health Systems Trust, summed up the major problems with the health sector as a lack of leadership and direction.

Although it adopted a national health plan a decade ago, it was only in 2003 that the government committed itself to rolling out an anti-retroviral plan to treat people with Aids. The first health minister, Dlamini-Zuma, clashed with her director-general, with the pharmaceutical industry and with tobacco companies, but succeeded in banning smoking in public places. She also pushed the idea of access to cheaper drugs and patents from drug companies, but was caught in a legal battle with the pharmaceutical giants until she left in 1999.

Both health ministers have come into conflict with Aids activists and health care professionals over the effectiveness of anti-retroviral treatment.

It took litigation by Aids activists against current Health Minister Manto Tshabalala-Msimang to force the department to make anti-retrovirals available in public hospitals to prevent the transmission of the virus from HIV-positive mothers to their unborn children. The minister continued to stall on the national rollout, making excuses about affordability and lack of capacity. But finally last year the Cabinet forced Tshabalala-Msimang to implement a national anti-retroviral treatment plan for people with Aids. It remains the department's major challenge. The new ARV rollout plan aims to treat almost 500 000 people while strengthening the health care sector.

The good news is that non-governmental organisations, international agencies and corporations in various provinces have filled the vacuum and forged ahead with ARV treatment. Western Cape leads the pack with 2 000 people given access to ARVs at 16 public sector sites. Gauteng is next in line with five hospitals rolling out ARVs from April this year. The rest of the provinces lag behind, with many still in the preparatory phase of training health care workers and treatment literacy for patients. There are still inequalities in provinces, even in delivery of ARVs to prevent mother-to-child transmission or to treat rape victims. Making matters worse: the Human Sciences Research Council estimates that some 16,3% of health workers are living with HIV, while at least 6 000 of them may be dying every year from Aids-related illnesses.

The department failed to ensure the training of sufficient health care providers to implement its Termination of Pregnancy Act. This has resulted in early burnout and high stress levels among existing workers. Second-trimester termination services are also dependent on the presence of a medical doctor, which makes it difficult for women to access these services.

South Africa has joined Mozambique, Swaziland and Zimbabwe in a regional effort to fight malaria. The ministry has also combined its tuberculosis programme with the HIV/Aids rollout plan, which has gone a long way towards recognising the impact of the co-infection. But South Africa still remains one of the 22 countries with a high rate of TB, and people here are still dying from this treatable disease.

The Health Department faces the implementation of three pieces of legislation which will put the ministry back into the ring. These are the Regulations relating to a Transparent Pricing System for Medicines and Scheduled Substances (Medicines and Related Substances Act of 1997), Social Health Insurance (Medical Schemes Act of 1998) and the Certificate of Need (National Health Bill – still to be signed into law by the President).

The National Health Bill aims to implement a "certificate of need", forcing doctors to justify where they intend to practise. While the Bill has the laudable aim of providing the same standard and quality of health care for all, it may well encourage young medical professionals to decide that where they intend to practise is overseas. To encourage health practitioners to stay in South Africa, the government entered into an agreement with the United Kingdom in October 2003 that would allow doctors and nurses to earn pounds and then return home. The department will need to prioritise the offer of incentives for doctors and nurses to work in rural areas and build their morale to ensure that the backbone of successful delivery is maintained.

The need for an introduction of national health insurance has begun gaining momentum, almost 14 years after it was first discussed. It is expected that it will now be implemented in 2006.

A Bill pushing through regulations to bring down the price of medicines was in the pipeline in mid-2004, while new regulations aimed at making the pricing system of drugs more transparent have resulted in outrage by the players in the pharmaceutical sector.

Department of Home Affairs

President Thabo Mbeki's Cabinet shake-up after the 2004 election, in which Mangosuthu Buthelezi was ousted as minister in favour of African National Congress stalwart and former deputy minister Nosiviwe Mapisa-Nqakula, is expected to revive the moribund and politically isolated department. All the top jobs are now occupied by members of the African National Congress.

But the department still has plenty of problems, some – but not all – the legacy of a lack of cooperation between the former minister and his directors-general.

DG Barry Gilder arrived in 2003 as morale in the department was at rock-bottom. It was said to be understaffed by 1 500 people and losing experienced managers, while there were allegations of widespread corruption.

The efficient running of the department had undoubtedly been impaired by the breakdown in relations between Buthelezi and Billy Masetlha, a former ANC intelligence operative.

Buthelezi claimed his former DG repeatedly made decisions without consulting him and had filled 153 departmental posts without ministerial approval. A committee chaired by Deputy President Jacob Zuma was set up to break the impasse but was unsuccessful.

Buthelezi and Masetlha disagreed on most important issues, among them the cost of the suggested new computerised national identification system, or "smart card". Buthelezi told Parliament in 2000 that the "smart card" would cost an estimated R2,5-billion to implement, but Masetlha said in 2002 that estimates were "nowhere near R2-billion at all". Masetlha claimed his assertion was based on a detailed study, while Buthelezi's estimates in 2000 were not.

Masetlha refused to leave his desk after his contract had expired. A report from the auditor-general released in late 2002 found that

Masetlha's term of office was scheduled to end in June 2001, and that the Cabinet's extension of his term for another year was invalid.

The embattled Immigration Bill was another major issue. The IFP threatened to walk out of Cabinet in March 2001 after reports that the Presidency planned to wrest control of the process of drafting the Bill, presented to Cabinet a year earlier. A major point of dispute was the Bill's proposal for an immigration service outside the public service. The immigration service would fall under a board, which would be chaired by the Home Affairs Minister, and public servants would be transferred to it to deal with issues such as work and residence permit applications. The immigration service would be a statutory body, like the South African Revenue Service. Eighty-three amendments, two years and a court battle later between the former minister and the President, the Bill has still not seen the light of day – and the concept of a board has been scrapped.

The new minister, and the new director-general, will inherit both these issues, but when taking up the DG's post Gilder knew it was not going to be a smooth ride. He publicly acknowledged the mess in the department and later drew up a turn-around strategy, which he presented to the media – only for Buthelezi to claim that he had never seen it.

Other issues have nothing to do with departmental infighting, but a lot to do with corruption. The department has been plagued by reports of corrupt officials who demand bribes from illegal immigrants in exchange for South African documents.

The immigration staff has also been accused of brutality against illegal immigrants and of blocking asylum for Zimbabweans. In the first nine months of 2003, South African authorities arrested and deported 41 000 Zimbabweans. The South African government claimed that only 1 471 people had formally applied for political asylum since 1994 – but Zimbabwean immigrants interviewed in South Africa insisted the low number indicated the difficulty they had to go through when applying.

The director-general, Barry Gilder, is a BA graduate of the University of the Witwatersrand, where he was a prominent member of the National Union of South African Students. He went into exile in 1976 and joined the ANC in London. Three years later he joined the ANC's armed wing, Umkhonto we Sizwe, and received training in the former USSR.

Between 1983 and 1989 he headed the ANC intelligence branch in Botswana. He returned to South Africa in 1991, joined the South African

Secret Service, and was appointed general manager: foreign offices. He rose to the position of deputy director-general in 1996. Four years later he was appointed deputy director-general: operational services at the National Intelligence Agency.

Department of Housing

The ANC fulfilled its election pledge to build a million new houses, even if it took the government six years instead of the promised five, but progress on that front appears to be grinding to a halt.

The amount of subsidy has now been linked by the department to a formula taking inflation into account, and it is set to increase annually. A main problem seems to be a controversial policy that requires a huge section of the population trying to access a housing subsidy (which ranges from R25 800 for people earning between R800 and R1 500 a month, to R8 600 for those earning up to R3 500) to save R2 479 in order to qualify. Those who make less than R800 don't have to show they can save, nor do those who earn more than R2 500. That leaves families in the middle, and they're finding it a near-impossible task. It's also near-impossible for developers, because although the savings requirement has been mandated, no one seems to know how it works.

Not surprisingly, developers are now building instead for those who aren't required to save, which also includes the indigent aged, disabled or ill. The people's housing process, where the poor can offer sweat equity instead of rands and cents to qualify, is also gaining ground; the department has so far approved 250 000 subsidies worth about R5-billion.

Practitioners claim the department has shifted its focus from low-income housing for the poorest of the poor, where the greatest need is, to social housing for families who have an income between R2 500 and R3 500. The department has concentrated a large proportion of its resources there, commissioning studies, reworking policy, encouraging the establishment of housing institutions. It's largely rental stock, and has its own built-in problems, including the reluctance of many tenants to pay and, consequently, the shaky footing of many social housing institutions.

But critics say even if those were solved, social housing can soak up only a small portion of the housing backlog, and thus does not deserve all the departmental attention it is getting.

Although 1,6-million houses have been built since 1994, which is a monumental accomplishment, in 2003 the Department of Housing put the backlog at 2,2-million households. Census figures show the population increased by 2,1% between 1996 and 2001, making urgent the need for housing.

Moreover, instruments devised to deal with the housing crisis have run up against powerful forces.

The Community Reinvestment Bill, for example, would have handled the lack of finance for low-income housing by compelling banks to "extend their lending to the lower end of the market". The financial sector has come up with its own version, a section of the Financial Services Charter, which makes that kind of lending decision voluntary.

The low quality of many of the 1,6-million subsidised houses built since 1994 is unfortunate, since all houses delivered via the subsidy are supposed to be warranted by the National Homebuilders Registration Council, a body set up for this function.

Many of these problems appeared during the tenure of Mpumi Nxumalo, director-general since 1997.

It was on her watch that the department came up with the disastrous savings requirement, and focus shifted from the poorest of the poor to social housing, largely rental. Housing practitioners complain of her arrogant style, which would, they say, perhaps be acceptable if it were not coupled with an apparent failure by her department to follow through.

Nxumalo appears well qualified for her post, with a degree in town planning from the University of Coventry in the UK and time spent working for the Coventry City Council, the London Docklands Development Corporation and the Borough of Southwark before taking up a post as director-general of housing in Gauteng, where she spent two years before being moved up to the national post.

In public, she talks an inspirational game: Inner city decay can be reversed. One way to deal with informal settlements is to make rural areas more attractive. The department's Rural Housing Loan Fund "has continued to focus its efforts on the further development of ... retail lenders". If progress was slow in 2001, when she praised the work done by the Fund, it was due, among other things, to a "rural context [and] the lack of capacity at local level".

She has a point. Housing delivery is a competency shared by all three levels of government, and it involves more players than mere housing departments. So if shacks are mushrooming the length and breadth of the country, it is not entirely the fault of the national department.

This year, the department has promised to "strengthen its ability to assist provinces and other spheres of government to spend their allocated funds in order to speed up delivery". It will also focus on corruption and fraud in the housing process.

With a new minister in charge, who is likely to have some new ideas on how to tackle housing delivery – and the solid credentials and political clout to see her ideas implemented – the department may yet find a way to house the poorest of the poor while continuing to look after the housing needs of the rest of its constituency.

Intelligence

This secret world allows only glimpses into its workings and educated guesses as to its successes, failures and scandals.

The South African political and economic landscape is awash with intelligence activity. This deluge of spying flows not only from the sometimes competing efforts of the statutory agencies – the National Intelligence Agency, the South African Secret Service, the intelligence division of the South African National Defence Force, and the Crime Intelligence division of the South African Police Service – but also from the activities of numerous private security companies, both local and multi-national, and the local and regional stations of foreign powers. The United Kingdom, for instance, is reputed to have deployed one of its largest spying operations outside Russia in South Africa. France has agents of influence here that date back to the apartheid era, and has long regarded its influence in Africa as vital to its commercial and geopolitical interests. The United States has kept a watch on South Africa's significant Muslim community as a potential haven for Islamic extremism, while South Africa's strategic role in Africa is also important to the US's growing African oil interests.

Both the Directorate of Special Operations (the Scorpions) and the South African Revenue Service have what amount to an independent intelligence-gathering and analysis capacity.

Added to this is the Presidential Support Unit, headed by former SASS director-general Billy Masetlha, which, while not quite President Thabo

Mbeki's private intelligence unit, offers independent analysis and is reputed to bypass reporting structures to take raw reports, for instance from Defence Intelligence.

Before the formation of his support unit, Mbeki is known to have used the international private intelligence firms CIEX and Kroll on occasions to provide independent assessment and quality control of advice from his own statutory bodies. The access granted to private companies has caused considerable unhappiness in the local intelligence community. Both CIEX and Kroll have strong historical links with British intelligence.

Formal reporting lines are supposed to flow via the intelligence minister, who has a ministerial secretariat and, below that, via the National Intelligence Coordinating Committee, which is supposed to facilitate the sharing of information from all four main agencies, and to set targets and priorities. According to insiders, this mechanism has begun to work reasonably well.

The NIA is responsible for domestic and counter-intelligence. The SASS serves as the foreign intelligence department of the government; its mission is to conduct intelligence in relation to external threats, opportunities and other issues that could affect South Africa's interests.

Whether all this secret information is much good to anybody is another question.

Certainly, well-targeted raids and prosecutions by the South African Revenue Service have improved corporate tax compliance, but on at least one occasion, involving an investigation of tobacco smuggling, the service has encountered legal problems flowing from collaboration with private security companies.

Intelligence failures (such as the US agencies' failure to pick up warning signs of the 9/11 attacks) tend to be more visible than successes. Nevertheless, the neutralisation of the terrorist threats posed by People Against Gangsterism and Drugs and the extreme right-wing Boeremag are regarded as indications that the intelligence community is doing its job, despite competition between NIA and Crime Intelligence for credit.

Especially with regard to African peacemaking efforts, Defence Intelligence has tended to compete with SASS and is reputed to have better access to the President.

A degree of overstepping each other's boundaries was exposed by reports in 2000 of attempts by Defence Intelligence to recruit local journalists as sources. It is also rumoured that NIA sent its own team to comb through the police investigation dockets pertaining to the Boeremag treason trial.

Such competition is almost a built-in feature of the system. Although it can lead to turf battles and duplication, it also offers a certain amount of useful mutual oversight – the watchers watch each other and occasionally leak dirt on their competitors.

This is important because the level of statutory monitoring of these bodies has been rather weak.

When new intelligence legislation was designed after 1994, South Africa's dark history of executive intelligence and dirty tricks led to the introduction of a number of checks and balances, including a multi-party parliamentary oversight committee and an inspector-general of intelligence.

The committee, currently chaired by the African National Congress's Siyabonga Cwele, has been fairly active. However, it has adopted a conservative stance across party lines, and has given little sign of seriously challenging actions by the intelligence agencies. It has not raised concerns, at least in public, about the aggressive approach apparently taken by the agencies with regard to activist social organisations, such as the Landless People's Movement. Instead, it chose to criticise attempts by Judge Joos Hefer to subpoena witnesses from the intelligence community to assist his commission of inquiry into allegations that National Director of Public Prosecutions Bulelani Ngcuka was an apartheid spy. In doing so, it backed a controversial legal stance by the agencies that placed intelligence essentially beyond the reach of judicial scrutiny.

The committee's annual reports to Parliament are devoid of operational detail that might allow observers to infer what the country's intelligence agents are doing to earn their keep, or whether they are respecting citizens' rights.

That oversight role was to have been performed by the inspector-general, yet South Africa has been without such a monitor for most of the ten years since 1994. Wrangling over conditions of service saw the first nominee, advocate Lewis Skweyiya, withdraw his bid. Government dragged its heels over finding a replacement. The nominee, Fazel Randera, was appointed in May 2000, but only sworn in a year later. He lasted a few months before resigning for unexplained "personal reasons". The third nominee, Zola Ngcakani, was only sworn in at the beginning of 2004.

Ngcakani, a civil engineer, is an intelligence insider who served as a senior official under former intelligence minister Joe Nhlanhla.

The powerful position of coordinator of intelligence (the National Intelligence Coordinating Committee chair) is occupied by the obscure MJ Maqetuka, whose public profile is almost non-existent.

The director-general of the NIA is Vusi Mavimbela, a former ANC department of intelligence and security regional commander who served as a special adviser to Mbeki when he was deputy president between 1994 and 1999.

Hilton Dennis, who served as the head of the ANC's counter-intelligence investigation unit in Lusaka prior to 1990, currently leads SASS.

The general commanding Defence Intelligence is Mojo Motau, a former chief of MK intelligence, while Crime Intelligence is headed by Ray Lalla, a former operative within the ANC's elite Operation Vula structures.

Over the past five years the civilian agencies, NIA and SASS, have undergone considerable reorganisation, with at least three major shake-ups leading to a degree of re-structuring fatigue.

The services have also continued to have disciplinary problems. NIA operatives, including at least one senior manager, have been accused of moonlighting for their own commercial interests.

The political battle between supporters of Deputy President Jacob Zuma and those who backed the corruption probe of Zuma by Ngcuka also appeared to cause ripples in the NIA, where Zuma, himself a former head of ANC intelligence, was perceived to have support.

Lindiwe Sisulu, who took over as minister following the retirement of Joe Nhlanhla owing to ill health, was vigorous in promoting modernisation and specialisation, for instance pushing through the establishment of an Intelligence Academy and a specialised communications security body.

Sisulu promoted a culture of delivery that helped to bring together agents from the old guard and the liberation forces, and also drew on outside input for advice. This included liaison particularly with British intelligence, which some purists in the community regarded as "too close".

She set up an advisory structure that drew on the expertise of retired members of the old apartheid-era agency, NIS, and also made NIA more open than it had ever been, establishing a website, making the names and photographs of its top officials public, and even promoting the agency in advertisements.

Sisulu's transfer out of Intelligence in Mbeki's new Cabinet in April 2004 came as something of a surprise. Her replacement by Ronnie Kasrils is believed by some observers to be connected to the perception that she allowed the agencies to drift too close to Zuma during his conflict with Ngcuka. Other insiders say that Sisulu was rather too independent and outspoken in her post, but that the move has less to do with her personally than with Mbeki's desire to see that no individual becomes entrenched in this powerful position.

Department of Justice

New brooms sweep clean – a point new minister Brigitte Mabandla and new deputy Johnny de Lange are likely to be ready to prove. Both arrive with legal backgrounds and a keen understanding of the profession and the system. Unsurprisingly, however, the tasks for the ministry and the department are enormous.

The transformation of the justice system presents a multiplicity of challenges – not least because realising the civil and political rights enshrined in the Constitution depends on the efficient and effective operation of the justice system.

The broad mission of the Department of Justice is to render an "accessible, fair, speedy and cost-effective system of justice, in the interest of a safer and more secure South Africa". For this mission to be fulfilled, however, the Justice Ministry cannot act alone; it needs to act in tandem with, inter alia, the Ministries of Safety and Security and Correctional Services. The way in which relevant ministries have been clustered is an administrative attempt to facilitate effective inter-departmental and ministerial cooperation, and ultimately delivery to citizens of their constitutional rights.

The Justice Department under new political management faces a few serious challenges, a relic of the past couple of years.

The passage of the Child Justice Bill, for instance, remains on the "to do" list.

Departmental briefings and public hearings by the justice and constitutional development portfolio committee on the Child Justice Bill were held in 2003. The Child Justice Alliance, spearheaded by the Community Law Centre's Children's Rights Project, has been one of the main drivers behind the legislation. The main thrust of the Bill is the protection of the rights of children in trouble with the law, in line with the Constitution and international law.

The Bill aims to ensure that the criminal justice system is adapted in a manner which enables it to deal with the individual child offender. One of the central features of the Bill, as the Alliance points out, namely diversion, is recognised as a significant means of protecting child offenders, where appropriate, from the harsh formalities of the criminal courts and providing them with an alternative route to accepting responsibility and making amends for the harm that they have caused.

The question of diversion is a tricky one and also one which involves coordination between the Department of Justice and the Departments of Finance and of Social Development. In addition, the challenges of the Bill once passed will be for the Justice Department not only to implement it but also to provide the requisite training, particularly for magistrates and prosecutors who will be at the coalface of implementation. One of the Justice Committee's key concerns was the affordability and feasibility of the legislation.

Parliament between 1994 and 1999 scrapped more than seven hundred pieces of race-based legislation. Much of this work was in fact done by De Lange's work-horse justice portfolio committee. The Promotion of Equality and Prevention of Unfair Discrimination Act (the "Equality Act") is a further attempt to redress the deeply entrenched history of systematic inequalities in South Africa stemming from both colonialism and apartheid. Its aim is also, though, to facilitate the establishment of a system of equality courts which would make it simpler and more cost-effective for individuals to bring cases before the court should they have suffered discrimination.

The Equality Act presents an implementation challenge for the department, which is currently calling for submissions relating to the Act's regulations. Two high-profile cases brought in terms of the Act – one in which a black person was denied entry into a club in downtown Cape Town, and the other an incident of racism between pupils at a Western Cape school – have been speedily dealt with. The test for the efficacy of the legislation will be whether "lower profile" cases will be able to be heard and dealt with as speedily.

The Equality Act also attempts to address new forms of discrimination such as those based on sexual orientation and HIV status. Preliminary research conducted between October 2003 and February 2004 by the Political Information and Monitoring Service at the Institute for Democracy in South Africa, to establish how effectively the Equality courts are implementing the Equality Act, found that most of the courts, although equipped with furniture and computers, did not yet have much trained staff. Forms were often not available in languages other than English, and in almost all jurisdictions the public was unaware that Equality courts existed.

The transformation of the legal profession is another thorny issue; the stakes are high, with entrenched interests in a profession which remains largely conservative and somewhat resistant to wholesale change. De Lange is likely to see the passage of the draft Legal Practice Bill as one of the department's major challenges. The draft Bill has been the subject of much discussion within the profession. It provides for the establishment of the South African Legal Practice Council, and sets out the requirements for the registration, enrolment and admission of legal practitioners. Provision is also made for the registration of paralegal practitioners.

Many within the profession have expressed reservations about the "opening up" of the profession which the draft Bill pushes for. Black lawyers make up about one-sixth of the total number of lawyers in South Africa.

The juniorisation of the staff of prosecutors remains a serious problem. While able to attract entry-level lawyers, it is difficult to hold on to those who have learned the ropes and then invariably leave to join a more lucrative private practice. In many cases, the cooperation between the police and prosecutors is found wanting. It is not unheard of to find a prosecutor and a detective meeting for the first time when the police officer is on the witness stand.

And although judges have been accused by De Lange of being overpaid and underworked, the reverse could not be truer. Other than judges of the Constitutional Court who have two researchers each and at least one foreign intern at any given time, High Court judges have complained that there are only two researchers working for the entire Bench. A sole researcher works for all the judges in the Supreme Court of Appeal.

Moreover, conditions at some of the courts are appalling – lifts that do not work, restrooms and other public spaces that are filthy, corridors and courtrooms that are either too hot or too cold.

Sometimes the prestige of being a judge is overwhelmed by the reality that whatever one is earning, one could be raking in much more in private practice. As a result, at least one Constitutional Court judge left the bench for private practice, saying he could not raise a young family on a judge's salary of about R500 000 a year.

The way in which these and other pressing problems are dealt with will be a test for the legal system itself, those who work in and around it and, most importantly, for its "customers", namely those who depend on the system for the implementation of their rights.

Department of Labour

The Department of Labour can be proud of having put in place some of the best labour legislation in the world.

And, the new labour policies have not resulted in jobless growth, labour experts believe, even though unemployment persists.

Statistics show that the level of unemployment in South Africa has more than doubled, from 2,2-million in 1994/6 to 4,5-million in 2003. The official unemployment rate in the first quarter of 2004 stood at 28,2% of the economically active population.

Although the unemployment figure dropped 3% from the previous 31%, the 2004 unemployment figures from Statistic SA shows that the number of discouraged work-seekers rose by 1-million between March and September 2003.

Poor employment growth appears primarily due to a shift in the kind of labour required by an economy more and more dependent on skilled or semi-skilled workers, and the department is tackling that problem.

To develop the skills among the workforce that the current economy requires, the department introduced 25 sector education and training authorities. These sectoral training agencies represent the most important attempt to address the skills crisis that hamstrings the South African economy.

The Minister of Labour, Membathisi Mdladlana, set a target of 80 000 learnerships and apprenticeships when he launched the department's national skills development strategy in February 2001.

However, this target looks unattainable so far, given a series of management problems in some of the Setas. The Setas receive an annual budget of R3-billion from a tax levy imposed on all companies; but in 2003 it emerged that in their three years of existence, the Setas had failed to disburse about one-third of their budget, or R3,2-billion.

The problems within the Setas prompted Mdladlana to introduce amendments to the Skills Development Act, giving him more power to influence the work of the skills agencies and to hold them to tighter account. Under the new amendments, it will become mandatory for Setas to enter an annual service level agreement with the Department of Labour. This will define performance targets in relation to the implementation of the skills development strategy, and detail reporting requirements.

Another major stumbling block to skills development is a certain amount of tension between the Education and Labour Departments. "Philosophically, the tension seems to pit the educationalists against the vocationalists. The national skills development strategy is clearly an attempt to elaborate skills empowerment through vocational measures. Indeed, this is the elegance of a demand–driven strategy," says Paul Lundal, a senior researcher at the University of Cape Town.

Implementing the skills development strategy is not the only challenge facing the department. While the Department of Labour has made conspicuous progress with regard to the Labour Relations Act, the Basic Conditions of Employment Act and the Unemployment Insurance Act, the outlook for advancing the Employment Equity Act remains bleak.

The 2002-2003 report by the Commission for Employment Equity, released in June 2004, showed that private sector managers in South Africa remained overwhelmingly pale and male, with whites continuing to dominate the plum positions. The report reveals that in the 7 000 firms analysed, blacks (Africans, Coloured people and Indians) occupied only 22% of top management positions.

The conclusions were drawn from employment equity reports submitted by companies to the labour department, in line with the Act, which requires companies employing more than 150 people to submit such reports yearly.

However the department is beginning to see some gains made under the Labour Relations Act, as the country continues to record a significant drop in the number of industrial strikes. Labour analyst Andrew Levy's strike report for 2003 shows that the number of man days lost in South Africa due to strike action fell from 945 000 in 2002 to 700 000 in 2003.

The Unemployment Insurance Fund has shown significant improvement since the department introduced amendments to the Act in 2002 as part of what it described as a turnaround strategy to make the fund financially sustainable. Key elements of the strategy included institutional reform, revised legislation and information technology.

As a result of the turnaround strategy, the Fund recorded a surplus of R1,4-billion in August 2003.

The Congress of South African Trade Unions says the Fund discriminates against national and provincial public service employees. Government argues that there is no need for public servants to get benefits from the Fund as they are already getting much better benefits than received by those in the private sector. But Cosatu believes that having public servants as UIF contributors will add to the stability of the fund, and the UIF looks likely to be a contentious issue between the union and government in 2004.

The department in mid-2004 lost its long-term director-general, Rams Ramashia, who cited differences with his minister.

This was not its only loss of capacity. The department appears to be running short of inspectors to implement certain laws, such as sectoral determinations which prescribe minimum wages, and employment conditions for vulnerable workers who do not fall under bargaining councils.

Department of Land Affairs

After 1994 the new government added the portfolio of Land Affairs, to address the skewed land ownership in South Africa. The Department of Land Affairs is responsible for deeds registration, cadastral surveys, surveys and mapping, spatial planning and information, land reform and land restitution. This new department had to develop new policies, and new laws were necessary to give effect to those policies.

The government's land programme, spelled out in a White Paper published in June 1997, envisions a threefold strategy. Firstly there is restitution, where people deprived of their land after 1913 owing to racial bias and without proper compensation can claim their land back. Secondly there is redistribution where the government is reforming land ownership in South Africa on a willing-seller willing-buyer basis.

Lastly there is security of tenure, governed by three laws including the Extension of Security of Tenure Act that protects farm workers and labour tenants from summary eviction.

The government wanted to transfer a third of the 85-million hectares of cultivable land to South Africa's black majority by 2005. The pilot land reform programme was created in 1994, with an office in each province operating under an agency agreement with the provincial government.

Though the land reform programme started off slowly, the past two years have seen a significant acceleration in areas such as land restitution. In the past decade about 700 000 people had received 3-million hectares of land worth R808-million through the government's restitution and redistribution programme, according to the Land Affairs Department.

This included about 800 000ha returned to people who had lost their land owing to apartheid. Another 1,5-million hectares was bought up and redistributed among the poor for residential and productive purposes, while 773 000ha of state-owned land was also handed over. Nearly 20 000 emerging farmers have benefited to date from the redistribution of about 400 000ha of land earmarked for agricultural development.

Under Agriculture and Land Affairs Minister Thoko Didiza, the department has not only focused on handing land over to the disadvantaged, but also empowering them. Though critics accuse Didiza of neglecting the poor, the department's view is that you cannot simply dump people on a piece of land and expect them to survive. Thus the department has initiated programmes like land redistribution for agricultural development that will help communities to farm productively and create their own livelihoods on their newly acquired land.

The main objective of the programme, in line with the Department's mission to provide access to land and to extend land rights to previously disadvantaged communities, is to redistribute white-owned agricultural land to black people in a sustainable way.

The most controversial issue at the moment is the Communal Land Rights Bill, intended to secure the tenure of people living under traditional leaders. One of the government's most pressing dilemmas is how to give the one-third of all South Africans living on communal land the tenure security demanded by the Constitution, without stirring up the hornet's nest of traditional leadership.

Initially the Bill was criticised by traditional leaders for taking away too much of their powers. After amendments, however, critics of the Bill raised fears that the traditional leaders will take land from the people and sell it to developers, because much of the power will once again rest in their hands. At the end of 2003 a wide range of organisations asked Parliament not to pass the Bill, but their protests were in vain. The

National Council of Provinces unanimously approved the Bill in February 2004, paving the way for the President to sign it into law.

The Bill has also come under fire for putting too much power in the minister's hands. But she has defended this, saying she will be able to protect communities' interests better this way.

Gilingwe Mayende is the current director-general in the Department of Land Affairs. He was appointed in 1999 when Thoko Didiza took office as minister. He succeeds Geoff Budlender as director-general.

Department of Minerals and Energy

The Minerals and Energy Department has undertaken what is arguably the most radical alteration of the South African economic landscape since the formation of the Union of South Africa in 1910. The Minerals and Petroleum Resources Development Act, passed in 2002, effectively nationalised the country's buried wealth.

The Act takes ownership of mineral deposits away from mining houses for the first time in 100 years and vests it with the state. The mining rights are now issued on periodically reviewed 30-year leases. This has given government leverage to drive transformation in the mining industry through instruments such as the Mining Charter.

The Mining Charter commits the industry to radically change the complexion and composition of ownership and management of the companies; transfer skills to people previously denied opportunities; and treat host communities in a dignified manner.

But this piece of legislation, while it remains one of the highlights of government's transformation agenda, is by no means the only driver of change brought about by the department, nor is it the most contentious. Minerals and Energy also governs the sector that put in place the first charter: liquid fuels. And it proved to be the first in a long road to transforming the energy sector.

Government is in the process of establishing a single regulator for the energy sector overseeing liquid fuels, gas, nuclear and electricity industry regulation. The biggest challenge in this area is the restructuring. The power utility, Eskom, is a successfully corporatised, efficient entity which in 2003 declared a dividend of R549-million. The utility now has to undergo restructuring that will see it cease to participate in the distribution arena, while generation functions will be partially privatised and opened to competition. All this is to happen while Eskom prepares to invest more than R50-billion over the next five years rehabilitating power stations and building South Africa's first new power station in 20 years.

Government showed that it would not blindly support Eskom's endeavours at the expense of the consumer when it refused the energy utility a 8,5% increase in tariffs. Eskom had sought the increase on the grounds of its planned investments. The National Electricity Regulator approved a 2,5% increase, a decision bravely upheld by the Department of Minerals and Energy after Eskom appealed.

The liquid fuels industry is also undergoing radical change. Last year saw the expiry of a memorandum of understanding and "blue pump" agreement between Sasol and the five major oil companies. The memorandum ensured that petrol giants bought some of their crude oil from Sasol, while the agreement allowed Sasol to host a pump at a station. Now Sasol is in the process of launching its own petrol stations in a market that is perceived as overtraded and where government intends to reduce the number of petrol stations.

The department's greatest asset is its top leadership. Director-general Sandile Nogxina is a rigorous advocate, well versed in matters of policy. And then of course there is its political head, Phumzile Mlambo-Ngcuka: a gracious yet tenacious figure who does not wilt under pressure from vested interests. As she prepared to start her second term, she lost a capable lieutenant in her spokesperson Khanyo Gqulu, who had been with her since her days as deputy minister of trade and industry.

National Treasury

It's hat-eating time for the cynics who warned we were all headed for the poorhouse when Trevor Manuel assumed stewardship of the Ministry of Finance in 1996.

Manuel steadied the listing ship he inherited at the Department of Finance and steered it to the safety of shore. The Treasury is the nerve centre of any organisation, especially government, and to leave it in weak hands invites plunder and bankruptcy. The pre-1994 government had run up a fiscal deficit in excess of 8% as old friends rode off into the sunset, their saddlebags stuffed with cash. The incoming African National Congress government agreed to this as the price of liberation.

Inland Revenue (now South African Revenue Service) was plodding and inefficient, and tax-dodging surpassed soccer as the national sport.

Under apartheid, national finances had been allowed to run amok. One has to go back to the 1960s to find a time when unswerving fiscal rectitude guided government policy. This was a period of strong economic growth, minimal budget deficits, low inflation, limited exchange controls and a stable currency. With this came an admirable national credit rating.

The National Party government preferred weak, malleable men at the Treasury helm who would nod in agreement when apartheid's economic fantasies, such as the Qwa-Qwa homeland, Mossgas and Bophuthatswana, came begging for funds. They would arm-twist the Reserve Bank into lowering interest rates to furnish the illusion of prosperity when galloping inflation called for credit tightening.

The African National Congress, much as it might have wanted to continue the spendthrift ways of its predecessor, decided to bite the bullet and bring order to the nation's finances in the interests of longer-term prosperity.

The Department of Finance's ten-year scorecard looks something like this:
- inflation is down from 14% in 1993 to about 4% in 2004;
- long-term interest rates are down from an average 16% in the late 1990s to less than 10% in 2004, thereby reducing the cost of government borrowing;
- the budget deficit is down from 8% in 1992 to 1,5% in 2002 and 2,4% in 2004;
- the ratio of public debt to Gross Domestic Product is down from about 55% in the early 1990s to 46%; the medium-term aim is to reduce this to well below 40%;
- the Reserve Bank operates independently of government;
- income and corporate tax rates are down;
- revenue collection is vastly improved;
- exchange controls have been relaxed, and the nation's foreign exchange reserves are on the mend.

With this has come a vastly strengthened rand – 54% up against the US dollar between December 2001 and May 2004 – and a much improved sovereign credit rating, which makes it cheaper for government and big borrowers to tap overseas credit markets.

These achievements have come at a price – that of slow economic growth. True, growth under the ANC government has averaged over 2% a year, well above the 1,5% in the 1980s as oxygen wheezed from the lungs of the apartheid economy. But this is nowhere near the 6% growth rate envisaged in the ANC's Growth, Employment and Redistribution (Gear) programme, and none of the economic gains of the last decade have had any impact on the country's 32% unemployment rate.

The United National Development Programme criticised the government in early 2004 for its obsession with low inflation when a third of the workforce has no jobs. Inflation-targeting wins applause from the rich nations, but developing nations are fast breaking ranks with the International Monetary Fund brains trust from which such policy proposals emanate. The UNDP also recommended a managed depreciation of the rand to generate additional export earnings, which would in turn create employment.

The news on the jobs front is not all bleak, and the real sizzle is yet to come, argues FNB chief economist Cees Bruggemans. Growth rates approaching 4% are in sight, provided we race to fill the looming skills void and steer clear of external shocks such as the Asian financial meltdown of the late 1990s. With growth rates like this, the economy will create about 100 000 new jobs a year.

South Africa got a taste of this in the mid-1990s when growth rates shot to 3,5% before being gunned down by a succession of emerging market crises, capital flight and sharply higher interest rates. The economic fundamentals are in far better shape today, so the prospects of a return to rampant inflation and interest rates of 10% or higher are more remote than they have been in more than a decade.

Economists heaped praise on Trevor Manuel and the Department of Finance for striking a balance between social spending and fiscal discipline. Government braved attacks from the left for placing inflation-targeting and reduced budget deficits ahead of poverty alleviation, but the increase in the 2004 budget deficit, to 2,4%, shows its social conscience still has a beating heart. Much of the increase is earmarked for social services and poverty alleviation.

The slow progress of privatisation – the 2003 listing of Telkom on the JSE Securities Exchange notwithstanding – suggests the government, with one eye on its left flank, has yet to resolve its internal ambivalence over the sale of state assets. Accelerated privatisation would allow government to scale down its public borrowing and reduce its annual interest bill, yet it is haunted by the prospect of job lay-offs and excessive profiteering in privatised entities. Hence its emphasis on "restructuring" state assets, with clauses binding new owners to job retention and service delivery.

The department scores high marks for introducing three-year planning cycles to provide greater predictability in budget preparation, and its tightening of public finance management. The Public Finance Management Act, signed into law in 1999, regulates public financial management so that finance managers are held accountable and discharge their duties transparently and efficiently.

All in all, not a bad performance from a government crammed with activists and revolutionaries. The nation's finances are in far better hands than was the case under the National Party, and the long-awaited era of economic prosperity may be just around the corner.

Department of Provincial and Local Government

Provinces depend on national coffers for up to 90% of their revenue, much of which is transferred for specific projects and infrastructure development. Regular meetings between the national minister and his nine provincial counterparts have ensured the provinces run more or less smoothly.

But local government remains a headache. With municipal debt running at an estimated R26-billion, and often-repeated concern about the lack of skills and capacity at municipal council level, the third tier of government – expected to deliver minimal free basic services – finds restructuring and its new duties somewhat overwhelming.

Perhaps it is not surprising: in the ten years after the first democratic elections, local government has been most affected by restructuring. And a flurry of legislation has redefined what councils must do and how they must do it. This includes the introduction of the executive mayor system now in place in all of South Africa's six metropoles: Johannesburg, Cape Town, Tshwane (Pretoria), Ekurhuleni (East Rand), Ethekwini (Durban) and Nelson Mandela (Port Elizabeth).

Some 2 000 racially segregated councils inherited in 1994 were reduced to 800 by 1996 and, in 2000, to 284. All had to redefine their role to become what national government calls "developmental local government", in line with the 2000 Municipal Systems Act which obliges councils to "move progressively towards the social and economic upliftment of local communities and ensure universal access to essential services that are affordable".

While municipalities have been placed in the frontline of fighting poverty through, for example, the provision of free basic services, their patchy delivery record has raised concern.

Instead of consulting communities directly before writing their integrated development plans, for example, some councils, particularly in rural areas, pay consultants. With billing systems often in disarray, even in large metropoles like Johannesburg, many of the smaller municipalities dip into their capital budget to finance the running of the council.

And then there are the complaints against councillors — from invisibility and ineffectiveness to corruption — repeatedly raised in national government imbizos. Complaints even surfaced during President Thabo Mbeki's 2004 election canvassing.

Such difficulties, alongside a lack of coordination between provincial and national departments and municipalities, also emerged as key concerns during a tour of councils countrywide by the parliamentary provincial and local government committee in 2003.

The department, keenly aware of what is, at times, a haphazard interaction among the three spheres of government, aims to improve this through new inter-governmental legislation to be tabled in Parliament during 2004.

For now it wants to smooth relations through a new system of transferring national finances to local government: the municipal integrated grant. Worth R15-billion over three years, it is aimed at infrastructure construction at municipal level.

Further challenges are on the cards with new property rates legislation which standardises the rates councils can collect — currently a tangle of 131 different laws — and the implementation of strict budgeting and financial reporting requirements under the 2003 Municipal Finance Management Act.

That new system will be phased in over several years. But, if a pilot project involving all metropoles is anything to go by, it may not be a smooth process. Some of South Africa's biggest urban councils were unable to comply with the new reporting and budgeting requirements.

However, the department has put much hope in a plethora of nationally-sponsored local government support programmes, including making IT available for billing and budgeting, training and skills improvement and better revenue collection.

Director-general Lindiwe Msengana-Ndlela has brought a hands-on approach and a focus on good governance. Her style is inclusive: her business cards also feature her contact details in Braille, an unusual touch for a civil servant. She is also a published author with three adult education readers.

Shortly after taking office in August 2000, Msengana–Ndlela announced the establishment of an anti–corruption unit. And within a year after a municipal viability indaba jointly convened by her department and the ministry, a number of government departments had coughed up R1,4-billion of the money they owed municipal councils. Of the R26-billion debt, government departments owe 6%, business 30% and individuals the remainder.

The government has set 2005 as a deadline to complete the local government overhaul. Its targeted poverty alleviation initiative in 21 rural and urban development nodes, identified by the President in 2001, will continue until 2010.

Meanwhile, the department must also pay attention to the prickly issue of traditional leaders. The Traditional Leadership and Governance Act, which aims to democratise their rule, was passed in 2003 after being what officials described as "consulted to death".

But many amakhosi are left feeling unappreciated; they had wanted a constitutional amendment to set out their powers.

The national government has passed this hot potato down to the provinces. The department must ensure each province passes its own traditional leadership legislation, and it must establish the new structures required under the national framework law. This includes district traditional councils, which are key to the new communal land rights regimen, and an appeal body to resolve leadership disputes.

With such challenges at hand, it is no wonder that officials frequently retreat into government-speak like "infrastructure provisioning", "inter-governmental fiscal transfers reform programme" and "revenue enhancement … specialised and targeted interventions".

Department of Public Enterprises

Public Enterprise is often referred to in jest as the Department of Privatisation. In 1994, the Office of Public Enterprises was established to champion and direct the restructuring of state-owned enterprises to ensure optimum economic and development impact.

The restructuring exercise is governed by a framework agreement signed in 2000. But restructuring predates that. It was kick-started in 1997 through a sale of six SABC radio station licences. The most recent exercise was the sale of a R2,5-billion stake in cellular phone company MTN. Restructuring has to date brought in excess of R35-billion, though this is tapering off. From 2004 to 2006 the Treasury expects R2,4-billion a year in proceeds from privatisation.

The department says the need for restructuring comes from the legacy of apartheid – highly unequal and racially based services, poverty, and a massive rural-urban divide. The reasons for reforming the state-owned enterprises included improving access of the historically disadvantaged to services such as telecommunications and electricity, increasing efficiencies and reducing costs, and using the revenues earned to reduce public debt.

Union activity has been a big thorn in the side of the department. Former minister Jeff Radebe met with fierce resistance from the South African Transport and Allied Workers Union. The union forced the government to change its thinking on restructuring Spoornet in 2002.

In 2003 the clash was over the concessioning of the Durban port, a conflict that was still not resolved by mid-2004. A committee, including representatives of labour and government, which had been looking at restructuring the ports had not met since late 2003, when it had hammered out an agreement in which the union agreed only to consider private sector involvement of some kind. The agreement however was never signed off by either side, and in theory the process continues. In the meantime, concessioning of operations at the country's ports has been put on hold.

One objective the department was able to meet very successfully was the reduction of public debt by R24-billion. Commercialisation and or partial privatisation has led to the reduction in public debt by raising funds from the private sector, thereby reducing pressure on the fiscus, and creating an environment for competition.

But the department also rates the creation of an entrepreneurial class of those interested in restructuring activities, the opening up of some industries to competition, and the widening of share ownership as visions they have reached.

State-owned enterprises are championing the cause of black economic empowerment. Last year Transnet awarded a R4-billion fuel supply contract, half of which was to BEE entities.

Government considers the strategic deployment of the procurement budgets of state-owned enterprises as an instrument of BEE. The department has been tasked with accelerating the restructuring of these enterprises in an integrated and coherent manner, to promote economic growth and socio-economic development. The primary aim of the restructuring programme is to redress the imbalances accentuated by the legacy of apartheid – not just racial, but also gender.

One of the most audacious restructuring exercises was Telkom's initial public offering in March 2003. The exercise was meant to raise R30-billion for the Treasury at the height of the telecoms boom three years ago. When it was undertaken, the amount fell far short. But as an investment Telkom has done well. From a listing price of R28 in March, the price has shot up to more than R60 on the back of the successful containment of costs and solid performance by subsidiary cellphone company Vodacom.

The World Bank's global development finance report has ranked Telkom's initial public offering in fourth place in a list of the 25 largest international deals done by firms in developing countries.

Yet restructuring frequently runs into administrative and legal problems, as the privatisation of Komatiland forest and Alexkor diamond mine shows. The department had to revive the sale of the R570-million Komatiland forest after it was derailed by allegations of corruption against a department official.

Diamond mining operation Alexkor's star is on the rise, the company having reported two consecutive years of operating profit. In August 2003, then-minister Radebe announced that the company had made an operating profit of R63,9-million from its mining operations, an increase from the operating profit of R16-million in 2002. That followed losses of R197-million between 1996 and 2001.

But the privatisation of Alexkor was dealt a blow when the Constitutional Court ruled that the Richtersveld community has a legitimate claim to the land where Alexkor was prospecting for diamonds. The government has been trying to sell a majority stake in Alexkor and had shortlisted three empowerment groups – Pan African Gems, the New Alexkor Consortium and Dimeng Diamond Holding – as potential buyers of the 51% stake.

The sale of Eskom's electricity-generating is clouded in uncertainty. Thirty percent, or R30-billion, was earmarked for privatisation and a third of that to empowerment groups. But shortly after the 2004 election victory, the African National Congress called for the sale to be put on hold and for a rethink of the restructuring and privatisation programme.

Transnet, the transport and logistics parastatal, has been strengthened by the appointment of former director-general of finance Maria Ramos to head the corporation, just ahead of government's plans to invest heavily in bolstering the country's infrastructure.

The first of these will be a R14-billion revamp of its subsidiary Spoornet.

Department of Public Service and Administration

Shrinking South Africa's largely wasteful and inert public service into a professional and cost-effective machine has hamstrung the Department of Public Service and Administration since 1994.

In 1998, a blueprint for restructuring the public service was provided by the Presidential Review Commission, a statutory body established in 1996 to investigate problems in the public service. It recommended drastic steps such as the dismantling of some government departments and creation of new ones. However this report remained a paper tiger until 2000 when a resolution to prune the number of public servants through a three-phase process was signed.

By September last year the first phase – to match personnel to the human resources and skills needs in the public service – was completed with the slashing of 135 995 public service posts. Public servants were given the choice either to take voluntary severance packages or to be redeployed into other areas of the government. Today the public service employs 1 031 594 people. With regard to their share in the public service sectors, 61,4% are in the social services (health, social development and education), followed by 16,5% in criminal justice, 14,7% in the government, and 7,4% in defence. Phase two will deal with the excess employees (20 958) who were not accommodated during the redeployment. They will be placed into special training programmes, and currently a framework is being developed to facilitate this re-skilling.

In addition, the department and the National Treasury have developed a business plan to review all public entities reporting to national government departments, excluding constitutional bodies and commissions. Currently there are 336 public entities. Last year Cabinet approved the rollout of community development workers in four provinces – Gauteng, Eastern Cape, North West and Limpopo – who are trained to bridge the gap between government services and the people.

They will assist with matters such as birth certificates, IDs, social grant applications and small business start-ups. The department has also developed a national strategy to mitigate the impact of HIV and Aids on service delivery.

A public service anti-corruption strategy has been approved by Cabinet for implementation over a three-year period. To buttress it, new anti-corruption legislation has been introduced in Parliament and there are processes being implemented to assess government departments' capability to deal with corruption. An incentive scheme has been introduced to inculcate a culture of performance among public servants.

In the same vein, however, the senior management service, which was established to develop quality managers and professionals by regulating their financial interests, has been a failure as only 20% have declared their interests under asset register requirements. The overall goal of the SMS is to implement an employment strategy to recruit, but most importantly to retain and develop, managers and professionals in the public service. This initiative was established to plug the drain of public officials to the private sector by offering them competitive salaries and training in the public sector. The SMS has implemented mechanisms to improve interdepartmental mobility of senior managers, for example directors-general, so that they shift to other jobs within the public sector rather than moving into big business for new challenges.

The department is a harbinger for employment equity – 68% of its management is black and 26% are women. About 0,1% are disabled. The minister, Geraldine Fraser-Moleketi, wants to up black management to 75%, women to 30%, and disabled people to 2% by 2005.

While all these strategies paint a rosy picture, the department is still heavily reliant on outside consultants at great cost to the state. After ten years of capacity development programmes, questions remain about why the public service, which spent R111-million in salaries last year, cannot take care of its own needs.

Department of Public Works

The department has been in existence continuously since the creation of the Union of South Africa in 1910. It continues to be responsible for the provision and management of all government-owned buildings, including prisons, police stations, magistrate's courts, military bases and office accommodation of all national departments.

After 1999, then–minister Jeff Radebe swopped portfolios with Stella Sigcau, who had been minister of state enterprises. After the 2004 elections, she keeps the same post.

In line with government's overall objectives, Radebe had begun a process of expanding the department's core function of maintaining state-owned properties towards job creation and black economic empowerment. Under Sigcau, this approach has been continued: working through public/private partnerships, with a central focus on rural development and community projects that create employment, especially for youth, the disabled and women.

This aspect of Public Works has grown enormously with the Expanded Public Works Programme, launched in April 2004. The intention of the programme is to reach one million unemployed workers over the next five years, offering temporary employment and some training on government projects where labour-intensive methods can be brought into play. Public Works will be the overall coordinator of the programme, which cuts across departments.

Public Works' own infrastructure projects will come in for the major portion of the EPWP budget; R15-billion will be used to hire and train people to build rural and municipal roads, install storm-water drains and water and sewer pipelines, and renovate schools and clinics. In addition, R4-billion will go to the Department of Environmental Affairs and Tourism to increase paid participation in such programmes as Working for Water; R600-million to the Department of Social Development to create jobs in early childhood development and community-based health care; and an amount still to be determined to Trade and Industry for funding the development of a range of small businesses and cooperatives.

Dealing with emergencies also seems to be part of the department's responsibilities. Within Sigcau's first year, for example, she faced several crises: in 2000, a fire ravaged the department's central office in Pretoria, causing damage estimated at R1-million. In the same year, floods devastated several provinces, especially Limpopo, Mpumalanga, the Eastern Cape and KwaZulu-Natal, causing an estimated R2,5-billion damage to roads and bridges. Sigcau chaired the interdepartmental ministerial emergency construction committee. Floods also did massive damage in neighbouring Mozambique, and Sigcau chaired the RSA emergency reconstruction committee, a sub-committee of the disaster management committee, which involved representatives from South Africa, Botswana, Mozambique and Zimbabwe.

In 2000, the "Clean and Green" project was launched, to mobilise communities into participating in environmental planning and fighting poverty by improving their immediate environment.

Strategic employment programmes for women in construction were launched in Mpumalanga and Limpopo, as well as a toll-free ethics hotline to encourage the public to report incidents of bribery and fraud by departmental officials.

However, although the department makes a point of choosing small suppliers and contractors whenever possible, it does not always pay them on time. According to the National Treasury, government contracts stipulate payment within 30 days, but the department can take up to a year or more to pay these struggling entrepreneurs. Those who cannot carry the costs themselves simply go under. Public Works this year prioritised timeous payments.

Restoration and upgrading of many township police stations and construction or restoration of magistrate's courts (Kroonstad, R13,76-million; Blue Downs outside Cape Town, R20-million) around the country was undertaken, as well as the construction of several community centres and schools, especially in rural areas.

From 1999 to 2004, the department invested over R383-million in KwaZulu-Natal alone, initiating 1 000 infrastructure projects and creating 39 924 jobs, 44,8% for women and 42,3% for youth, second only to the Eastern Cape, where R364 626 262 was invested in 809 projects.

A new maximum security prison, Kutuma Sinthumule, reputed to be the largest of its kind in the world, is being built on behalf of the Department of Correctional Services at Louis Trichardt – now Makhado – in Limpopo, at a cost of R345-million. Along with Mangaung Maximum Prison near Bloemfontein, these two prisons are private finance initiatives, by consortiums between South African and international private companies which run similar initiatives in the United States, the United Kingdom and Australia.

Empangeni Prison was refurbished at a cost of R33-million. A super-maximum prison, the first of its kind in South Africa, Egongweni Correctional Centre in Kokstad, was built at a cost of R314-million. A black woman contractor won a contract worth R19-million for the repair and maintenance of Leeuwkop Prison near Johannesburg. By March 2003, R188-million in contracts for 75 projects had been awarded to female-owned enterprises.

In 2002, an HIV/Aids awareness campaign in the construction industry was initiated.

In 2001-02, the department recorded 100% expenditure of its capital works budget for the first time in its long history, as well as 100% of its poverty alleviation and rural infrastructure development budget. The 2003 annual report is not yet available.

In February 2002, Sigcau appointed a new director-general, Themba James Maseko, to replace Tami Sokuto, who joined the private sector at the end of his three-year contract.

Maseko is a former CEO of Sifikile Investment Holding and a past managing director of Simeka Management Consulting, as well as former director-general for the Gauteng Department of Education between 1995 and 2000. When an MP, he served on various parliamentary committees including education, public enterprises, justice, and the bill of rights for the new Constitution. Maseko has BA and LLB degrees, as well as an MBA. He also completed the senior executive programme jointly offered by the Universities of Harvard and Witwatersrand.

Department of Science and Technology

The Science and Technology half of the erstwhile Department of Arts, Culture, Science and Technology developed a multitude of programmes during the decade it shared a ministry – in fact, gobbling up well over half the budget allotted for these unlikely bedfellows. So it was well set up to go out on its own.

There is a good balance here: an educationist as minister and a physicist – who had run the combined department until it was split in 2002 – as director-general, thus covering both ends of the spectrum. The deputy minister is an agriculturalist, adding knowledge of a more down-to-earth application of both science and technology.

Education first: The department intends to cooperate with the Department of Education on a range of projects, among them offering educators a chance to upgrade their skills in teaching maths, physical and life sciences, engineering and computer studies; and giving learners ways to improve their performance in some of those subjects. It also plans the placement and support of learners in key strategic economic sectors, among other initiatives.

The National Science Week will continue; since 2000, it has been publicising careers in science, engineering and technology for young people.

An institute for the promotion of sciences – a Bill was still in the drafting stage in mid-2004 – defines "sciences" as "natural sciences, engineering sciences, medical sciences, agricultural sciences, social sciences, indigenous sciences, technology, all aspects of the innovation chain and indigenous technologies". The institute would advise the minister, raise its own money, and create programmes to promote science and technology throughout the country.

A national research and development strategy, adopted by Parliament in 2002, will increase the proportion of the national budget spent on R&D. It also focuses basic science on areas where South Africa has an edge over other countries: human palaeontology, indigenous knowledge and astronomy.

In line with the last-named discipline, South Africa is bidding to have a major astronomical project, the $1-billion square kilometre array radio telescope, built in the Northern Cape, with some of its components made in South Africa. The telescope, which will require complex computing and information processing systems, will be 100 times larger than any receiving surface currently in existence. The winning bids will only be announced in 2006.

The department's director-general, Dr Robert Adam, earned a BSc Honours in chemistry from the University of Cape Town, and honours and master's degrees in theoretical physics from Unisa, the last two while he was in prison in the 1980s for his participation in the armed struggle; and a doctorate, also in theoretical physics, after his release. He was a post-doctoral fellow at Vrije Universiteit in Amsterdam, then joined the University of Natal's Department of Physics before his appointment in 1995 as chief director in the then Department of Arts, Culture, Science and Technology, from which he moved steadily up the ranks.

Department of Social Development

The Department of Social Development has not yet found the balance between grants and empowerment – understandable in a country where so many people live in dire poverty.

Most of the department's energy and funds are going to grants. NGOs accuse the department of paying too much attention to alleviation of poverty through the almost exclusive mechanism of grants, and not spending enough funding on other areas such as skills development. However, the need for grants – in fact, the need for a Basic Income Grant to meet the core needs of the deeply impoverished – is often brought to the department's attention by the same organisations.

The reliance on grants has another aspect which the department is currently trying to resolve: the billions of rands of fraud already occurring.

In a sad scenario, the more the department tries to eliminate abuse of the system, the more it cuts off needy people who do not have the ability or the understanding to apply for the documents to qualify for the money that will make their lives marginally easier. This double-edged sword means that some of South Africa's poorest of the poor are slipping through the social safety net.

The legacy of poor rural South Africans is often traced back to the legacy of apartheid and the need for employment that saw black men move to the cities for work as part of the migrant labour system. An insufficient rural service delivery, inferior levels of Bantu education and broken homes as a result of forced migration still plague the department.

Criticism at provincial level is often aimed squarely at the more rural provinces – and these are also the poorest provinces that desperately need the department's intervention.

Four years ago, the department underwent a name change, becoming the Department of Social Development instead of the Department of Welfare.

The name change indicated a desire to be more than a source of welfare; a more holistic and integrated approach was required to shake off the legacy and create a "better life" for society's poor and marginalised people. The name change also indicated the department's commitment to the agenda of social transformation, which is a constitutional imperative.

The department's main task is to reduce poverty, at the same time promoting social integration. It has been set the daunting task of ensuring that all South Africans may shelter under the umbrella of welfare services and social protection, creating an environment that reduces poverty. Programmes are implemented based on research. The department also registers non-profit organisations and holds them accountable.

Despite desiring public accountability, departmental officials respond to attacks from the non-governmental organisation sector by urging the NGOs to work in partnership with them, and not to go running off to the media. The department desires a much more cohesive relationship with NGOs, faith-based communities, the business sector, organised labour, and other role-players.

The department aims to build self-reliance within communities through empowering them. With the current system, this is not immediately feasible but may in time lead to less reliance on grants to stem the tide of poverty.

Currently, 7,7-million people receive grants annually, at a cost of over R34,8-billion each year. This figure has increased from 2,6-million beneficiaries in 1994.

The department's budget for the last financial year (2002/2003) indicates that they had R650 251 000, almost R130-million of it allocated for "normal operational expenditure", while the remainder was allocated to projects. Food relief was allocated 45% of this money. HIV/Aids was allocated less than 10%, poverty just under 20% of the funds, and social security improvement was budgeted at 5%.

Other items on the Social Development budget were HIV/Aids, food and poverty relief, and social security improvements.

The department's 2004 budget saw the extension of the Child Support Grant receive the bulk of monies, at just under 60%. The department aims to have extended the grant to include all impoverished children under the age of 14 by the next financial year.

This is a three-step process: children under nine came into the net in 2003, and in 2004 children under 11 were included. The department says it is ahead of its targets and has already extended the net to a further 3,3-million children. Seven million children are expected to benefit from the extension by mid-2005.

There have been glitches: officials in some provinces refused admittance to the programme to children under nine. And, the critics say, children who reach the maximum age according to the old requirements but would again become eligible in the new financial year are not being kept on the system, causing unnecessary paperwork – and anguish to recipients of the grant.

The largest number of children who are currently falling out of the net are those who, due to inefficiencies within Home Affairs, lack the correct documents. By liaising closely with Home Affairs and the Department of Education to provide documents and ensure that all children are given the chance to register, the department has taken a step forward to alleviate the backlog.

But this step forward will be undermined if they continue to operate without enough resources. The department's director-general, Vusimuzi Madonsela, who was appointed on a three-year contract in May 2003, announced the establishment of a social development agency early in 2004. The agency is expected to tackle the problem of under-resourced provincial departments by taking over grant administration in 2005.

The National Social Security Agency will take over what was a provincial responsibility on a budget of R60-billion per annum, and will relieve provinces of administration tasks, allowing them to focus on other aspects of poverty alleviation.

Sport and Recreation South Africa

South Africa is one of the few countries that dignify sport with its own full ministry, but the role played by sports boycotts in the apartheid years meant it was unlikely that a post-1994 government was going to leave this particular field to the players. That said, the area's lack of real significance is tacitly acknowledged by the fact that, below the ministerial figurehead, the most senior official is a single deputy director-general, currently Denver Hendricks.

The more-publicised issues of the past ten years – such as recalcitrant rugby officials, the cricket bribery saga and corruption in soccer – have been dealt with by the ministry, leaving the department to concentrate on less glamorous but more important tasks.

Sport and Recreation South Africa sees the removal of the "substantial disparities between advantaged and disadvantaged communities in terms of access to sport" and sporting facilities as one of its key functions. It is limited in its objective in that most of the biggest and best sporting complexes in the country are in private hands or owned and controlled by professional sports bodies that seem loath to share their facilities with other codes.

One of the department's tasks is to create, maintain and upgrade multi-purpose sports facilities, and to recruit and train people to manage these facilities.

The department currently has three statutory bodies to assist with the delivery of sport and recreation. These are the South African Sports Commission, the South African Institute for Drug Free Sport, and the South African National Boxing Control Commission (reconstituted as Boxing South Africa). The last-mentioned of these was formed in 2002 to bring some order to boxing, and is unlikely to remain under direct government aegis once it has proved it can stand on its own feet.

The Sports Commission is the most active arm of the department. Among its tasks are arranging events such as the Traditional Games, and keeping track of compliance within sports that have a racial quota system. The Traditional Games aims to ensure the survival of non-professional sports – ranging from stick-fighting to jukskei – whose continued existence is threatened by a lack of media attention and corporate funding.

The commission establishes yearly targets to ensure that all sports and recreation bodies achieve their affirmative action objectives. These targets apply down to grassroots level, and are not merely for elite sportspeople. Sanctions for non-compliance can include withdrawal of state funding or a ban on international competition.

There are also many non-governmental organisations, such as the National Olympic Committee of South Africa, Disability Sport South Africa, and national sporting federations, that are partially or wholly dependent on Sport and Recreation South Africa for funding. All sporting codes and their national federations must be registered with the department in order to participate in events at full international level or award national colours. Teams and individuals can approach the department for funds for development, training or participation in competitions.

The department also has a say in the awarding of television rights for national and international events. It can – in conjunction with the broadcasting authorities – decide that an event, say the Olympic Games or soccer World Cup, is of national interest and then insist that that event be broadcast on free-to-air channels.

The department has an annual budget of about R55-million and seeks to increase this to about R120-million with funds from poverty relief programmes. With this extra money it hopes to raise the level of participation in organised sport among the broad population from the current 7% to 20%. Its emphasis will be on getting previously marginalised groups, particularly black women and the disabled, involved in sport.

It also aims to take a more active role in streamlining efforts and pooling resources to support South African competitors in international events. A substructure within the department deals with funding of athletes and teams.

The department has committed itself to use sport to effect positive change within South African society. It recognises the influence sportspeople wield within their communities, and has encouraged organisations and individuals to throw their weight behind social-conscience initiatives such as the fight against HIV/Aids.

The ham-fisted actions of former minister Ngconde Balfour have often overshadowed or even negated the work done by his department. For example, his frequent high-profile rows with the rugby and cricket authorities over quotas belie the steady progress being made at grassroots level to fully integrate these sports. Annual reports from regional to provincial level are made available to the media and any other interested parties detailing compliance with clearly stated targets.

Without a loose cannon at the top it might be possible for SRSA to achieve its objectives. Its small but dedicated team is enthusiastic and efficient.

Department of Trade and Industry

The Department of Trade and Industry has devoted the last decade to restructuring a closed economy and can be broadly described as being responsible for two key areas. The first is to act as a custodian of South Africa's trade position in the world economy. The second is to be the engine of the domestic economy by stimulating small business, guiding the structural composition of the economy, and facilitating economic transformation. Over the past ten years, the department has displayed an ability to be very good with the big picture but poor on detail.

The department is led by one of the longest-serving directors-general, Alistair Ruiters. Under his stewardship it went through drastic image revamp and restructuring. These have at various times been fraught with acrimony and morale-sapping uncertainty. Business Day once ran an editorial accusing the department of using spin to hide malaise. Ruiters now frequently expresses satisfaction that the restructuring is complete. Some of its visible and lasting changes include a call centre to offer services like business and investment advice, and a department mindset that treats economic citizens as customers. Yet a view persists that the changes were nothing more than institutional tinkering that did not add value.

The greatest successes have without a doubt been on the trade and export front. South Africa now enjoys preferential trade status with both the European Union and the United States through the Africa Growth and Opportunities Act. However, it seems unlikely to tire in its campaign for a fairer trading system to change the world. From Seattle in the United States to Cancun in Mexico, wherever World Trade Organisation delegates gather, treaties are drawn and deals are made, South Africa is looked upon to champion the cause of the poor.

One of the country's most celebrated successes in exports is in the vehicle component manufacturing sector. In 1995, the government put in place the Motor Industry Development Programme. The programme is aimed at encouraging car parts exports through incentives. Vehicle component exports grew for seven consecutive years after the programme's inception to reach R22,9-billion in 2002, before falling 7% to R21,3-billion in 2003.

The last great achievement of the department in the first decade of freedom has been to legislate the deracialisation of the economy by putting in place the Broad-based Black Economic Empowerment Act, two years after it was initially mooted. The Act seeks to promote economic empowerment by encouraging ownership by historically disadvantaged South Africans. It also encourages empowerment through skills transfer and sourcing goods and services from black- and female-owned suppliers.

Yet for all its successes the department is frequently criticised for its programmes' failure to create jobs. The decade ahead thus presents major challenges in both policy and implementation, domestically and abroad.

The first major area of glaring failure has been the lack of an environment that helps small and medium enterprises to thrive. The department's finance institutions, like finance guarantor Khula Enterprises, have been spectacular failures, when it comes to supporting small business. South Africa ranks consistently low on surveys like the University of Cape Town's Graduate School of Business Global Entrepreneurial Monitor Survey, which measures small business activity in developing countries.

Observers note that the failure of small and medium enterprise is not solely due to government. It is largely due to the banking sector's conservative mindset. Economist Iraj Abedian attributes the banking sector's inertia to historical evolution. He argues that South African banks were created to safeguard surpluses of mining houses, whereas their counterparts in Europe were created with a venture capital mindset, which demands that they take risks.

One way the government can help small business is to cut down the clutter of bureaucracy one has to go through to register a small business or keep it operational and compliant. Two examples on how the DTI has failed to grapple with detail are gambling and liquor trading laws.

The social ills of mushrooming casinos are an increasing scourge, and yet the proceeds – while they have yielded benefits to some – have not reached the poor. The lottery, continually generating lucky millionaires, still continues to elude the good causes it seeks to serve, and in cases where charities are reached, the money is either inadequate or late.

On the long-awaited liquor Bill, the department clashed with brewers twice in recent years. A major area of difference is the industry's insistence that the department legalise areas in black townships which account for a high proportion of clear beer consumption, while the department's fixation remains breaking the industry three-tier system that sees production, distribution and wholesale held by a single entity.

The department also needs to examine the structure of industry. There is growing evidence that there is concentration of power in industries like chemical and steel manufacture that tends to make downstream industry suffer through practices such as import parity pricing.

And industrial clusters such as the one found in the Ekurhuleni Metropolitan in Gauteng need to take higher priority and receive more support. Research from the Corporate Strategy and Industrial Development Research Project at Wits University have found that a low proportion of firms in this cluster – said to be the highest concentration of industry in Africa – know of or use government incentives available.

Department of Transport

The Department of Transport got off to a good start in 1994, with struggle stalwart Mac Maharaj in the driving seat. Maharaj left government after the 1999 elections to pursue his own interests in the private sector. In his place came Dullah Omar, who had been minister of justice. When Omar, suffering from cancer, became so ill he could no longer work – he died a month before the 2004 elections – the then-minister of public enterprises Jeff Radebe stepped into the breach, and has now inherited the portfolio.

Omar's term of office was not characterised by any innovation; he held the department's ship steady on the course laid down by Maharaj. Several projects initiated during Maharaj's reign – among them the "Arrive Alive" campaign – continued or were completed. The road death rate, especially over holiday periods, began to drop. Credit–card–style drivers' licences were successfully introduced, although the department had to extend deadlines several times to accommodate recalcitrant drivers and the volume of registrations.

The independent statutory bodies and arms–length departmental agencies set up during Maharaj's term continue to function well. They include the Airports Company of South Africa, which owns and operates South Africa's nine principal airports; the National Road Agency, tasked with developing, maintaining and managing the country's 72 000-km national road network; the National Ports Authority, which oversees development and maintenance of all ports and harbours, playing a vital role in facilitating international trade; and the South African Civil Aviation Authority, which carries on, despite a nepotism scandal that, among other factors, lost Authority head Trevor Abrahams his job.

However, several pieces of enabling legislation, such as the National Ports Authority Bill, have been stalled for some time, and one of the first tasks Radebe will face will be to give new momentum to these, and to oversee their course through Parliament.

Work on transforming the National Traffic Information System – NaTIS – which has been in operation since 1991 into eNaTIS, has continued. The electronically linked system is intended to coordinate input about vehicle and drivers' licences from all nine provinces. The old paper-based system was thoroughly inefficient, and eNaTIS, touted as the solution to ongoing crime and corruption in the issuing of, in particular, vehicle licences, should improve matters, though progress towards full implementation has been remarkably slow.

The issuing of vehicle and drivers' licences is the responsibility of municipalities, which act as the government's agents, nominally under the oversight of provincial governments. However, it is ultimately the department's responsibility to coordinate the national system, so the rapid implementation of eNaTIS remains an imperative.

Negotiations to bring the informal minibus taxi industry under control have faced several obstacles. Government's attempt to introduce a larger, safer vehicle as a standard has not been universally welcomed by taxi owners and drivers, and it now looks as if the entire taxi recapitalisation plan is going to be scrapped. Efforts to reconcile the often–violent rivalries between owners of taxi fleets have also only met with moderate success. Overall, attempts to regulate this industry have reached a stalemate.

There have been amendments to several existing Acts, and a number of new transport-related Bills have been introduced through parliamentary committees. Much of this work awaits the attention of the new minister.

While still acting minister, in August 2003 Radebe appointed Wrenelle Stander director-general of the department, the first black woman to hold this post. She comes well qualified – she served in high-level posts at the Air Traffic Navigation Services Company and the Minerals and Policy Centre, and was the transport department's general manager for aviation and maritime regulation.

Department of Water Affairs and Forestry

In 1994 the department was faced with a legacy in which at least 14-million South Africans, particularly in rural areas, had no access to safe drinking water, and 21-million had no access to basic sanitation. Women and children often had to walk long distances to fetch water from rivers or boreholes. Further, there was no umbrella body to manage supply and distribution of water nation-wide; this had been managed at a provincial level, and separately in the former homelands.

The department was tasked with bringing South Africa's water management into line with the new Constitution, which explicitly provides access to food and water as a social right. The Constitution also states that South Africans have the right to a healthy environment, which entails protection of the environment and use of its resources in a sustainable manner.

To facilitate the coordinated management of water, the National Water Act was passed in 1998. The Act takes into account that South Africa is a dry country (only 30 nations worldwide have less water per person). The Act has therefore nationalised the total water supply – a move not popular with the agricultural sector. It also sets aside sufficient water, in any catchment area, to meet the needs of the people in that area, as well as to meet the ecological needs of rivers and wetlands.

The department also implemented a "free basic water" policy, in which households are entitled to 6 000 litres of water a month free. This is funded by an exponential rates scale, in which the more water used per household beyond the free quota, the more expensive it becomes.

The outgoing minister of the department, Ronnie Kasrils, has said that nearly 10-million people now have access to clean water who did not have it in 1994. This means that South Africa is theoretically ahead of the target set at a meeting of the United Nations in 2000, where 100 heads of state committed to halving by 2015 the number of people lacking safe water. The department estimates that it will have eradicated the backlog of infrastructure for water by 2008, and sanitation by 2010.

The Municipal Services Project, a joint Canadian–South African organisation that monitors municipal delivery in South Africa, questions the department's figures. Quoting only "researchers", the MSP nonetheless points out that project failure because of broken pumps, lack of funds to maintain pumps, damage to mains, and non-payment of tariffs resulting in cut-offs mean that it is possible about 70% of the projects which have been launched since 1994 are no longer operational. The MSP concludes that more research is required to see what is working and what isn't.

In an address to the Water Institute of South Africa conference in May 2004, the director-general of Water Affairs and Forestry, Mike Muller, concluded that in the poorer areas, from the Eastern Cape to far north Limpopo, "there are water schemes that are not delivering water because the electricity bill has not been paid [or] because there is no staff to maintain the pumps and motors." Lack of trained staff was the most critical problem, he said.

Service and delivery are to be decentralised to local government in 2004. To this end municipalities will receive grants from the department, which has warned that these are "not an early Christmas present but a heavy responsibility". The department will work with municipalities to help them use the money to end the bucket-toilet system and the backlogs in water supply and sanitation. The bucket system, often poorly managed, is blamed for most outbreaks of cholera.

The department has been following the revised protocol for river management drawn up by the Southern African Development Community, and has signed various agreements with neighbouring states for studies and management of resources such as the Limpopo river and the Maputo basin.

The management of state forests has been transferred to commercial concerns and, in some instances, South African National Parks, but structured in a way that benefits rural communities through jobs and income. The restructuring is intended to facilitate black empowerment by allowing previously disadvantaged communities a share in ownership and control of the forestry companies.

The department has been instrumental in involving South Africans at all levels in its projects and educating them as to the value of natural resources. An example is the Working for Water project which aims to eradicate water-greedy exotic species; because they are exceptionally tough and proliferate very successfully, they take over and destroy sensitive indigenous environments.

The department created temporary jobs for 20 000 people in the physical removal of declared alien species, but it also worked to educate and win the support of the large and lucrative plant and garden industry. Campaigns such as Waterwise Gardening, which encourages South Africans to plant indigenous dry-adapted species in their gardens rather than thirsty exotics, have also been successful in raising public awareness about water as a valuable resource.

The director-general, who has held the post since 1997 after joining the department in 1994, expressed "delight" with the appointment of the new minister, Buyelwa Patience Sonjica, following the April 2004 national election. Sonjica chaired the portfolio committee on water affairs and forestry from 1999 to 2003, and "is not coming into the department cold", Muller has pointed out.

Muller, who has been called one of the mandarins of the democratic bureaucracy, was educated in Swaziland, and studied engineering in the UK. He worked in London local government, and joined the Mozambique government's National Water Agency in 1979, and the Development Bank of Southern Africa in 1988. He helped prepare the Reconstruction and Development Programme of the democratic South African government in advance of the 1994 elections.

3

Commissions and the Constitutional Court

Commission on the Restitution of Land Rights

The work of the Commission on the Restitution of Land Rights, established in terms of the Restitution Act of 1994, focuses on providing equitable redress and restoration to victims of dispossession, particularly the landless and the poor. In doing so it contributes towards the equitable redistribution of land in South Africa. It also facilitates development initiatives by bringing together all relevant stakeholders, especially provincial governments and municipalities.

The commission has a deadline: by 2005 it must meet the president's directive of resolving all land claims. The task is not taken lightly, but by the beginning of 2004 it had settled only some 60% of the claims lodged with it.

In the beginning the commission adopted a judicial approach, but it soon became clear that the court-driven process was taking too long. Amendments to the Restitution Act in 1999 gave the minister of land affairs and agriculture the power to make awards based on negotiated settlement agreements. The department says the amendments have resulted in a phenomenal and exponential increase in the number of claims settled.

Another controversial amendment to the Restitution Act was passed at the beginning of 2004. It gives the minister the power to expropriate land from farmers who are unwilling to sell and pay them an estimated value of the farm. Farmers' unions such as AgriSA have called it draconian.

At the end of 2003, 800 000ha had been returned to their original black owners through the restitution process. Between 1995 and the end of 1998, 79 649 claims had been filed countrywide. By February 2004, about 47 000 claims had been processed.

Land restitution received a budget of R854 914-million in the 2003/2004 financial year. The commission employed 342 workers in 2004, and planned to increase the number by 150 to help speed up the programme.

Last year the commission focused on settling rural land claims, which constitute 20% of the total and are more challenging than urban claims. Often they include difficulty in obtaining relevant documentation and information, unresolved disputes, unregistered and unsurveyed land rights, and poor infrastructure, which often hampers accessibility.

Tozi Gwanya heads up the commission. His professional career commenced in 1975 with a post as a clerk in the Transkei Department of Education. The year 1994 saw him becoming the director of the Africa Cooperative Action Trust, and five years later he was appointed regional land claims commissioner for the Eastern Cape. In 2003 he was appointed chief land claims commissioner.

Commission for Gender Equality

It is not clear what the achievements of the Commission for Gender Equality have been as it fails to report adequately on its own work. Valuable research has apparently been done on submissions to Parliament, dealing with legislation which impacts on gender relations, but the work of the Commission's parliamentary office was ignored even by its own annual report.

While the Commission has undertaken a campaign on the theme of women and poverty, non-governmental organisations working in this field question what they have done to intervene effectively in this matter. Good work has apparently been done, such as providing gender mainstreaming training for provincial government departments, but this is difficult to quantify. A few commissioners are apparently working hard, but the rest seem unsure of their role and mandate.

The Commission has failed to intervene in a range of significant gender issues. These have instead been left to NGOs to deal with, such as the justice for women campaign, provision of post-exposure prophylaxis drugs for victims of sexual assault, maintenance, and the rollout of anti-retroviral drugs.

Some suggest it suits government to have a weak commission staffed with party functionaries, and that this has been proven by the CGE's singular failure to challenge the African National Congress on any issue at all, from the President's jokes about beating up his sister to the appalling levels of gender violence being committed against the women of Zimbabwe. It has, however, taken up the exoneration of sexual harassment charges of the South African ambassador to Indonesia with Foreign Affairs Minister Nkosazana Dlamini-Zuma.

The CGE has not always been as confused and ineffective. It was set up in 1997 with a tiny budget – at R17-million for 2004, it still has the smallest budget of any commission – but a huge mandate to advance gender equality in all spheres of society, and it went about its task with a vengeance.

It was chaired by former struggle activist Thenjiwe Mtintso, with gender activist Colleen Lowe-Morna as CEO. Together the pair formed a formidable team, with Mtintso considered a paragon of leadership virtues, and Lowe-Morna a savvy activist adept at raising the profile of the commission through strategic engagements with civil society, the media and government.

But two years later Mtintso was redeployed by the ANC to become the party's deputy secretary general. Many saw the loss as a fatal blow, particularly when she was replaced by the elderly Joyce Piliso Seroke, generally referred to in gender circles as a gracious lady but not a dynamic leader.

With the departure of Mtintso, tensions rose between the commissioners and the secretariat, which consists of highly skilled gender experts hired by commission committees. Many commissioners felt threatened by the skills of the secretariat staff, and this resulted in major infighting, with commissioners attempting to interfere in the day-to-day management of the CGE instead of focusing on the larger issues around the vision and mission of the commission. Commissioners also proved resistant to upgrading their skills – in fact a programme in which they were offered an opportunity to go on attachment to the Equal Opportunities Commission in the UK failed to attract even one application.

This tension culminated in the effective constructive dismissal of Lowe-Morna, who came back from a trip to find she had been locked out of her office. She won a court battle, and the CGE's subsequent appeal, and was awarded two years' salary plus legal costs, at a cost to the taxpayer of over R1-million. She was replaced by Elize Delport, one of four members sacked from the board of state-owned diamond mine Alexkor for neglecting their trustee responsibilities.

The Commission continued to lurch from crisis to crisis with the controversial appointment of Zith Mahaye, which sparked a probe by the Public Protector into the alleged irregularities in his appointment. The Protector dragged its feet and the probe never actually got under way, but attracted a lot of negative publicity. Mahaye resigned and was replaced by Bafana Khumalo in an acting capacity. (The current CEO is Chana Mojake.)

Word is that the government's ten-year constitutional review – in which it will evaluate the work of various commissions – is being done "semi-secretly" based on public documents but without any engagement with the CGE. There is speculation that the various commissions may be amalgamated along the lines of the Australian Human Rights and Equal Opportunities Commission, with specific desks dealing with gender, disability, employment, etc., a move that would appear to require a constitutional change. Meanwhile the CGE has secured funding from the European Union for a three-year project, along with the South African Human Rights Commission and Public Protector's office, to bolster links with civil society and develop a coordinated mobile office to allow the organisations to go into provinces such as KwaZulu-Natal, Limpopo and Eastern Cape and do work on public education and monitoring.

Human Rights Commission

Many of the challenges faced by the Human Rights Commission are similar to those that have dogged other Chapter 9 institutions. Most of these difficulties arise from structural problems: the now familiar tensions between the secretariat (made up of highly skilled experts) and the commissioners (who are essentially political appointees).

Set up to promote, protect and monitor human rights, the HRC was launched amid high hopes and ideals, and staffed by the best and brightest human rights lawyers in the country. As with the Commission for Gender Equality, the structural tensions led to infighting, stifling of talent, and high staff turnover. Critics often raise questions about the relevance of the Human Rights Commission and its perceived failures to act on issues that top the public agenda.

The chairperson of the Commission is Jody Kollapen, a man who inspires affection and respect throughout civil society. Kollapen, a lawyer by training and one of the leading lights of Lawyers for Human Rights, joined the Commission a year after it was launched.

Before becoming chairperson he spearheaded the commission's campaigns on xenophobia and prisoners' rights, and devoted much time to educating journalists on human rights issues, encouraging them to see all stories through a human rights lens. A gentle soul who has devoted his life to the struggle for human rights, he is seen as having a more conciliatory style than his predecessor, Barney Pityana, who launched the now-infamous inquiry into racism in the media.

Kollapen is credited with attempting to make the Commission a happier place to work. Unfortunately these attempts have not been entirely successful, as the droves of staff who continue to leave will attest: most blame the CEO, Lindiwe Mokate, claiming she is an autocrat who runs the Commission like her own personal fiefdom.

Kollapen feels that much of the criticism levelled at the HRC is due to unrealistic expectations of the commission by a public unaware of its many successes. He acknowledges that the Commission has lost profile and doesn't publicise its work sufficiently, but says a clear distinction must be made between monitoring, which is the Commission's function, and delivery, which rests with government.

He says the role of the HRC is to highlight deficits in capacity and delivery, and to lobby around these and, if necessary, to litigate. He says the Commission has often been able to make meaningful interventions. An example was its work in the Eastern Cape, where people were unable to access social grants because they did not have identity documents and did not have the money to travel to town and apply for these documents. The HRC intervened; it successfully prevailed upon Home Affairs and Social Welfare to travel to these areas with mobile units and process applications. Kollapen says that while this kind of work is not well publicised, this sort of action is also not as comprehensive as it should be.

He acknowledges that the HRC doesn't engage in much litigation but points out that the Commission's enabling legislation makes it clear that conciliation and mediation are the preferred methods to resolve disputes, and that a high proportion of disputes referred to commissioners are resolved through this approach. Kollapen is clearly reluctant to be seen as complaining about the HRC's budget allocation, but stresses that they do what they can with the resources they have.

The Commission has identified socio-economic rights and equality as its two major areas of focus, but Kollapen is quick to point out that the commission should not become complacent about civil and political rights, which are still areas of contestation. For example, serious issues such as crime or terrorism have a tendency to make one amenable to limiting civil rights. While rights may be limited in certain circumstances, this cannot be done arbitrarily, but requires a pragmatic yet principled approach.

Socio-economic rights are seen as the major challenge, and Kollapen warns that citizens may develop a warped sense of democracy if they have the right to vote but don't enjoy the basic socio-economic rights, such as food and shelter.

Socio-economic rights, however, are more complex and difficult to implement, linked as they are to government policies, capacity and resources, and therefore not just a matter of enforcement.

Socio-economic rights are also open to differing interpretations in terms of their content. He stresses that while they are included in the Bill of Rights and government has a legal obligation to deliver them, they are subject to progressive realisation, and the pace of this realisation, as well as the minimum content of the right, need to be the focus of lobbying and advocacy (e.g. the benchmark set for the right to access to water is a tap 200m away from the house). Once there is agreement on content, then monitoring can begin.

As a national institution, the HRC has an influential role to play in government policy with a view to reducing poverty. Kollapen says courts are often being forced into making policy, even though they are loath to do so, when the Constitution is contravened. This has fiscal consequences for government (e.g. the recent ruling on permanent citizens being given access to social grants). Providing a basic income grant would be one way of providing social security, but would not discharge the obligation, he adds.

Kollapen appears unfazed by the rumours that the various Chapter 9 commissions – among them gender, youth, and human rights – may be amalgamated. He says there is an argument to be made for such a move, as there are areas of overlapping jurisdiction and all the commissions suffer from resource constraints. The major considerations should be advancing human rights and using public funds optimally.

Independent Electoral Commission

The watchdog of South Africa's elections, the Independent Electoral Commission (IEC), is internationally renowned for its rigorous protection of South Africa's most sacrosanct democratic tool – every voter's cross.

At the helm of one of this country's greatest challenges – to link one election day, nine provinces, about 17 000 voting districts and about

20-million registered voters – are two stylish and savvy women: Dr Brigalia Bam, the chairperson of the IEC, and advocate Pansy Tlakula, the chief electoral officer.

The IEC is a permanent body established in terms of the Electoral Commission Act of 1996. It is a publicly funded body and is accountable to parliament, but it is independent of government.

During the 2004 elections it spent about R790-million. Broken down, this amounts to about R240-million on administration costs such as salaries, and R400-million on logistics, such as setting up voting stations and counting centres.

The IEC has five full-time commissioners, appointed by the President, whose brief is to deliver free and fair elections at all levels of government – national, local and provincial. The primary functions of the IEC are to divide the country into voting districts, register eligible voters, make logistical arrangements for smooth running on election day, and count, verify and announce the election results.

During the 2004 election there were 17 000 voting stations, up from 14 500 in 1999. Statistically, 3 500 voters should pass through each voting station. This controls bottlenecks in busy areas, such as inner cities and informal settlements.

Also during the 2004 elections, the IEC employed 215 000 volunteers, who were trained to manage these voting stations. However, to ensure continuity for future elections, the IEC is busy developing a learnership in managing elections, which will be registered under the National Qualifications Framework.

The IEC has successfully conducted three general elections: the country's first democratic election in 1994, the 1999 election and the 2004 election. It has also managed the 1995 and 2000 local government elections and a number of by-elections.

South Africa uses a proportional representation voting system based on political party lists at the national and provincial levels. A registered political party receives a share of seats in parliament in direct proportion to the number of votes cast for it in the election. Voters don't vote for individuals, but for a political party, which decides on members to fill the seats it has won. Voters cast two ballots: one for the election of the 400 members of the National Assembly, the other for the election of the 430 members of the nine provincial legislatures.

The gargantuan task of drawing the boundaries for the voting districts is done by one of the world's most extensive Geographic Information Systems. The GIS produced over 75 000 electronic and colour scale maps in 1999 which set out the voting districts. This system allows the IEC to among others keep track of the movement of informal settlements. Given South Africa's high illiteracy rate and the fluidity of its labour market, the voting districts act as residential addresses for roughly 60% of the population who do not have fixed abodes.

Essential to the IEC's anatomy are Party Liaison Committees which function at all three levels of government. They act as discussion forums for the different political parties.

If political parties have any complaints on election day, regarding the voting process or the election outcome, they lay a complaint at the IEC head office in Pretoria where a settlement is reached through mediation. In the case of a stalemate the complaint is taken to the electoral court to be settled. In 1999, out of a few hundred complaints, only three went to court.

Brigalia Bam is steeped in politics, and her career is a polyglot of business, human rights, education and women's development. She is efficient and her conversations sparkle with epigrams.

Born in Tsolo in the Eastern Cape in 1948, she trained as a teacher and then pursued her studies abroad at the University of Chicago where she read communications. During the 1950s and 1960s she worked in the education, health and welfare sectors in South Africa. Then she moved to Switzerland where she worked for the World Council of Churches, and later served as the Africa Regional Secretary and Coordinator of Women's Worker Programme for the International Food and Allied Workers Association in Geneva.

Since her return to South Africa in 1988 she has served on the SABC, Murray & Roberts Engineering, Global Dialogue and ABSA boards. She was a commissioner on the South African Human Rights Commission, and chairperson of the Open Society Foundation. She is the Chancellor of the University of Port Elizabeth and the founder and president of the Women's Development Foundation. She has served on the IEC since the 1999 elections when she was a deputy chief electoral officer.

Advocate Pansy Tlakula is softly spoken, unassuming and razor sharp. She took over as CEO at the beginning of last year. She came from the Human Rights Commission where she had been a member since 1995.

Before that she was the executive director of the Black Lawyers Association. She is the former chairperson of the Council of the University of the North West, which has since merged with Vista University Sebokeng Campus and the University of Potchestroom. She serves on the boards of several NGOs.

Judicial Service Commission

The JSC is charged (by section 174(2) of the Constitution) with the transformation of the higher judiciary to a more demographically and gender representative bench than the one it inherited in 1994. It interviews candidates and makes recommendations to the President. In the case of the Constitutional Court, the JSC must nominate three more people than the number of seats vacant, and the President makes the final selection; in the case of the Supreme Court of Appeal and the High Court, the President endorses the JSC's nominations.

The Commission is also empowered (by section 178(5) of the Constitution) to advise the national government on any matter relating to the judiciary or the administration of justice.

It has, say observers, succeeded remarkably well in its transformation role, given that the pool of suitably qualified people from which it can select is small and there is no great temptation for high-earning commercial lawyers in private practice or the corporate world to give up comfortable, lucrative jobs to struggle, in the case of the high courts, at least, in bleak chambers in poorly equipped courts for considerably reduced incomes.

The intense vetting process candidates have to undergo at the hands of the JSC makes the prospect, for many, doubly unattractive.

Nonetheless, the complexion of the judiciary has changed considerably. By April 1993, the country had 69 black judges – 58 men and 11 women – 122 white male judges and 13 white female judges spread across the Constitutional Court, the Supreme Court of Appeal and the High Court.

Prior to the creation of the Commission in 1994, judges were appointed by the Cabinet from the ranks of senior practising advocates. The Commission was created to enable greater democratic control over the appointment process. The membership of the JSC is therefore representative of the executive, Parliament, the judiciary and the legal profession. Members include the Chief Justice, the Minister of Justice, practising advocates and attorneys, legal academics, parliamentarians designated by the National Assembly (three of whom must be members of opposition parties), and members of the National Council of Provinces.

It is, inevitably, dominated by African National Congress members and supporters, but, though some believe there are political considerations involved in some of its appointments, it cannot be described as a "lackey" of the ruling party.

Part of the perception problem lies in the fact that although the JSC has introduced a degree of transparency unknown in the past to the appointment of judges, conducting public hearings that are open to the press, its criteria for selection are not clear and some of its appointments (and some of its non-appointments) are considered puzzling. It has been described as "a bit of a mysterious body that has failed to make itself transparent" and as "doing an incredibly important job in the murky half-light cast by its own rules of procedure". This makes it difficult to study, and its workings almost impenetrable to interested outsiders. The hearings are not open to the electronic media, curricula vitae are not made available, and verbatim transcripts can only be obtained at huge cost.

Undeniably, though, it is an important body that has made a considerable impact on the judicial system.

Public Service Commission

The Public Service Commission is an independent statutory body established in 1996 to monitor, investigate and evaluate human resources practices within the public service and to report on these to Parliament and provincial legislatures. Despite its role as a public service watchdog, the Commission is better discernable by its inactivity than its activity.

It has 14 commissioners chaired by Professor Stan Sangweni, who has recently been reappointed, but is described by a leading academic as "ineffectual and a lackey of the executive". The same is said to apply to his commissioners, who fetch salaries in excess of R550 000 each per year.

Despite the notoriety of corruption in the Eastern Cape government, for example, the public service commissioner in that province has neither reported nor investigated a single incident of corruption or maladministration.

The PSC is structured around six areas. The first is professional ethics and risk management, which deals with corruption on an ethical level. The second is special investigations, a unit which investigates cases of corruption at all government levels. The third is management and service delivery improvement. The fourth is labour relations, which monitors employment equity practices in the public service. The fifth is human resource and development; and the sixth is senior management and conditions of service, which evaluates the performance of senior managers.

Despite its function to report incidences of corruption, malpractice or underperformance to Parliament and provincial legislatures, the PSC has yet to develop any systematic monitoring mechanism to meet these responsibilities. It is currently developing such a mechanism, but even if it did possess such a tool, its success would be dependent on the degree of political will by the PSC to investigate cases of corruption and maladministration. Today that political will is worryingly diluted.

This is also where a number of structural considerations could also mitigate against the independence of the PSC. Firstly its budget (during the last financial year it was R57-million) is determined by the Minister of Public Service and Administration, Geraldine Fraser-Moleketi; yet the department is one that the commission is supposed to monitor. Secondly the PSC's 14 commissioners, although appointed by the President, are nominated by the minister and by provincial premiers, whose performance they will also have to monitor.

The 14 commissioners include Koko Mokgalong in the head office in Pretoria, David Mashego in Mpumalanga, Mawandile Msoki in the Eastern Cape, Dr Ralph Mgijima in Gauteng, and Kenneth Matthews in the Northern Cape.

National Youth Commission

Established in 1996, the National Youth Commission was formed to act as an internal government lobby group to ensure youth issues remain high on government's agenda.

According to its mandate, the Youth Commission is supposed to ensure that policy making, across the board, is sensitive to the needs of young people between 14 and 35 years.

But in recent years the organisation has been slated for inaction, failure to achieve its goals and mismanagement of funds, as senior staff reportedly received inflated salaries but failed to deliver.

The troubled organisation has had to whittle down its number of commissioners from 18 to five, and has had to streamline it operations to prove it is worth the R13-million budget that it is allotted annually.

It is currently headed by Jabu Mbalula. Born and educated in the Free State, Mbalula has long been involved in the youth activism movement; he served on organisations such as the Congress of South African Students and then National Education Coordinating Committee. He is also a member of the national executive committee of the African National Congress Youth League.

Mbalula was appointed to his second three-year term last year. He and the other commissioners are appointed by the President on the recommendation of the parliamentary joint monitoring committee on the improvement of the quality of life of children, youth and people with disabilities. Head offices are in Pretoria, with provincial structures in eight of the nine provinces.

In mid-2004, the Youth Commission believes it is turning the corner on its problems and can rise to the challenge of its mandate – which, stresses a spokesman, is to guide policy making and not necessarily to be involved in the implementation of specific projects.

Earlier this year, the commission held nationwide imbizos or meetings to bolster awareness about the organisation, to gauge the sentiments of the youth, and to create platforms for young people to articulate their needs and feelings. Priority issues that were identified include greater involvement for the youth in economic development, combating unemployment, and the need to nurture an Aids-free generation.

The Youth Commission spearheaded the formulation of the national youth development policy framework which was adopted by Parliament in 2001. Now it says that 2004 has to be the year of implementation and for the organisation to intensify its lobbying and advocacy work as set out in the policy framework's implementation vehicle, the national services programme.

Four key areas of development have been identified in the programme. The first focus is on skills development including life skills, economic skills and entrepreneurial skills. Secondly the programme seeks to ensure that young people participate in the development of their communities.

Thirdly youth will be encouraged to be part of nation building, and finally they are to be steered towards cultivating a sense of patriotism.

The Commission has also identified four youth target groups: those in higher education; those involved in further education and training; unemployed youth, and those who are in conflict with the law.

The Youth Commission says it works closely with its sister organisations in civic structures, and insists that the parallel roles of a statutory government body and those from the NGO sector are necessary to guarantee that South African youth are not ignored and their voices are heard, loud and clear.

Constitutional Court

A little over nine years after its official inauguration on 14 February 1995, South Africa's Constitutional Court moved into a magnificent permanent home on the site of the old Johannesburg Fort, one of the symbols of the apartheid era.

With its 11 judges, selected and appointed by the President from a list of nominations from the Judicial Service Commission, the Constitutional Court occupies the apex of the judicial system. It is headed by the country's Chief Justice, currently Judge Arthur Chaskalson who was the court's first president until the roles of President of the Court and Chief Justice were merged in 2001.

Since its inception the court has operated under two different constitutions, the text of one of which it was called upon to certify; has developed an extensive body of jurisprudence; and is respected worldwide for the quality of its judgements. It finds itself, by constitutional mandate, in the centre of not only the legal but also the social and political transformation of South African society.

In its nine years the court has handed down more than 200 decisions, some of which have made a considerable impact (not always positive) on the lives of segments of society ranging from death row prisoners through terminally ill patients to homosexual couples. In one of the court's earliest decisions the death penalty was abolished on the grounds that "the rights to life and dignity are the most important rights and the source of all other personal rights".

Socio-economic rights triumphed in the famous Grootboom case, in which the court ruled that the state housing programme was not reasonable – a ruling that led to an amendment of the government's housing policy. A reluctant Department of Health was forced to change its decision on the provision of the anti-retroviral nevirapine to HIV-positive pregnant mothers, and the Independent Electoral Commission was instructed to ensure that prisoners were given the opportunity to vote in the 2004 general elections.

On the other hand, one man died and others surely will after the court was unable to order the provision of renal dialysis in a state hospital because it was reluctant to "interfere with rational decisions taken in good faith by the political organs and medical authorities whose responsibility it is to deal with such matters".

Broadly speaking, the decisions of the court can be divided into three categories. Two of these seldom make headlines. They are the cases that deal with the technical issues of the court's own procedures and powers, and those that deal with the Constitution's division of political power among the various organs of state and spheres of government.

The best-known aspect of the court's work falls into a third category – human rights cases. The court spent much of its time in its first few years dealing with the remnants of the apartheid statute book. Now, with most old-order legislation out of the way, its human rights decisions have begun to focus on other issues: the common law and the socio-economic rights cases.

A crucial test of its success is its relationship with the other branches of state – a relationship which has been adroitly managed by Chaskalson.

Informed observers have described the relationship between the government and the court to date as cordial. The more cynical among them believe it is a little too cordial, and see the court as tending to lean in favour of the government. They query the outcome should the two bodies go head to head on any major rights issue. To date, with few exceptions (the case, brought by the Treatment Action Campaign, for giving anti-retrovirals to pregnant women in state hospitals being an obvious one), there has been little reason for the Constitutional Court to test itself against a government that has not tried to take any action against the rule of law that might confront the court with a constitutional crisis.

Even its detractors would find it difficult to decry the undoubted achievements of the Constitutional Court and the effect of the 207 judgements handed down between April 1995 and December 2003.

One of the most important of these achievements is that it has invigorated the whole legal system, and constitutional values are beginning to trickle down from the Supreme Court of Appeal to the high courts and, most importantly, to the magistracy. Magistrates now receive judicial training that teaches them about the Constitution; an education that will hopefully redound to the benefit of those who appear by their hundreds and thousands in the lower courts.

4

Political Parties

African Christian Democratic Party

Heavy on family values and biblical mores, the party likes to make much, during parliamentary question time, of claims that 12-year-olds are now given condoms and instructed how to have sex.

The party's seven MPs blame the HIV/Aids pandemic and crime on government laws and policies. At the heart of South Africa's moral degeneration are the legalisation of abortion and gambling, the recognition of same-sex partnerships, and the relaxation of censorship laws, which has led to the flourishing of pornography.

The ACDP stands for conservative Christian principles, including the return of the death penalty, and respect for marriage and the family. "With the concept of multi-party democracy in the air, Christians from all over the Republic recognised the need for a party that would not only represent Bible-believing Christians, but also those who have a high regard for moral values," the ACDP website proclaims.

With this in mind, the party was established in December 1993. Just 100 days later it had secured enough votes for two MPs and three seats across all nine provincial legislatures.

As the only party to vote against South Africa's Constitution in 1996, the ACDP recently called for the county's supreme law to be amended to recognise Christian values. It has always rubbed the party up the wrong way that in South Africa the Constitution is the supreme law, rather than the Bible. The ACDP wants to raise "a new generation of God-fearing leaders".

The party has been gaining more support in recent elections. In the 1999 national elections, it tripled its number of National Assembly representatives to six and acquired its first seat in the National Council of Provinces. In the 2004 elections, its representation in the National Assembly grew to seven after the ACDP complained to the Electoral Court that 2 666 votes attributed to Azapo had actually been cast for the ACDP – a view the court agreed with.

Born in Pretoria, ACDP leader Reverend Kenneth Meshoe initially studied to be a teacher at the University of the North, then at Tennessee

Bible College. He joined an outreach project under American evangelist Reinhard Bonnke and in 1980 became an associate evangelist.

By March 1988 Meshoe and his wife Lydia, currently an MPL in the Gauteng legislature, formed the charismatic church, Hope of Glory Tabernacle, in Vosloorus on the East Rand.

Now over 4 000 strong, the church in late 2003 opened an assembly hall. Its prayer and fasting campaign to end violence in Vosloorus on Johannesburg's East Rand has been recorded in Meshoe's book Operation Pushback.

Lydia Meshoe remains active in Women of Destiny, an ACDP-aligned community development group formed to implement, as the party blurb says, ACDP policies by "applying the Biblical principles". This includes child-care facilities, feeding projects and assistance to people living with HIV.

Over the past five years in Parliament, the party has formulated its own policies. Some of them are somewhat odd – like making prisoners on parole wear brightly coloured overalls so that communities can identify them. Others, like housing policy, are actually not far removed from current government policies. The underlying thread, however, is a biblical sense of justice, retribution and the centrality of family to society.

African National Congress

The African National Congress has succeeded in turning itself from a national liberation movement into a governing political party, but the transformation has left the party marked with a myriad of large and small political divisions.

One of the main dividing lines in the post-apartheid ANC is seemingly between those who have gone into government and those who have chosen a political role outside of the state.

Confronted with the realities of running a country and kick-starting its social development and economic growth, many of those in the ANC who took up elected positions, or were appointed to posts in government, adopted an increasingly technocratic approach to South Africa's challenges. Depending on whom you speak to, perhaps the best example of this was government's Growth, Employment and Redistribution strategy, essentially a relatively conservative economic policy which limited state spending and severely restricted the budget deficit.

The result was that while the ANC in government won widespread praise for its astute handling of South Africa's finances, the country spent relatively little on social and economic development programmes during the ANC's first ten years in power. Some attention was given to social grants, the provision of water, housing and school lunches for primary school learners, but the impact on the lives of ordinary people was somewhat more paltry than had been expected.

This frustrated allies of the ANC – like the Congress of South African Trade Unions, the South African Communist Party and many non-governmental organisations – who have many members in the party's ranks. They believed the representatives of the ANC in government were failing to implement its political mandate – to use all of the available resources of the state to rapidly tackle poverty and underdevelopment in South Africa. Their more traditional view of the mandate of the ANC often found widespread popular support among their members.

However, while the divisions over economic and social development strategy spilled over into very public spats between Cosatu, the SACP and the government, ANC officials in party headquarters maintained relationships with their allies and nursed the strains in its ranks. While ANC and South African President Thabo Mbeki was talking about the ANC becoming a smaller, professional political party, many in its ranks were objecting to what they perceived as an end to its tradition of open debate in its ranks.

ANC secretary-general and former National Union of Mineworkers general secretary, Kgalema Motlanthe, is widely believed by those close to the organisation to have played a key role in keeping the ANC – and its allies – together during these tense times by bridging the gap between those who felt shut out of ANC and government policy-making and those in Cabinet and other state structures.

After the ANC's national conference in 2002, when government began to feel that the country's fiscal situation was strong enough for it to begin to expand state spending, the tensions among the allies began to ease. However, differences between those in the ANC and its allies who would like to see a much more expansionary fiscal policy, and those in government who are still relatively conservative, continue.

ANC MPs, especially those in parliamentary oversight committees, have found themselves facing the competing demands of being loyal party members while needing to hold government accountable for the actions of the executive. Although the majority of ANC parliamentarians simply fell into line behind the executive on matters of legislation and governance, there have been some significant exceptions, and many ANC members have actively fought to uphold an independent role for the legislature.

These are only some of the many personal and political differences and divisions which are present in today's ANC. However, in a hangover from its days as a liberation movement, the ANC will very seldom publicly admit to differences in its ranks, even when these differences are an open secret. The party vigorously defends the public perception of its unity.

Divisions in the ANC are nothing new, and its greatest strength has always been its ability to accommodate them. While other organisations split, and split again, until their factions were so small as to be irrelevant, during its struggle against apartheid and through its years in exile the ANC maintained its unity. While in exile from the 1960s to its unbanning in 1990, former ANC president Oliver Tambo kept the organisation unified while it campaigned to bring down the apartheid government through international sanctions, internal mass actions and limited armed struggle.

By the early 1980s, the ANC had established itself, in the international community and among the majority of South Africans, as the "sole legitimate representative of the people of South Africa", according to the slogans of the time.

The organisation went into negotiations to end apartheid in South Africa confident of the support of the overwhelming majority of South Africans. Despite the reservations of many in its ranks, largely those who supported the concept of a revolutionary transfer of power instead of a negotiated settlement, and despite some setbacks during the negotiations process, the ANC kept its popular support while negotiating an end to white rule. Since 1994, the ANC has won South Africa's three general elections and two local government polls with ever-increasing majorities, although off ever-decreasing turnouts.

While many tend to put the ANC's overwhelming political support down to its being credited with liberating the majority of South Africans from apartheid, too little recognition is given to the fact that the ANC government has also received recognition for its promises and attempts, however limited, to improve the living conditions of poor South Africans, and is consequently being rewarded at the polls.

227

The next challenge for the ANC is the selection of the president who will succeed Thabo Mbeki, presently serving his last term as party leader. The organisation is due to hold its next national conference, where the new president will be elected, in 2005.

In 2002 the ANC declared itself a social democratic party.

Azanian People's Organisation

Azapo remains on the fringes of the political landscape even if its president, Mosibudi Mangena, is in Cabinet. Azapo did not participate in the multi-party negotiations at the Convention for a Democratic South Africa or in the first democratic elections in 1994. It changed its stance for the 1999 elections, in which it scored 0,2% of the vote to get one National Assembly seat for Mangena.

President Thabo Mbeki's January 2001 announcement that the Azapo MP had been appointed as Deputy Minister of Education sparked a constitutional headache. And within party circles it was hotly debated whether Mangena should take up the post; in some party circles it was felt that the offer was a personal one, rather than one extended to Azapo.

Azapo, wanting to maintain its parliamentary presence, ordered Mangena to resign as MP. A constitutional amendment was passed to specify that a deputy minister could be appointed from outside the National Assembly in certain circumstances.

So Mangena was sworn in and Azapo deputy president Pandelani Nefolovhodwe became the party's sole parliamentarian.

He was nearly joined by a colleague after the 2004 elections, but the Electoral Court ruled that 2 666 votes attributed to Azapo had actually been cast for the ACDP – and so Nefolovhodwe is, once again, a lone voice.

The quietly spoken MP battles to make an impact with the one minute speaking time allocated to him. This became clear in a 2003 parliamentary debate on Pan Africanist Congress founder Robert Sobukwe, during which the African National Congress appropriated him as their own.

Azapo was launched in 1978, from the remnants of the Black Consciousness Movement spearheaded by Steve Biko in the 1970s. Strong on African leadership, the party calls for all land to be state-owned; it also wants free education and health care under a strong socialist state.

In recent years Azapo has criticised government's black economic empowerment initiatives and legislation as creating a small black elite at the expense of the working class.

Azapo politics have often been marked by internal fights and fractiousness.

In August 2002 dissidents broke away to form the Black Consciousness Forum, at least partly due to Mbeki's courting of Azapo and Mangena's appointment.

But in wider political circles, the appointment had been seen as a gesture of cross-party cooperation and a sign of the increasing influence of the black consciousness principle of encouraging African leadership within the ruling party. The presidency already employs another leading Azapo member, legal adviser Mojanku Gumbi, who is said to have significant influence. Several other Azapo appointments to government posts have followed.

Azapo says those unhappy with the recognition of its members' skills have already defected, leaving the party unified.

For several years various attempts have been under way to form a united front with other black consciousness organisations. Before the December 2000 municipal elections there was a memorandum of understanding with the Socialist Party of Azania, an earlier break-away group from Azapo, and the Pan Africanist Congress of Azania.

Talks to form a more permanent black consciousness front are continuing, so far without success despite policies and attitudes shared by all three political parties. Despite such upheavals, Mangena has led the party since 1994. And it appears that participating in formal politics has whetted the appetite for bigger things. In December 2002 the Azapo central committee decided "to mobilise for an Azapo government in 2009".

Democratic Alliance

South Africa's official Opposition is confident of expanding its appeal. But there has been a price to pay: the Democratic Alliance is seen as having lurched to the right.

Party leader Tony Leon's recent call for the reinstatement of the death penalty is seen as symptomatic of this. Although the DA allows a free vote, the endorsement has alienated many. It was sharply and publicly slated by liberal stalwart Helen Suzman, founder of the DA's ancestral Progressive

Party. In 1969, during her long solo stint in Parliament, Suzman brought a private member's Bill to abolish the death penalty.

Echoing the DA's move to the right were the party's 2004 election candidate lists, featuring an increased number of former Conservative Party and old guard National Party members. Despite a stated intent to shed its image as a white party, the DA has failed to produce a pool of black public representatives.

For the April 2004 elections, the DA formed a "Coalition for Change" with the Inkatha Freedom Party and claimed it would win 30% of the vote. The DA's support − 9,5% in 1999 − did increase, but not by much: the party scored 12,3% on its own, with the coalition chalking up just around 20% of the poll. The DA described the result as a "qualified success", then embarked on a bit of soul-searching to determine why its black support was only 2%.

The official Opposition, with 50 seats in the National Assembly, is widely regarded in government circles − and elsewhere − as the party of "white rage". Vocal in its criticism of government policies, laws and foreign relations − particularly over the government's apparent support for Zimbabwe President Robert Mugabe and, more recently, Haiti's ousted President Jean Bertrand Aristide − the DA is often and, many say, unfairly − characterised by the African National Congress as unwilling to accept black leadership.

Unapologetically free market, the DA has slammed much of even moderate trade union legislation it sees as pro-worker. It has criticised legislation to promote black economic empowerment.

And it has led the charge against an ANC two-thirds majority.

Relations between DA leader Tony Leon and President Thabo Mbeki are icy; exchanges between the DA and ANC in parliamentary debates are vicious.

The DA came into being in mid-2000 with the marriage between the then Democratic Party and the New National Party. Its forerunner was a post-1999 election coalition between the two parties in the Western Cape, aimed at combining their polling support of just over 6% and 38,39% to keep out the ANC, even though the ANC had won more votes (42%) than either party.

The alliance was criticised by Suzman and left many others uncomfortable. But Leon was in a commanding position, and he pursued the merger with vigour.

Under his leadership, the DP in 1999 replaced the NNP as official Opposition, with 38 seats in the National Assembly. That was a far cry from the seven it had won with 1,7% of the vote in the 1994 poll. The exceptional boost was largely attributed to voters' response to the "Fight Back" campaign. At the time the party ignored the negative reaction among many black South Africans, who interpreted it as "Fight Black".

Confidence was bolstered in the December 2000 municipal poll, the first election the DA contested, with victory in key Western Cape councils. But it did not last. By late 2001 the NNP had withdrawn, after securing a cooperation agreement with the ANC in return for defection legislation. Under the new legislation, lawmakers were allowed a brief period to "cross the floor" to other political parties, thus altering the balance of power in some areas.

During the municipal defection period in late 2002, many of the Western Cape municipalities, including Cape Town, came under ANC-NNP rule. But the DA maintained that its ex-partner had only regained a minority of its former members. This, party officials said, was a sign that the DA was seen as credible at the grassroots.

By that time the DA had adopted many of the crowd-catching NNP strategies: bussing in supporters, bopping music, Cape minstrels and a plethora of party paraphernalia like T-shirts, flags and caps. The so-called "Houghton liberals", the party's core base, were horrified.

But with successful inroads into the Coloured vote, the DA increasingly focused on townships. The party now regularly scores around 11% in township by-elections, or a 100% increase, according to its officials, but it has not been able to translate these victories into a national critical mass. Much credit has been given to Western Cape provincial legislature leader Helen Zille, who has worked extensively in Cape Town's townships. Teaching herself isiXhosa, the former education MEC has been vital in establishing viable DA township branches. After shaking up the provincial Education Department – she was education MEC from 1999 to 2001 – the former Rand Daily Mail political reporter headed for national politics in Parliament. Her no-nonsense, hands-on attitude is one of the party's major drawcards.

What remains lacking is a visible black leader. The highest-ranking black member of the DA is Joe Seremane, the national chairperson, who joined the DP in 1998, serving as MP in the National Council of Provinces. In 1999 he took up a front-row bench in the National Assembly.

Seremane was a member of the Pan Africanist Congress and spent six years on Robben Island for recruiting – he had organised cadres to leave South Africa – before being deported to the former Bophuthatswana homeland in 1969. In the 1980s, he was director of Justice and Reconciliation in the South African Council of Churches, and after 1994 was appointed chief land claims commissioner, a post he held for four years. Seremane hit the headlines when he tried to uncover how his brother Timothy died at the ANC's Quattro detention camp in Angola in the late 1980s. It was claimed Timothy Seremane had been beaten, tortured and executed. The issue arose before the truth commission in 1997 and again in late 1998 when ex-camp commander Mthunzi Gabriel Mthembu applied for amnesty, but was never satisfactorily explained.

Although hard-working, Seremane appears to play second fiddle to Leon, and he continues to take flak for sitting in the Opposition benches at Parliament.

In early 2003 the DA shed its last link to the old liberals who had formed the DP after a series of break-ups and mergers in the late Eighties. Following the floor-crossing period, the party was officially known in all legislatures as the DA. In the process it gained another nine senior NNP MPs, who were unhappy about cooperation with the ANC, and lost one MP.

The DA's "Coalition for Change" – touted as an alliance of democrats – has been perhaps the most visible manifestation of its vain attempt to prevent an ANC full house in provinces and two-thirds majority in Parliament. Bruised at its failed merger with the NNP, and despite its lukewarm showing in the 2004 poll, the DA sees the future of strong opposition politics in cooperation agreements like this one.

Freedom Front Plus

Chasing an Afrikaner homeland, the FF+ nevertheless has increasingly come to grips with the New South Africa, and is using the country's constitutional bodies and laws to push for Afrikaner rights.

It successfully invoked the Constitution's language equality clause to ensure census forms were available in Afrikaans, laid a complaint with the South African Human Rights Commission against the use by the Landless People's Movement of the slogan "One Farmer, One Bullet", and took the issue of farm murders all the way to the United Nations.

In late 2003 the FF+ successfully negotiated behind the scenes for South Africans temporarily abroad to be able to cast their ballots in the 2004 elections.

After all, they saw a potential few thousand votes for the FF+ at stake, according to the party's youth group, which has been active in London for several years.

The party needed the extra votes. Its seats in the National Assembly were slashed from nine in 1994 to three just before the 2004 elections – and after the elections, back up to four.

The Freedom Front added the "+" as it worked to consolidate the conservative Afrikaner vote. The FF first absorbed the Conservative Party, whose long-serving leader Ferdi Hartzenberg finally retired in February 2004, and the Afrikaner Eenheidsbeweging, which had lost its sole MP ten months earlier during the floor-crossing period.

The party believes many disgruntled Afrikaners who voted for the then Democratic Party in 1999 are set to return to the volk. That despite the setback in its campaign to highlight farm murders: a commission of inquiry found these were criminal acts, not politically motivated as the FF+ had claimed.

The FF+ has turned to styling itself as the vehicle for what party leader Pieter Mulder calls "an angry new generation of young whites". The party, which has repeatedly called for the abolition of affirmative action, wants at least a cut-off date for it, with those who entered school in 1992 and are set to write matric at the end of 2004 no longer subject to employment equity requirements. The FF+ has found fertile grounds of support at the University of Pretoria, where it has led the students representative council for several years.

But the face of conservative Afrikaners has taken a battering following the arrests of right-wing Boeremag members charged with plotting to overthrow the state. Ten years later, memories were resurrected of the pre-1994 election bombing spree by right-wingers intent on disrupting the first democratic poll which they regarded as threatening their survival as a distinct cultural and language group.

It had been exactly those perceptions that drew the party's first leader, General Constand Viljoen, out of retirement in 1994 to negotiate with the African National Congress. The Afrikaner Volksfront fell apart as the CP-sponsored drive to boycott the first democratic elections gained dominance. Instead, Viljoen formed the FF and contested the poll.

The FF came fourth in 1994 with 640 000 votes, but this was slashed to 0,8% in 1999. In 2001 Viljoen returned to cattle farming and paprika harvesting in Mpumalanga.

Dr Pieter Mulder took over the reins. The former communications lecturer and department head at Potchefstoom University, who had represented the town in Parliament since 1988, was a co-founder of Viljoen's FF.

During the Constitutional Assembly negotiations, Mulder was widely credited as a key player in getting cultural and minority rights, mother-tongue education and the principle of territorial self-determination written into the Constitution.

With his brother Corné at his side, Mulder has been at the heart of the FF+ drive to – as the party puts it – "constructively work within the constitutional framework" while chasing the Afrikaner homeland dream. The underlying tenet appears to be that conservative does not mean racist.

So while Mulder criticises South Africa's so-called quiet diplomacy on Zimbabwe and calls for a plebiscite on the return of the death penalty, there appears to be a certain respect within government circles for his approach. The result? It is easier for him to meet key leaders than it is for, say, the leader of the official Opposition.

With South Africa celebrating ten years of freedom, the FF+ says that this has not necessarily translated into justice for all communities. Instead the party under its "Programme for Hope" wants to pursue greater security for minority rights.

Despite little progress on Afrikaner self-determination, the dream continues: Carel Boshoff, linked to Orania, the experimental informal Afrikaner settlement, was on the FF+ election candidate list, although too far down to make it to Parliament.

Independent Democrats

Less than a year after Patricia de Lille left the Pan Africanist Congress, the party she founded touts itself as clean, critical, outspoken and independent – much like the characteristics ascribed to its leader.

The 2004 elections appear to have confirmed its appeal: on its debut, the ID scored better than many of the established parties, emerging as fifth largest with 1,73% of the national vote, giving it seven seats in the National Assembly and one in the National Council of Provinces. It not only narrowly outscored the New National Party nationally but outdid it even in some of the NNP's Western Cape heartlands, like Swellendam and Beaufort West.

Disenchantment among liberals with the Democratic Alliance, faith in De Lille's public image and disgruntlement with other political parties are factors in her success. The ID emerged strongly in the Northern and Western Cape, fared well among Coloured and white voters, but had little impact on the African vote, despite the fact that its leader cut her political teeth as an Africanist.

De Lille says her party will now focus on fine-tuning policies to give effect to the ID's election slogan: "More voice for your vote".

She is central to the ID. Although provincial and national structures have been established in a whirlwind of activity, it remains her face and reputation as a feisty politician who does not mince her words that carries the party.

A wide range of her personal network – academics, non-governmental organisations, lawyers and other well-placed individuals – came in early with advice, time and cash. And those who have come aboard have secured people in their own networks.

Yet some of the choices of leaders like Themba Sono in Gauteng and Lennit Max, the former provincial police commissioner, in the Western Cape have raised eyebrows. Max has been widely criticised for not doing enough in the Western Cape's fight against crime, although he blames a lack of resources. Sono, a former member of the Democratic Alliance, was blamed for opportunism and accused of giving positions to pals. Anger over his alleged actions sparked a walk-out during the party's leadership elections in Gauteng.

"I'll be the new ID of South Africa," quipped De Lille when she announced the launch of the new party in early 2003. She wants not simply to criticise for criticism's sake, but to be "an effective, principled political voice", to hold government to account and focus on bread-and-butter issues.

And that is something she knows about. As one of seven siblings, growing up the daughter of a Beaufort West school principal in the Karoo was not easy.

Grassroots concerns were also central to her as an Africanist trade unionist in the 1970s and 1980s. When the PAC was unbanned in 1990, De Lille officially joined. She was among the group which pushed, successfully, for the party's participation in the multi-party negotiations at the Convention for a Democratic South Africa and in the elections. In 1994 she arrived in Parliament as one of its five MPs.

Once there, she continued to speak out, raising the first alarm bells over irregularities in the multi-billion rand arms deal.

In early 1998, in Parliament, she named five ANC Cabinet ministers who she said had been identified as having spied for the apartheid state. She was promptly suspended, took Parliament to court – and won. These court proceedings also gave rise to the re-writing of Parliament's powers and privileges legislation, passed at the end of 2003, which unambiguously set out and tighten the rules of conduct in the House, leaving parliamentary privilege more or less intact but closing the odd loophole.

In mid-2000 De Lille successfully approached the courts to improve the lot of a group of juveniles detained in overcrowded, disease-infested conditions at Pollsmoor Prison. That one of the youngsters had murdered her sister did not deter her.

It was to De Lille a group of parliamentary women employees turned with sexual harassment claims. She persuaded them to lay charges, and the accused manager was eventually dismissed. De Lille was also the first politician to publicly take an HIV/Aids test.

When De Lille left the PAC some felt betrayed, noting that the party had allowed her to speak out, even when her views were contrary to PAC policies, and allowed her to become a force of her own.

The United Democratic Movement came to legislative office in 1999 on a whirlwind similar to the ID's in 2004, also riding to some degree on the reputation of its leader. The reversal in its fortunes hold salutary lessons for De Lille: she must spend time on policy formulation (the party has few identifiably different policy measures, and she is equivocal on the death penalty); build other leaders; and establish a more polished party infrastructure, if the ID is to grow.

New National Party

"Survivor" was an apt description of the NNP – until the 2004 election.

After the NNP's pitiful showing – 1,65% of the national vote, which entitles the party to a mere seven seats in a Parliament the party controlled with overwhelming numbers for nearly half a century – the only question left is why the NNP has not dissolved.

The party faithful put on a brave face. For now the NNP may continue to lurk on the national political landscape. Its cooperation agreement with the ruling African National Congress has become its lifeline, even though its supporters have resoundingly rejected the pact and deserted it in droves.

Despite the endorsement by former president FW de Klerk of the cooperation agreement, it was a difficult message to sell to voters. In some areas of the Eastern Cape, even the perpetually conflicted Pan Africanist Congress won more votes than the NNP, and so did the new kid on the block, the Independent Democrats.

The pact with the ANC had seemed to be the ticket for the NNP's resurrection, following the loss of two-thirds of its support in 1999 and an acrimonious divorce from the Democratic Alliance in late 2001. What had seemed to party leaders as the answer to opposition politics – a merger of two small parties – quickly turned sour. NNP leader Marthinus van Schalkwyk increasingly found himself in the cold, while DA leader Tony Leon asserted his primacy as leader of the Opposition.

The numbers supported Leon's role. The Democratic Party had come out tops in the opposition field during the 1999 poll, while the NNP's support had slipped from 20% of the vote to 6,9%. Only in the Western Cape did the NNP emerge with substantial polling support (38,39%), largely based on working-class Coloured votes.

The deal begun to unravel just as NNP structures had given way to the DA's.

At the heart of the trouble was the DA Cape Town mayor, Peter Marais, formerly NNP, who was accused of using fake names on petitions in his attempts to rename two of Cape Town's oldest streets after Nelson Mandela and FW de Klerk. In the uproar that followed, Van Schalkwyk backed Marais, even though he himself had suspended Marais two years earlier for flirting with the ANC. Leon wanted Marais out, ridding the party of the source of the bad publicity.

In a crafty political poker game, Van Schalkwyk secured a cooperation pact with the ANC by November 2001.

The NNP's spin doctors have been hard at work ever since, describing the party as "a voice in government" and explaining that cooperation is working, despite differences with the ANC, for example on the death penalty, which the NNP wants restored.

And De Klerk has publicly endorsed the pact, saying he made a mistake by taking the then NP out of the Government of National Unity in 1996.

Van Schalkwyk has been at the helm of the party since September 1997, shortly after the party was rebranded as "New". With his boyish looks, he was dubbed "Kortbroek" (short pants) by a University of Stellenbosch professor, as he struggled to fill the shoes of FW and his legacy.

The National Party was formed in 1914 to represent Afrikaner interests. After a series of splinters and re-unifications, the "purified" NP came to power under DF Malan in 1948. Soon thereafter it started implementing grand apartheid with a series of key laws like the Group Areas Act and Immorality Act.

In 1961 South Africa withdrew from the Commonwealth in reaction to criticism of apartheid. By that time the Broederbond, a secret Afrikaner society spanning government, business, the judiciary and academia, was the determining influence.

By the 1980s apartheid was dressed up as "pluralism", "own affairs" and "power sharing". Several homelands had already come into being, and in 1983 a tricameral parliament, for whites, Indians and Coloured people and excluding Africans, was opened amid boycotts and protests by anti-apartheid activists.

The NP under PW "Groot Krokodil" Botha rapidly increased security force spending to crack down hard on civil anti-apartheid protests, as one state of emergency followed another. But his verligte successor, FW de Klerk, unbanned the liberation movements on 2 February 1990, setting afoot a negotiated transition.

A decade later, Pik Botha – who under the NP had been the world's longest-serving foreign minister – urged that the NNP be allowed to die off, and promptly joined the ANC. His call echoed that of Roelf Meyer in 1997 before the key NP constitutional negotiator resigned to co-found the United Democratic Movement.

Van Schalkwyk has often stated that the news of his party's death has been announced prematurely. Certainly he has benefited from keeping it alive: although he is no longer Western Cape premier, he has been named to the national Cabinet.

Pan Africanist Congress of Azania

Bizarre positions on a range of issues – for example, calling for the amputation of criminals' limbs – and perennial leadership battles have made it difficult for most people to take the Pan Africanist Congress seriously .

But there is a hard push behind closed doors to sort out once and for all the factionalism and back-stabbing which has riddled the PAC since its unbanning in 1990. The December 2003 leadership election debacle has opened the eyes of even the most blindly loyal PAC members.

Furious behind-the-scenes manoeuvring meant those presidential hopefuls accused of fomenting division and resorting to strong-arm tactics are out. This includes ex-secretary general Thami ka Plaatjie, who led a 2001 land invasion at Bredell, outside Johannesburg, and Limpopo leader Maxwell Nemadizivhanani.

Motsuku Pheko may not be the leader of first choice, but he's the man who led the still-wobbly PAC into the 2004 elections. His new deputy, Themba Godi, is said to be hands-on and straight-talking, keenly aware of the need to rebuild strong party structures instead of wasting hot air in leadership contests. He took up the parliamentary seat vacated by ex-president former Methodist bishop Stanley Mogoba, who gracefully retired to focus on church matters.

Discreet bridge-building to rally members behind Pheko has continued through 2004. He used Human Rights Day, commemorating the killing of 69 PAC anti-pass protesters at Sharpeville, to call on members to raise their grievances within the party.

The party believes it has the historical and political credentials to vie with the African National Congress. The PAC was formed in April 1959 as a breakaway faction from the ANC; its leaders believed the Freedom Charter's protection of minority rights stemmed from a persuasive influence of white South African communists. The PAC was led by Robert Sobukwe until his death in 1978.

The PAC believes in the return of land to indigenous people: hence its support for Zimbabwe's land invasions, regardless of human rights abuses and the misappropriation of land by Zimbabwean cabinet ministers. Other policies appear a bit thin on the ground. The PAC wants an end to the privatisation of water, electricity and other community services. While it proposes a R500 monthly grant to indigent families, there is little indication how it would raise the cash.

Yet the PAC has a strong community track record when it has been able to respond to grassroots concerns. Its health spokesperson, Dr Costa Gazi, has been outspoken on the HIV/Aids pandemic, digging into his own pocket to buy anti-retrovirals for indigent patients when he worked at the Cecilia Makiwane Hospital near Mdantsane. His comments that failing to provide nevirapine to pregnant women was tantamount to manslaughter incurred the ire of health department officials. Disciplinary charges and protracted legal wrangling followed. Gazi subsequently retired and now serves as PAC councillor in the Amatola region. He was briefly expelled from the party when his name appeared – without his permission, he said – on another party's list just before the April 2004 elections, but was restored to the fold shortly afterwards.

Financial straits and a lack of viable party structures bedevil the PAC, which in the early 1990s has lost key leaders like Dikgang Moseneke, who was appointed to the Constitutional Court, and the outspoken Patricia de Lille, who, although she did not always voice party policies, nonetheless ensured some publicity for the PAC before leaving during the floor-crossing period in early 2003 and forming her own party.

In 1994, the PAC obtained five National Assembly seats despite a haphazard and belated election campaign. But in 1999 this was cut down to three when it scored just 0,7% of the vote, and with De Lille's departure it was left with only two – back up to three after the 2004 poll.

The PAC has struggled for a long time to come to terms with the new South Africa. It joined the multi-party negotiations at the Convention for a Democratic South Africa at the eleventh hour, even though its armed wing, the Azanian People's Liberation Army, continued to attack soft targets while talks were under way in the early 1990s.

Festering sores remain in the PAC psyche. The small house on Robben Island where Sobukwe was imprisoned from 1960 to 1969 has fallen into disrepair, while renovations were made to the main prison blocks where high-profile ANC members were jailed. That seemingly deliberate neglect rankles with the PAC. Also, dozens of Apla members remain in prison for what the party insists were political crimes. Many of those did not apply for amnesty after the head of Apla, Letlapa Mphahlele, refused to participate alongside many white apartheid generals in the process. But as a general amnesty has been ruled out by government, this grievance continues.

South African Communist Party

The South African Communist Party is struggling to make the transition from an elite vanguard, with direct access to the highest levels of power in the ruling African National Congress, to a political party with broad popular support. This change has become necessary because the party's political power and influence has waned as the ANC in government has adopted increasingly conservative economic policies. While the ANC and the SACP were in exile, the party acted as the intellectual power-house of the liberation movement, with its leaders often at the forefront of debates around strategy and tactics to overthrow the apartheid government. And its contacts in the former Soviet Union bloc were often sources of vital political and material sustenance for the SACP and ANC. Virtually all the senior leaders of the ANC, at the time, were members of the SACP.

However, the fall of the Soviet Union broadly coincided with the liberation of South Africa. The SACP suddenly found itself the guardian of a seemingly discredited ideology – and no super-power backing – at a time when an ANC government needed to put in place social and economic development policies aimed at improving the living standards of South Africans.

Faced with these challenges, the ANC government very quickly adopted relatively conservative social and economic policies, apparently in line with those favoured by market economies. The SACP, which continued to press for more radical transformation programmes, railed against these relatively conservative policies. This had the effect of creating tensions with the ANC government and weakening its historical ties with the liberation movement. Ironically, the SACP's response to government policies was muted by the fact that a number of serving ANC cabinet ministers were also in the senior leadership of the party.

The SACP also tried to play a bridging role between the ANC and the other ally in the tripartite alliance, the Congress of South African Trade Unions – which was vehement in its opposition to these government policies. But, as tensions in the alliance grew, the SACP subsequently found itself effectively sidelined by the government and, because it has only ever contested elections on an ANC ticket as part of the alliance, without a significantly independent political voice or profile. The party also found its most high-profile leaders in Cabinet, formulating and implementing the government policies the SACP was opposing.

Perhaps as a result of all this, the party under SACP secretary-general Blade Nzimande has begun to try and build its own political profile. In 1994 Dr Bonginkosi Emmanuel Nzimande, who holds a PhD in sociology, traded his post at the Education Policy Unit at the then University of Natal for Parliament. There he ably chaired the education committee until 1998 when he left to take up the reins at the SACP.

Nzimande has emerged as a key role-player in the Financial Sector Campaign Coalition. Arising from one of the SACP's Red October campaigns – the month dedicated to socialist action in recent years – the campaign is credited with speeding up moves towards a financial sector transformation charter.

In December 2003 the Young Communist League was relaunched; it had crumbled during the years the party was banned. Although the SACP denied it, the League was seen in many quarters as an attempt by the party to begin developing a young political cadre independent of the ANC.

The party is also working to uphold the legacy of Chris Hani, one of the SACP and ANC's most popular leaders, assassinated in 1993. The party commemorates the anniversary of his death and has established the Chris Hani health trail (April 2002) and the Chris Hani anti-poverty trail (April 2003). The SACP still wants socialism in South Africa, and its focus on the poor and working class remains unwavering. This is perhaps why the SACP remains popular at grassroots level, even though its support without the ANC has not been tested.

The SACP was formed in July 1921 under the name of the Communist Party of South Africa. It was the first non-racial political party in South Africa, and led the call for black majority government, saying this was the first step towards socialism in the country.

United Democratic Movement

The 2004 elections have been good to the UDM, which has more than doubled its National Assembly seats and scored – for the first time – a deputy minister's post.

The UDM had been having a rough time, bedevilled by defections to the African National Congress and the Democratic Alliance, as well as financial problems resulting from its successful court challenge in 2002 against floor-crossing legislation.

It won that court battle but lost the war when the provisions were rewritten, constitutionally correct, in early 2003. In the rush by MPs to join parties they thought would give them a better deal, the UDM lost the majority of its senior parliamentary caucus; of the 14 seats the party obtained in the 1999 election, only four were left.

With legal bills to pay, a decimated parliamentary allowance for constituency offices and a 2004 election campaign to fund, perhaps it was no wonder UDM leader Bantu Holomisa complained that big corporate donors were forgetting the smaller parties. Yet despite all the hurdles, in 2004 the UDM found itself with nine National Assembly seats, plus one in the National Council of Provinces. Moreover, when the Inkatha Freedom Party told two of its members offered deputy ministries not to take them up, one of those posts went to a UDM stalwart.

Still, its recovery is a long way from the public endorsement the UDM received ahead of the 1999 elections, some two years after its formation. Then pollsters were speculating the party could obtain up to 5% of the vote. And here came the first disappointment of the self-styled alternative to government: it got 3,4%, which translated into 14 National Assembly seats, a position as the Opposition in the Limpopo legislature, and representation in most others.

Six months later, in January 2000, co-founder Roelf Meyer, the leading New National Party constitutional negotiator, resigned from the UDM for the business world.

Holomisa struggled on. In the December 2000 municipal elections the party clinched control of one council (Umtata) as well as a sprinkling of councillors throughout the country. But most of the party's support continues to lie within the former Transkei homeland in the Eastern Cape.

The UDM is a broad church for such a small party; its adherents differ widely on a number of policies. But basically those who have stayed are disenchanted with mainstream politics. Its leader Holomisa, a former Transkei general, is seen as a good, principled man, but not necessarily a politician. He remains a popular figure, and has toured the length and breadth of the country to rally support.

The UDM, which bills itself as "the political home of all South Africans", punches above its political weight. It speaks out on HIV/Aids, corruption within government and the arms deal. As a rule, the UDM is sought after for comment on the Budget or foreign policy developments.

Relations with the ruling ANC have traditionally been frosty at best, deadly at worst, particularly ahead of previous elections in strongholds in the Eastern and Western Cape and the Umtata civil service.

In January 1999 UDM KwaZulu-Natal leader Sifiso Nkabinde was killed in Richmond. And with this fell away the party's visible presence there, even if critics had decried Nkabinde as little more than "a gangster". Nkabinde had joined the UDM at its launch after being expelled by the ANC for being "infiltrated by the apartheid security establishment", according to an ANC statement at the time.

Holomisa, too, had been expelled from the ANC. He refused to retract corruption claims he made at the Truth and Reconciliation Commission against Public Works Minister Stella Sigcau, widely believed to be in Cabinet not for her abilities but for her Pondoland royal and other connections. As punishment, he was expelled from the ANC in 1996 and stripped of his post as deputy minister of environmental affairs and tourism.

In 1987 Holomisa had led a bloodless coup in the Transkei, with the tacit support of the exiled ANC, deposing the deeply corrupt Matanzima brothers. He handed over to Sigcau, then deposed her less than three months later in another bloodless coup, again citing corruption.

On his watch, between 1988 and 1989, some 33 previously banned organisations were allowed to operate in Transkei. Holomisa went on to represent the ANC at the multi-party negotiations at the Convention for a Democratic South Africa.

Perhaps regretting the expulsion, the ANC has attempted the odd toenadering, but all have been rejected by Holomisa, who remains loyal to the party he helped give birth to.

Key focus areas for the UDM have long been job creation through public works and free anti-retrovirals for those who need them – both policies given life this year by the ANC – and unrelenting criticism of the controversial multi-billion-rand arms deal.

5

Trade Union Federations

Congress of South African Trade Unions

The Congress of South African Trade Unions is South Africa's most influential labour federation, not only because of its size, but because of its close – although sometimes acrimonious – alliance with the country's government, dominated by the African National Congress.

Today Cosatu, which has 19 affiliates, is one of the largest labour federations in the world, with a paid-up membership of about 1,8-million workers. However, changes in the South African economy – especially the reduction of their formal workforces by companies, and persistent unemployment – is shrinking Cosatu's membership. Cosatu affiliates have typically drawn their strength from full-time workers in mining, manufacturing and the public service.

Some labour analysts also point out that the federation needs an organisational and political overhaul to better meet the challenges of facing unions in a modern economy open to the buffets of the international market.

Despite the struggle it faces to hold on to its membership, Cosatu maintains its political weight because of its membership in a tripartite alliance with the ANC and the South African Communist Party. In a nutshell, Cosatu uses its membership to campaign for the ANC, especially during elections, in return – theoretically – for a hotline to government during important policy debates.

The bond between the party and the trade union federation, however, is built on more than a straight exchange of influence, benefiting both. There are bonds of a shared history in the liberation struggle, and of loyalty. Cosatu's general secretary, Zwelinzima Vavi, puts it this way: "We are the ANC and the ANC is us."

The problem in the alliance has been that while government is committed to "consulting" Cosatu, it has firmly reserved the right to make up its own mind about policy. Skirmishes in the alliance are basically a battle for the soul of the ANC.

The alliance was wracked with tensions for most of the period between 1996 and 2001, when government adopted a relatively conservative economic policy – strict caps on social spending, keeping the deficit down, and the restructuring (or privatisation) of state assets – and Cosatu demanded an expansionary budget from the state aimed at rapidly improving South Africans' living standards.

Although some tensions remain between the alliance partners, specifically around privatisation, relations have improved recently as government has increasingly felt able to open the spending taps, on the back of consistently better-than-expected revenue figures.

Part of the problem for the labour federation when it comes to disputes with the government is that its members remain firm supporters of the ANC – no matter what differences the Cosatu leadership has with the state.

A survey of Cosatu members conducted by the Sociology of Work Unit at the University of the Witwatersrand just before the 2004 election showed that 66% of workers still believe that the tripartite alliance is the "best way of safeguarding worker interests in Parliament". Nearly the same number said the alliance should continue beyond 2004. Only 18% said Cosatu should not be aligned with any political party, and 6% said workers should form their own party.

This does not mean that the federation has not been able to influence government policy on matters directly affecting workers. Throughout the past decade, Cosatu has held several national strikes: in 1995 against the lockout clause in the Constitution; and to press for job creation; and against privatisation in 2001. Cosatu recently proved its political clout by pressurising the ANC to review a proposed anti-terrorism Bill, noting the implications it had for strike action – because political protest could be defined as "terrorist activity" under the legislation.

In the coming years, Cosatu is likely to focus on getting government to meet the goals of its "2015 Plan". The main aim of this plan is to get the South African economy to create quality jobs. Other objectives are: to secure a living wage for its members, to bolster its membership, to monitor the progress of land reform, and to pressure the government to improve its HIV/Aids prevention and treatment programmes. The labour federation is also planning to include the growing informal economy in its ranks and to merge its affiliates into super-unions.

Cosatu's charismatic general secretary, Zwelinzima Vavi, began his working life in 1984 on the gold and uranium mines of South

Africa. In 1987 he was dismissed during the 21-day strike that rocked the Chamber of Mines, and he joined the National Union of Mineworkers as an organiser. In 1988 he became Cosatu's regional secretary for what was then the Western Transvaal. Before taking up his current position, he served as Cosatu's deputy general secretary from 1993 to 1999. An SACP member, Vavi sports a guyabera, the Cuban national shirt, and a photograph of Che Guevara hangs on his office wall. While the veteran unionist has developed a skill for the tough, high-level negotiations that characterise Cosatu headquarters life, he says it is still on the shop floor and at the rally where he is most comfortable.

Federation of Unions of South Africa

The Federation of Unions of South Africa is a largely white-collar union that has eclipsed the National Council of Trade Unions as the second-largest federation. It is a politically independent and non-aligned federation.

Its strategic model is more conservative than that of Cosatu, and it favours cooperative agreement among labour, business and the state.

Membership figures have see-sawed since its formation in 1997, when it had 450 000 members. This figure grew to 570 000 in 1999 and is currently 540 000. This fall in membership is attributed to jobless economic growth and to the increasingly skilled face of the workforce. Professionals are union-shy, and casual workers – a growing tranche of South Africa's labour force – are too poor to pay subscriptions.

The federation has 23 affiliates including the Airline Pilots Association of South Africa, the Jewellers & Goldsmiths Union, and the Real Workers Union. Compared to its rival, Cosatu, Fedusa's affiliates are rather minor in the trade union field.

Fedusa's showpiece is its learnership programme, which it has developed in line with the South African Qualifications Authority. Currently there are 145 people on the programme who are trained in the financial administration, paralegal and public relations fields.

The federation operates from two national offices. The head office is in Johannesburg, which includes an HIV/Aids and gender department. Its parliamentary department is situated in Cape Town.

Cesare Andrea (Chez) Milani, Fedusa's general secretary, holds a law degree from the University of Stellenbosch. In 1995 he obtained an honours degree in labour relations from Unisa. He is currently completing an MBA at the University of the Witwatersrand.

His career includes a stint as a labour lawyer from 1993 to 1994. From 1994 to 1997 he was a national legal adviser for the Hospital and Other Services Personnel Trade Union of South Africa. He was one of the founders of Fedusa in 1997, and is the federation's first general secretary.

National Council of Trade Unions

The status of the National Council of Trade Unions as the third-largest federation in the country has been a point of contestation in recent years.

The 20-year-old federation, with Africanist and black consciousness leanings, was formed in 1986 by a merger between the Council of Unions of South Africa and the Azanian Congress of Trade Unions. Nactu claims to have 22 affiliates with a membership of about 300 000.

But according to the Labour Bulletin, it is difficult to assess whether Nactu's membership figures are accurate, as the federation's most recent numbers are from its national congress in 2001.

Nactu's main affiliates operate in the chemical, construction, metal, transport and public sectors. Many analysts had expected Nactu to play a proactive role in influencing government policy. However, this role has largely been reserved for the largest federation in the country, the Congress of South African Trade Unions, as part of the tripartite alliance, with the South African Communist Party and the ruling African National Congress.

In the early stages of democratic rule, Nactu concentrated on building its own structures and recruiting membership. On the membership front, Nactu, like other federations, has made little progress. Labour analysts suggest the decline in union membership is due to a number of factors, including job losses and the casualisation of labour.

Despite these conditions, Nactu seems to believe that there is room for growth. The federation aims to record one million members by the year 2005.

Nactu draws most of its finance from membership, but in recent years it has been looking at other avenues to raise funds. Nactu Investment Holdings assisted the federation in 2000 when it was facing cash-flow problems – yet despite coming to the aid of the federation, the venture has evoked some controversy.

Long-time general secretary Cunningham Ngcukana left Nactu in May 2004 to assume a position as deputy director-general in the Presidency, working in the secretariat of the New Partnership for Africa's Development.

Mahlomola Skosana, formerly assistant general secretary, has since taken over the top job.

At the structural level, Nactu has been trying to merge different affiliates in the same sector into single industrial unions. This has been achieved despite political and organisational tensions among affiliates. One success was the merging of four affiliates to form the Municipality, Education, State, Health and Allied Workers Union. Nactu has also merged unions in the metal sector.

The federation prides itself on its great diversity of members, who are mostly at the lower end of the labour market. Its membership is located throughout the country, but it is strong in KwaZulu-Natal, Gauteng, Limpopo and Mpumalanga.

The federation's strong affiliates are the South African Chemical Workers Union, the largest agricultural union – the National Union of Farmworkers, the Building, Construction and Allied Workers Union, and the National Union of Food, Beverages, Spirit and Wine. The federation has the largest furniture union in Africa, the National Union of Furniture and Allied Workers.

There are key problems facing Nactu's affiliates. According to the Labour Bulletin, many of Nactu's unions are hampered by poor administration, which prevents them from even being able to collect subscriptions effectively from the companies they organise. There are also problems with union structures, and the unions are struggling to retain staff because of an inability to pay market-related salaries.

Acronyms

ANC — African National Congress
ANCYL — African National Congress Youth League
Apla — Azanian People's Liberation Army
ARV — anti-retroviral
AU — African Union
APLA — Azanian People's Liberation Army
Azapo — Azanian People's Organisation
BCM — Black Consciousness Movement
BEE — black economic empowerment
CBO — community-based organisation
CCMA — Commission for Conciliation, Mediation and Arbitration
Codesa — Convention for a Democratic South Africa
Cosatu — Congress of South African Trade Unions
Contralesa — Congress of Traditional Leaders of South Africa
DA — Democratic Alliance
Dacst — Department of Arts, Culture, Science and Technology (now split into two departments)
EPWP — Expanded Public Works Programme
FFC — Financial and Fiscal Commission
Fedusa — Federation of Unions of South Africa
Gear — the Growth, Employment and Redistribution macro-economic strategy
HRC — Human Rights Commission
HSRC — Human Sciences Research Council
Icasa — Independent Communications Authority of South Africa
Idasa — Institute for Democracy in South Africa
IFP — Inkatha Freedom Party
JSC — Judicial Service Commission
LPM — Landless People's Movement
LRC — Legal Resources Centre
MEC — Member of the Executive Committee (a provincial minister)
MJC — Muslim Judicial Council
MK — Umkhonto we Sizwe
Nadel — National Association of Democratic Lawyers of South Africa
Nactu — National Council of Trade Unions

NaTIS	–	National Traffic Information System
NCOP	–	National Council of Provinces
NEC	–	national executive committee
Nedlac	–	National Economic Development and Labour Council
Nehawu	–	National Education Health and Allied Workers Union
Nepad	–	New Partnership for Africa's Development
NGO	–	non-governmental organisation
NIA	–	National Intelligence Agency
NLC	–	National Land Committee
NNP	–	New National Party
NPA	–	National Prosecuting Authority
NWC	–	national working committee
OBE	–	outcomes-based education
PAC	–	Pan Africanist Congress
Pagad	–	People Against Gangsterism and Drugs
SACBC	–	Southern African Catholic Bishops' Conference
Saccawu	–	South African Commercial, Catering and Allied Workers Union
SACP	–	South African Communist Party
SADC	–	Southern African Development Community
SAHRC	–	South African Human Rights Commission
Salga	–	South African Local Government Association
SANDF	–	South African National Defence Force
SAPS	–	South African Police Service
Sars	–	South African Revenue Service
Saso	–	South African Students Organisation
SASS	–	South African Secret Service
SDI	–	spatial development initiatives
SNO	–	second national operator (for landline telecommunications)
SOE	–	state-owned enterprises
TAC	–	Treatment Action Campaign
TRC	–	Truth and Reconciliation Commission
UCT	–	University of Cape Town
UDF	–	United Democratic Front
UIF	–	Unemployment Insurance Fund
UNDP	–	United Nations Development Programme
UNHRC	–	United Nations Human Rights Commission
Unisa	–	University of South Africa
UWC	–	University of the Western Cape
Wits	–	University of the Witwatersrand

Think Tanks and Research Organisations

Africa Institute of South Africa (Aisa)
Aisa is dedicated to knowledge production, education, training and the promotion of awareness on Africa, for Africans and the international community. This is achieved through independent policy analysis, collection, processing and interpretation, and dissemination of information.

Address: Nipilar House, corner of Hamilton and
        Vermeulen Streets, Arcadia, Pretoria
Post: PO Box 630, Pretoria 0001
Phone: +27(0)12 328 6970
Fax: +27(0)12 3230 8153
Email: ai@ai.org.za
Website: www.ai.org.za

Agricultural Research Council (ARC)
The ARC's mission is to promote the agricultural and related sectors through research, technology development and transfer in order to enhance the natural resource base and environment, sustain a competitive agricultural economy, provide new economic opportunities, ensure high quality and safe food, and support an informed society.

Address: 1134 Park Street, Hatfield, Pretoria
Post: PO Box 8783, Pretoria 0001
Phone: +27(0)12 427 9700
Fax: 27(0)12 342 3948
Website: www.arc.agric.za

Alternative Information and Development Centre (AIDC)
The AIDC conducts research focusing on problems of debt, international trade, finance and microeconomic policy, and it implements an integrated strategy of lobbying and advocacy towards developing policies that can address poverty, unemployment and social inequality.

Address: 129 Rochester Road, Observatory 7925,
        Cape Town
Phone: +27(0)21 447 5770
Fax: +27(0)21 447 5884
E-mail: info@aidc.org.za
Website: www.aidc.org.za

BusinessMap Foundation

The mission of the foundation is to be a thought leader, providing independent knowledge and intelligence on economic transformation to shape debates and policy processes in civil society and the public and private sector.

Address: 28 Juta Street,
         Braamfontein 2001
Post: PO Box 157, Auckland Park 2006
Phone: +27(0)11 276 8460
Fax: +27(0)11 276 8462
E-mail: businessmap@businessmap.org.za
Website: www.businessmap.org.za

Centre for Civil Society (CCS)

CCS's aim is to promote the critical study of civil society as a legitimate and flourishing area of scholarly activity in South Africa and on the African continent. The centre also aims to promote partnerships for knowledge-sharing and capacity-building in civil society. It provides research grants to academics, research institutes, independent scholars, activists and civil society organisations in order to develop a critical mass of literature on the sector. It also undertakes post-graduate teaching and training for activists in civil society.

Address: University of Natal,
         King George V Avenue, Glenwood,
         Durban 4041
Phone: +27(0)31 260 2528/2874
Fax: +27(0)31 260 2458
E-mail: miller@nu.ac.za

Centre for African Renaissance Studies (Cars)

Cars is a research, teaching and publication graduate academic institution at the University of South Africa (Unisa) with a focus on African renaissance studies. Its mandate includes a focus on developing outward reach to the whole of Africa and diaspora Africa.

Address: Skinner Street, Pretoria,
         Tshwane Metro City
Phone:+27(0)12 320 3180
Fax: +27(0)12 320 3417
E-mail: malapo@unisa.ac.za

Centre for Development and Enterprise (CDE)

The Centre for Development and Enterprise is an independent policy research and advocacy organisation focusing on critical national development issues and their relationship to economic growth and democratic consolidation. CDE formulates practical policy proposals outlining ways in which South Africa can tackle major social and economic challenges.

Address: Pilrig Place, 5 Eton Road, Parktown,
        Johannesburg
Post: PO Box 1936, Johannesburg 2000
Telephone: +27(0)11 482 5140
Fax: +27(0)11 482 5089
E-mail: info@cde.org.za
Website: www.cde.org.za

Centre for Education Policy Development (CEPD)

CEPD's aim is to develop alternative education and training policies, which are aimed at promoting the principles of non-racism, equity, democracy, quality education and lifelong learning.

Address: 76 Juta Street, Braamfontein,
        Johannesburg
Post: PO Box 31892, Braamfontein 2017
Phone: +27(0)11 403 6131
Fax: +27(0)11 403 1130
E-mail: info@cepd.org.za
Website: www.cepd.org.za

Centre for Policy Studies (CPS)

The mission of the CPS is to influence policy debate and dialogue through producing research on the most pressing political and social policy issues in South Africa, particularly those surrounding governance and democratisation.

Address: 9 Wellington Road, Parktown,
        Johannesburg
Post: PO Box 16488, Doornfontein 2028
Phone: +27(0)11 642 9820
Fax: +27(0)11 643 4654
E-mail: portia@cps.org.za
Website: www.cps.org.za

Centre for the Study of Higher Education (CSHE)

The mission of the centre, which is the University of the Western Cape's Education Policy Unit (EPU), is to conduct research and analysis in the field of higher education policy studies, and to contribute to building capacity among researchers, policy-makers, planners and institutional personnel in this field. In undertaking this task, the CSHE seeks to contribute to political, economic, intellectual and cultural development and to the transformation of education and training in South Africa.

Address: UWC, Modderdam Road, Bellville
Post: Private Bag X17, Bellville 7535, Cape Town
Phone: +27(0)21 959 2580
Fax: +27(0)21 959 3278
E-mail: cshe@uwc.ac.za
Website: www.epu.uwc.ac.za

Centre for the Study of Violence and Reconciliation (CSVR)

The CSVR engages in conflict management and prevention, research and policy formulation, advocacy and lobbying, and runs various intervention projects. It works with a wide range of organisations, constituencies and stakeholders in both the governmental and non-governmental sectors.

Address: Braamfontein Centre, 23 Jorissen Street, Braamfontein,
        Johannesburg
Post: PO Box 30778, Braamfontein 2017
Phone: +27(0)11 403 5650
Fax: +27(0)11 339 6785
E-mail: info@csvr.org.za
Website: www.csvr.org.za

Community Agency for Social Enquiry (Case)

The Community Agency for Social Enquiry is an applied research non-governmental organisation, working in the socio-economic, political and developmental fields in South Africa. Case's work includes national, provincial and local surveys, focus groups, project and organisational evaluations, programme impact assessments, and policy and literature reviews.

Post: PO Box 32882, Braamfontein 2017
Phone: +27(0)11 646 5922
Fax: +27(0)11 646 5919
E-mail: director@case.org.za
Website: www.case.org.za

Council for Scientific and Industrial Research (CSIR)

The CSIR is a technological research, development and implementation organisation. Its aim is to foster industrial and scientific development, either by itself, or in partnership with public and private sector institutions, to contribute to the improvement of the quality of life of the people of South Africa. It achieves these through directed and multi-disciplinary research and technological innovation.

Address: Meiring Naude Road, Brummeria, Pretoria
Post: PO Box 395, Pretoria 0001
Phone: +27(0)12 841 2911
Fax: +27(0)12 349 1153
Website: www.csir.co.za

Development Policy Research Unit (DPRU)

The Development Policy Research Unit is part of the School of Economics at the University of Cape Town. It conducts research on labour markets, poverty and inequality. Its mission is to contribute to the quality and scope of public policy for industrial development in South and Southern Africa.

Address: 4th floor, Robert Leslie Social Science Building,
          Upper Campus, Rondebosch
Post: University of Cape Town, Private Bag, Rondebosch 7701
Phone: +27(0)21 650 5705
Fax: +27(0)21 650 5711
Website: www.commerce.uct.ac.za/dpru

Economic Policy Research Institute (Epri)

The institute analyses South Africa's socio-economic conditions and constructs sustainable economic policies that foster job creation and redistribution while supporting sustained economic growth and macroeconomic stability. Epri carries out research supporting the objectives of economic growth, job creation, and redistribution. The orientation of the research is largely macroeconomic.

Address: 3rd floor, Sanclare Building, 21 Dreyer Street,
          Claremont 7700, Cape Town
Phone: +27(0)21 671 3301
Fax: +27(0)21 671 3157
Email: info@epri.org.za
Website: www.epri.org.za

Electoral Institute of Southern Africa (Eisa)

Eisa's mission is to strengthen electoral processes, good governance, human rights and democratic values through research, capacity building and advocacy. The institute services governments, electoral commissions, political parties, civil society organisations and other institutions operating in the democracy and governance fields throughout the Southern African Development Community region and beyond. Its programme areas are democracy, conflict management and electoral education, electoral and political processes, and balloting and electoral services.

Address: 2nd floor, The Atrium, 41 Stanley Avenue,
          Auckland Park, Johannesburg
Post: PO Box 740, Auckland Park 2006
Phone: +27(0)11 482 5495
Fax: +27(0)11 482 6163
Website: www.eisa.org.za

Empowerdex

Empowerdex is an economic empowerment rating and research agency. The company's mission is to support both public and private sector entities in accelerating the economic empowerment process. Through research, Empowerdex aims to identify the market trends and quantify the impact and effects of economic empowerment policies and initiatives, so as to provide the government and the market with information to design and implement black economic empowerment policies.

Address: 1st floor, Nkonki Building, 3 Simba Road,
          Sunninghill, Johannesburg
Post: PostNet Suite 273, Private Bag X26, Sunninghill 2157
Phone: +27(0)11 234 7890
Fax: +27(0)11 234 5855
E-mail: info@empowerdex.com
Website: www.empowerdex.com

Freedom of Expression Institute (FXI)

FXI aims to protect and foster the rights to freedom of expression and access to information, and to oppose censorship. The FXI undertakes a wide range of activities in support of these objectives, including lobbying, education, monitoring, research, publicity and litigation, and the funding of legal cases that advance these rights. Its mission is to fight for freedom of expression and eliminate inequalities in accessing and disseminating information and knowledge in South Africa and beyond.

Address: 87 Argon House, Juta Street, Braamfontein,
Johannesburg
Post: PO Box 30668, Braamfontein 2017
Phone: +27(0)11 403 8403/4
Fax: +27(0)11 403 8309
E-mail: fxi@fxi.org.za
Website: www.fxi.org.za

Human Sciences Research Council (HSRC)

The Human Sciences Research Council conducts large-scale, policy-relevant, social-scientific projects for public-sector users, non-governmental organisations and international development agencies. Its research activities and structures are aligned to South Africa's national development priorities such as poverty reduction through economic development, skills enhancement, job creation, the elimination of discrimination and inequalities, and effective service delivery.

Address: 134 Pretorius Street,
Pretoria
Post: Private Bag X41 Pretoria 0001
Phone: +27(0)12 302 2999
Fax: +27(0)12 326 5362
Website: www.hsrc.ac.za

Institute for Democracy in South Africa (Idasa)

Idasa's mission is to promote a sustainable democracy in South Africa by building democratic institutions, educating citizens and advocating social justice. The primary objective is to build capacity for democracy in civil society and government.

Cape Town

Address: 6 Spin Street, Cape Town
Post: PO Box 1739, Cape Town 8000
Phone: +27(0)21 647 5600
Fax: +27(0)21 461 2589
E-mail: info@idasa.org.za
Website: www.idasa.org.za

Pretoria
Address: 357 Visagie Street (corner Prinsloo Street), Pretoria
Post: PO Box 56950, Arcadia 0007
Phone: +27(0)12 392 0500
Fax: +27(0)12 320 2414/5
E-mail: info@idasa.org.za
Website: www.idasa.org.za

Institute for Security Studies (ISS)
The mission of the ISS is to enhance human security in Africa. It achieves this through applied research and the dissemination of information that can inform decisions on critical areas of individual, national, regional and international security.

Address: 301 Lange Street, Block C, Brooklyn Court,
        New Muckleneuk, Pretoria
Phone: +27(0)12 346 9500/2
Fax: +27(0)12 460 0998
E-mail: iss@iss.co.za
Website: www.iss.co.za

International Union for the Protection of Nature (IUCN)
The mission of the International Union for the Protection of Nature, the world conservation union, is to influence, encourage and assist societies throughout the world to conserve the integrity and diversity of nature and to ensure that any use of natural resources is equitable and ecologically sustainable. Its aim is to build recognition of the many ways in which the livelihoods of the poor depend on the sustainable management of natural resources, and to give policy advice and technical support to global secretariats and the parties to international conventions.

Phone: +27(0)12 342 8304
Fax:+27(0)12 362 6990
E-mail: webmaster@iucn.org
Website: www.iucn.org

National Business Initiative (NBI)
The National Business Initiative acts at the intersection of the private and the public sector to contribute to political and economic stability and to enhance the country's competitiveness as a key to sustained growth. Its programmes target areas that promote job creation and skills development, such as those that facilitate and promote entrepreneurship

to sustain businesses and create jobs, and the public-private partnership programme facilitating finance and management of infrastructure and public services.

Address: 13th floor, Metal Box Centre, 25 Owl Street, Auckland Park,
    Johannesburg
Post: PO Box 294, Auckland Park 2006
Phone: +27(0)11 482 5100
Fax: +27(0)11 482 5507/8
E-mail: info@nbi.org.za
Website: www.nbi.org.za

National Institute of Economic Policies (Niep)

Niep is an economic research institute servicing non-governmental organisations and government with research, education and training in the area of economic policy.

Address: Ground floor, Broll Place, Carse O'Gowrie, Sunnyside Park,
    Parktown 2193, Johannesburg
Phone: +27(0)11 484 0784
Fax: +27(0)11 484 2324
E-mail: admin@niep.org.za
Website: www.niep.org.za

National Labour and Economic Development Institute (Naledi)

This non-governmental organisation, founded by the Congress of South African Trade Unions, undertakes labour and economic research. Its mission is to conduct policy-relevant research aimed at building the capacity of the labour movement to effectively engage with the challenges of South African society.

Address: 6th floor, Cosatu House, 1 Leyds Street, Braamfontein,
    Johannesburg
Post: PO Box 5665, Johannesburg 2000
Phone: +27(0)11 403 2122
Fax: +27(0)11 403 1948
E-mail: naledi@naledi.org.za
Website: www.naledi.org.za

Nepad Secretariat

The New Partnership for Africa's Development (Nepad) Secretariat coordinates the implementation of projects and programmes approved by the Heads of State and Government Implementation Committee (HSIC). Nepad is a programme of the African Union designed to meet its development objectives. Its priorities are establishing the conditions for sustainable development by ensuring peace and security, democracy and good political, economic and corporate governance. It also promotes regional cooperation and integration and capacity building.

Address: The Development Bank of SA, 1258 Lever Road, Midrand,
   Johannesburg
Post: PO Box 1234, Midrand, Halfway House 1685
Phone: +27(0)11 313 3716
Fax: +27(0)11 313 3450
E-mail: thaningas@nepad.org
Website: www.nepad.org

Trade and Industry Policy Secretariat (Tips)

Tips conducts research on trade and industrial policy and assists in harnessing relevant trade and industrial research for policy considerations.

Post: PO Box 87643, Houghton 2193
Phone: +27(0)11 645 6404
Fax: +27(0)11 484 4115
E-mail: info@tips.org.za
Website: www.tips.org.za

University of Fort Hare Education Policy Unit (EPU)

Fort Hare's EPU conducts research in the field of education with the aim of providing creative solutions to challenges in the education and training system in the country.

Post: Private Bag X1314, Alice 5700
Phone: +27(0)86 010 3626
Fax: +27(0)40 653 1554
E-mail: moyogmoyo@ufh.ac.za
Website: www.ufh.ac.za

University of Natal Education Policy Unit (EPU)

This EPU's mission is to intervene in the education policy process through advocacy and quality education policy research in order to transform education in KwaZulu-Natal in particular, and South Africa in general. The unit conducts research and engages in dialogue around education policy and practice. Its research focus areas are democratic school governance and management, resources for teaching and learning, rural schooling and school environment.

Address: 2nd floor, Main Tutorial Block, Mariannhill Road, Pinetown
Phone: +27(0)31 260 2607
Fax: +27(0)31 260 2118
E-mail: epunatal@nu.ac.za

University of the Witwatersrand Education Policy Unit (EPU)

The mission of the EPU at Wits University is to provide policy support, research and analysis to national and provincial governments, to function as a rapid response mechanism for decision-makers and policy-makers in education, to produce high-quality impact research, and to fulfil a resource and dissemination function.

Address: Room 146, 1st floor, Boyce Block, Education Campus
(formerly the Johannesburg College of Education),
University of the Witwatersrand, Johannesburg
Post: Education Policy Unit, University of the Witwatersrand, Private
Bag 3, Wits 2050
Phone: +27(0)11 717 3072/6
Fax: +27(0)11 717 3076
E-mail: motalas@epu.wits.ac.za
Website: www.wits.ac.za

Wits Institute of Social and Economic Research (Wiser)

Wits University's Wiser Institute aims to produce social and economic research of quality and relevance and then disseminate research findings in ways that will inform critical local and international debates.

Address: 6th floor, Richard Ward Building, East Campus, University of
the Witwatersrand, Johannesburg
Post: Private Bag 3, PO Box Wits 2050
Phone: +27(0)11 717 4220
Fax:+27(0)11 717 4235
Email: admin2@wiser.wits.ac.za
Website: www.wiserweb.wits.ac.za

BEE Legislation

Broad-Based Black Economic Empowerment Act

Purpose
To establish a legislative framework for BEE, to empower the minister to issue codes of good practice and publish transformation charters, to establish a BEE Advisory Council. To achieve the constitutional right to equality and promote the "economic unity of the nation".

Definitions
Black means Africans, Coloureds and Indians. Broad-based BEE means empowerment of all black people including women, workers, youth, people with disabilities and people living in rural areas through:
• increasing black management, ownership and control.
• ownership and management of enterprises, productive assets by communities, workers, co-ops, other collective enterprises.
• human resources and skills development.
• employment equity.
• preferential procurement.
• investment in enterprises owned and managed by black people.

Objectives
• Meaningful participation by black people in the economy, broadening the entrepreneurial base.
• Achieving a substantial change in the racial composition of ownership and management structures.
• Increasing the extent to which communities, workers, co-ops and other collectives own and manage enterprises.
• Promoting access to finance for BEE.
• Broad-based BEE will be measured by substantial black participation in the economy as measured. by ownership, management and skills development.

Functions of BEE Advisory Council
• Advises government, reviews progress on BEE, advises on draft codes of good practice, advises on draft transformation charters.

- President chairs the council with minister or director-general as alternative; three other cabinet ministers or DGs are second alternatives.
- Members must have expertise and be drawn from trade unions, business, community-based organisations and academia.
- Members will not be paid, but will be reimbursed for expenses incurred.

Codes of Good Practice
- Further interpret BEE for specific sectors, qualification criteria for preferential procurement, indicators to measure broad-based BEE.
- Set guidelines for drawing up transformation charters.
- May specify targets and period for achievement of targets.
- Must distinguish between black men and women.

Status of Codes
Every organ of state or public entity must take codes into account when:
- issuing licences, concessions or other authorisations.
- developing and implementing preferential procurement.
- determining qualification criteria for sale of state-owned enterprises.

BEE Strategy
- To map out an "integrated, coordinated and uniform" approach to BEE by all organs of state, public entities, the private sector, non-governmental organisation, local communities and others.
- To develop a plan of financing.

Transformation Charters
Must be published in Government Gazette if they
- have been developed by major stakeholders
- advance the objectives of the Act.

Source: Department of Trade & Industry; Parliamentary Portfolio Committee on Trade and Industry

The BEE Scorecard

Core component of BEE	Indicators	Weighting
Direct empowerment score		
Equity	% share of economic benefits	20%
Management	% black executives and/or executive board/board	10%
Human resource development and employment equity score		
Employment equity	Weighted by analysis	10%
Skills development	Skills spending as a proportion of payroll	20%
Indirect empowerment score		
Preferential procurement	Procurement from black–owned and –empowered enterprises	20%
Enterprise development	Investment in black–owned and –empowered enterprises	10%
Residual 10%		
Determined by sector/enterprise		10%

Source: The Department of Trade and Industry; BEE strategy document, 2003

Charters

Mining

Objectives

Make access to resources equitable for all South Africans, expand opportunities to black South Africans, expand and use the existing skills base, promote employment, and increase socioeconomic welfare of mining communities, promote the beneficiation of commodities.

Targets – Human Resource Development

- To increase learnerships from 1 200 to 5 000 by March 2005.
- Government to secure training for black staff overseas.
- Companies to undertake literacy and numeracy training, aiming for blanket coverage by 2005, implement career paths.

Employment Equity

- Employment equity placement at 40% within five years.
- 10% female participation in five years.
- South African subsidiaries of multi-nationals to focus overseas placement and training programmes on black South Africans.
- Identification and fast-tracking of talent pool.

Migrant Labour

- No discrimination against foreign migrant labour.

Socio-economic Conditions

Numerous clauses to ensure integrated development of mining communities, housing provision, conversion of hostels, promotion of home ownership, better nutrition.

Procurement

- Identify current levels of procurement from BEE companies.
- Commit to a preferential procurement programme in three to five years.
- Encourage big suppliers to form partnerships with black companies.
- Commit to developing BEE procurement capacity.

Ownership and joint ventures

Active involvement
Black–controlled: 50% + 1 vote
Joint ventures: 25% + 1 vote
Collective investment through employee share ownership programmes or unit trusts: majority ownership must be historically disadvantaged South Africans.

Passive Involvement
Greater than 0% and up to 100% ownership with no involvement in management.
General industry target: 26% black ownership in ten years. Stakeholders will meet in five years to review progress. Companies must report their progress on an annual basis, and reports must be externally audited.

Other Issues
Beneficiation: companies agree to assess current levels and set beneficiation.
Exploration and prospecting: government to provide support.
Licensing: score-card approach will facilitate the processing of licence conversions.
Financing: industry agrees to assist financing of BEE companies to the extent of R100-billion within the next five years to achieve 26% ownership target.

Tourism

Transformation Strategy for Tourism
To provide for:
Business linkages between established and emerging businesses, government procurement that takes into account factors other than price that will stimulate transformation, standards and targets that have to be documented, monitored, reported and evaluated. It provides for a rewards system whereby any organisation that exceeds expectations will be publicly rewarded and acknowledged.

Objective

To measure and change ownership, skills development and capacity. A first audit took place in April 2001. Ownership focuses on the number of previously disadvantaged individuals who own and control tourism-related businesses.

Skills development looks at the number of black and female employees with a working knowledge of operations in the tourism industry; capacity is the liability of new businesses to provide minimum acceptable service levels and the ability to compete in the current market.

Execution

• To develop a monitoring system to measure agreed targets.
• Reward/recognition programme for those who exceed objectives.
• Forum to link major tour operators and black tour guides.
• Audit of existing policies and practices within Department of Environmental Affairs and Tourism.

Marine Life Resources Act

Establishes a council to which fishing rights can be allocated for lease to people from previously disadvantaged backgrounds and to small and medium-sized enterprises.

Recommendations on empowerment in the fisheries policies includes expanding equity ownership in companies through: direct BEE investment, supporting small and medium enterprises by selling quotas to small-scale operators, unbundling, mergers and the formation of co-ops and other forms of formal commercial cooperation.

Previously advantaged companies can tender for fishing rights if they show: significant equity transfer to black and female persons and communities, broad transformation, recruitment and training to transform management, business skills transfer to black staff.

Marketing and Advertising Industry

The main aim of the charter, known as a statement of values, is to ensure that 51% of the aggregate equity of the industry is in the hands of previously disadvantaged individuals (PDIs) by 2006.

To reach this goal, the draft charter proposes:

- That adspend and procurement policies be transformed, that human resources of the industry be more representative of the country, that there be increased training and skills development programmes, that the local content of the industry be increased, and that the regulatory environment be made more conducive to transformation initiatives.
- Management and control of the industry should be in the hands of a group that is 70% previously disadvantaged individuals, 51% female and 3% disabled.
- A balanced scorecard must be developed for the industry.
- Adspend must reflect South Africa's population and the ownership of communication vehicles.
- Creativity and market segmentation must be considered in the South African context.
- The supply chain must reflect the country's economic concerns and help develop small, medium and micro enterprises and black-owned media.

The transformation of the industry is still under discussion. This process is being driven by a steering committee and a monitoring committee, made up of key stakeholders in the industry. Their aim is to speed up the pace of transformation in the industry.

South African Petroleum and Liquid Fuels Industry

The main aim of the charter is to ensure that 25% of the aggregate value of all entities that hold the operating assets of the country's oil industry is owned and controlled by historically disadvantaged South Africans (HDSA) within the next ten years.

To reach this goal, the charter provides for:

- HDSA companies to be given fair opportunity to acquire ownership in the infrastructure for movement and storage of crude oil, including pipelines and depots. Opportunities should also be created for HDSA companies to enter the liquid fuels retail networks and commercial operations.
- Oil refiners and synthetic fuel manufacturers to consider selling shares in their facilities to HDSA companies, including them as joint venture partners in any expansion or upgrades, and making refining capacity available to them through other mechanisms.

- HDSAs to have at least 9% interest in any licences for exploration and production in the country's off-shore area.
- Companies to investigate and implement internal and external financing mechanisms for giving HDSA companies equity ownership and consider engaging them in strategic partnerships.
- Participants in the industry to adopt supportive procurement policies which will facilitate the growth of HDSA companies. A list of preferred suppliers will be created and maintained by the government.
- The industry to commit itself to employment equity targets and undertake to build the skills of its employees.
- A constant process of consultation, monitoring, evaluation and reporting between government and the industry that will form the basis for annual forums.

ICT Draft

The Information and Communication Technology (ICT) working group submitted a third working draft of the ICT charter on 10 May 2004.

The main objectives of the charter are to promote and facilitate economic empowerment in the ICT sector by:

- Enabling meaningful participation of blacks in the growth of the ICT sector and in the national economy.
- Achieving a substantial change in the racial and gender composition of ownership, management and control structures as well as in the skilled and specialist positions of new and existing enterprises.
- Increasing the extent to which black women, communities, disabled persons, workers, cooperatives and the youth participate in all areas of the sector.
- Facilitating access to ICTs by black people, the rural and urban poor as well as other marginalised groupings.
- Providing skills development and training to black people.
- Providing an enabling environment for transparency, fairness and consistency when measuring and adjudicating on matters related to BEE in the ICT sector.

The working group consists of 30 representatives from industry associations, including the South African Chamber of Business, the Electronic Industries Federation and the Black IT Forum.

Preferential Procurement

The main objectives of this charter as they pertain to this indicator are to:

- Increase the amount of money spent on procuring from BEE enterprises; the focus should be on procuring from black-owned and black-controlled enterprises.
- Provide incentives for enterprises to procure from charter-compliant enterprises, thus ensuring the ripple effect of affirmative procurement is realised throughout the economy.
- Ensure that ICT and other skills that would otherwise be lost through, for example, retrenchments, are still made available to the sector and the economy.
- Establish a coordinated framework for the implementation of black supplier development programmes.

The Department of Trade and Industry, with non-profit organisations, has developed a database of BEE companies in the ICT and electronics sector to speed up the pace of procurement from black-owned and black-influenced companies. The database is meant to help established companies develop new value chains and provide BEE companies with a marketing platform.

Empowerment

Empowerment will be measured by ownership, skills transfer, employment equity, job creation and procurement. The chairman of the working group, Dali Mpofu of Altron, says an industry BEE scorecard should be weighted more strongly in favour of factors other than ownership, though equity is important.

Edited version of the BEE Act and current BEE charters.
For further information see the following websites:
www.dti.gov.za or www.ictcharter.org.za

Summary of the Department of Health's Operational HIV/Aids Treatment Plan

On 19 November 2003, the task team established by the Minister of Health following the 8 August Cabinet statement published an Operational Plan for Comprehensive HIV and Aids Care, Management and Treatment for South Africa. The plan is a blueprint for rolling out anti-retroviral (ARV) drugs and improving the health service by adding nearly 22 000 employees to the health-care system by March 2008.

It commits to implementing at least one service point providing treatment in every health district or metropolitan council in South Africa by the end of its first year of implementation, and to ensuring access to care and treatment in every local municipality within five years. There are concrete treatment targets: 53 000 people on treatment by the end of March 2004, and over 200 000 CD4 tests by then. The full plan is available on http://www.gov.za/issues/hiv/. What follows is a summary.

Section One: Prevention, Care and Treatment of HIV/Aids
This section commits the government to implementing a continuum of care, including voluntary counselling and testing (VCT), prevention of mother-to-child transmission (PMTCT), education, life-skills programmes, management of sexually transmitted infections (STIs), condom distribution, tuberculosis management, nutrition, psycho-social and social support, home-based care, and medical care and treatment by dedicated, trained medical teams.

People access these services through VCT centres, the PMTCT programme, STI clinics, primary health-care clinics, TB clinics, the South African Military Health Service and, notably, prisons. The plan envisages support for the implementation of this programme from NGOs and the private sector.

Prevention is the cornerstone of the government's approach to HIV/Aids, and new interventions such as treatment are seen as complementary to prevention. Adults who have a World Health Organisation stage IV illness or have CD4 counts of less than 200 and are symptomatic will be referred to district or regional hospitals to commence treatment if they are prepared and ready to take ARVs adherently, i.e. to adhere to a treatment regime.

Once they are initiated and stabilised on ARV treatment, nurses at the patients' clinic will handle monitoring and follow-up.

District and regional hospitals have been selected as the appropriate level for initiation and review of ARV treatment decisions in light of the following factors: 24-hour patient access; clinician availability; laboratory and diagnostic capability, either on-site or linked by a transportation system; pharmacy capability to secure and safely dispense ARVs; logistical support for regularly scheduled outpatient clinics; and clear consultation and referral lines both up to the reference hospitals and down to primary care facilities.

In selected circumstances, where access to a district hospital is limited, ARV initiation may occur at lower-level facilities and mobile clinics where the requisite expertise is available.

Men, women who can potentially have children, pregnant women and people who cannot take efavirenz (e.g. those with a psychiatric history) will be prescribed d4T, lamivudine and nevirapine. People who experience serious nevirapine side effects or have evidence of liver disease (i.e. hepatoxicity) will be prescribed efavirenz instead.

The second-line regimen for people who become resistant to these regimens is AZT, ddI and lopinavir/ritonavir (which most people still know as Kaletra).

Mechanisms for routine monitoring are included. Six-monthly CD4 tests are envisaged for patients on ARVs or with CD4 counts below 500. Patients not ready for ARVs, with CD4 counts above 500, will receive 12-monthly CD4 tests. Six-monthly viral load tests will be provided to all patients on ARVs and/or with CD4 counts below 200.

Children who have CD4 counts below 15% and are symptomatic or with a WHO stage IV illness with "at least one responsible person capable of administering" the child's medication will be able to commence treatment. The drugs used are the same as with adult regimens (although administered at different doses) except that lopinavir/ritonavir can be used in the first line instead of nevirapine or efavirenz. To encourage adherence, each patient will have access to counselling, be encouraged to develop personal treatment plans, join support groups and utilise a variety of other measures, including creating links with patient advocates.

There is much emphasis in the plan on nutrition, especially where patients have TB and HIV. Dieticians will be employed at district and service delivery level. Staff are to be trained in nutrition assessment. Elements to be included in counselling and education include basic nutritional education, including weight maintenance; food safety; food strategies that employ locally available foods; and the provision of appropriate recipes. Communities will be targeted with general information on nutrition, with particular emphasis on HIV and Aids-specific needs, and referral to home-based care programmes.

Children, people with TB and HIV, pregnant women, people with Aids and people who are malnourished will be given nutritional supplements. Infant formula milk may be available to newborn children for those who require it.

The plan recognises the importance of traditional healers in South African society, and makes suggestions such as:

(1) expanding dialogue between traditional healers and conventional medical practitioners;
(2) involving traditional healers in the programme through training;
(3) enhancing referral networks to include traditional healers;
(4) using enhanced quality-assurance mechanisms. Protocols with regard to the crossover between traditional healing and the treatment programme will be developed and piloted in at least two communities.

The plan also recognises the need to do more research on the effects of traditional medicines on HIV, and interactions between traditional and conventional medicines.

Section Two: Accreditation, Human Resources and Assessment
Provinces are responsible for selecting sites for accreditation. The national Strategic Management Team will be responsible for accrediting sites. Sites will have to redo accreditation once every two to three years.

For every 500 patients, the plan recognises that two doctors, four nurses, two pharmacists, two dieticians, one social worker, ten lay counsellors, two administrative clerks and two data capturers are needed.

A critical goal is to recruit 1 786 new employees by the end of March 2004. Training courses on HIV/Aids are envisaged, and the curriculum is described. Some of the other support systems for human resources include a mentoring system for counsellors and a phone-based clinical consultation treatment line. A detailed set of incentives for encouraging employees to join or stay in the public health system will be implemented, primarily from 2005 onwards.

The task team visited 77 service points (health facilities such as clinics and hospitals) including at least one in every health district. It estimated the number of patients that needed to be treated in each of these sites, and evaluated them to determine if they are ready for treatment rollout.

Section Three: Drug Procurement, Distribution and Laboratory Services

The plan envisages the establishment of a procurement negotiating team with a range of experts. The planned procurement procedure is detailed. The negotiating team will send out a request for proposals to pharmaceutical companies.

The drug distribution mechanisms envisaged by the plan are extensive, and include provisions for storage, security and inventory management.

The report estimates that investment is needed to improve the infrastructure of 90% of health facility pharmacies. Increased numbers of pharmacists are envisaged.

The plan envisages the National Laboratory Health Service as the institution that will conduct all monitoring tests. According to the Treatment Action Campaign, the laboratory health service's CD4 counting capabilities only exist in Johannesburg, Cape Town, Bloemfontein and Durban. CD4 sites will therefore be established in Nelspruit, Polokwane, Umtata, Ngwelezana, Port Elizabeth, Newcastle, Port Shepstone and Tshepong, the last three over a five-year period.

HIV antibody tests are inaccurate for determining the status of children under 18 months. PCR tests can do this, but they are not readily available and are much more expensive than antibody tests. The report recommends that a Paediatric Monitoring Task Force be established and charged with coordinating protocols for infant diagnostics and monitoring with the PMTCT programme and the National Laboratory Health Service.

Section Four: Social Mobilisation

This chapter proposes the implementation of a comprehensive communications and community mobilisation programme to ensure that administrators of all relevant government programmes, health care providers, people living with HIV and Aids, and their families and caregivers are knowledgeable about all key provisions and requirements of this plan, as well as their respective roles and responsibilities.

The communications plan also focuses on educating people who will be taking anti-retroviral drugs and their families on what to expect from the treatment and what they must do to make it successful. Finally, and of equal importance, the plan integrates prevention messages into programme communications.

The plan also proposes significant investments in community support programmes for those being treated for Aids.

The Government Communication and Information System will be an important partner in the implementation of this communication and community mobilisation strategy and plan.

Section Five: Information, Monitoring and Research

The plan makes extensive provision for information, monitoring and research, including a patient registration system (with mechanisms for keeping confidentiality), monitoring adherence and adverse drug reactions. The task team has put much effort into what are called "pharmacovigilance" activities.

The purpose of these activities is to assess the efficacy, side effects and optimal use of ARVs in the South African context. Pharmacovigilance activities will be conducted by the Medicines Control Council in conjunction with the national pharmacovigilance unit in Cape Town and pharmacology departments at the Medical University of South Africa and Free State University.

The report states that one of the aims of pharmacovigilance is to minimise the impact of misleading or unproven associations between adverse events and ARV therapy.

The plan recommends an extensive research programme, and there is a substantial research budget accompanying it. Some of the research programmes are:

• Determining optimal ARV use in the South African setting
• Detecting early resistance
• Collecting extensive epidemiological information
• Finding the best way to integrate HIV services with other health services
• Prevention research with an emphasis on sexual behaviour
• Examination of social issues with emphasis on the effect of HIV on families and women
• HIV and TB co-infection

- Opportunistic infections
- Optimal ARV efficacy and toxicity monitoring
- Nutritional issues
- Role of traditional and complementary medicines
- Patterns of progression to Aids in the South African population
- Mechanisms for improving the immune system

The plan states the following key research questions:

1. What is the role of traditional and complementary medications in the context of HIV care and ARV treatment?

2. What are the gender-specific differences in the natural history of HIV disease and response to treatment? (For the former, a natural history cohort of HIV infected and untreated should be established.)

3. What are the metabolic complications of ARV treatment in the South African population?

4. Does micronutrient supplementation improve clinical disease outcomes for people living with HIV and Aids?

5. What is the cost-effectiveness of ARV treatment in South Africa?

6. What are the optimal models of care for urban and rural health care facilities?

7. To what extent can one identify markers of good outcome of treatment in the early stages of intervention? Likewise, can one define markers of bad outcome that can allow for early intervention to improve outcome?

8. What is the overall effect of the HIV and Aids care and treatment programme on access to health care?

9. What is the impact of the HIV and Aids care and treatment programme on attitudes of health care providers, and on retention of health care workers?

10. Various research questions are identified in other chapters of the Operational Plan, such as chapters on pharmacovigilance, traditional medicines and nutrition.

Section Six: Management and Budget

The management section of the plan includes a detailed schedule for implementing the plan and describes the structure responsible for it. The director-general of the Department of Health heads a strategic management team composed of various clusters (e.g. HIV, Aids and TB cluster, maternal child and women's health cluster, pharmaceutical services, etc.)

All the clusters have some role in the programme, but it is to be driven by the HIV, Aids and TB cluster. The plan budgets for increased resources for the team to ensure it has the capacity to implement the plan.

A treatment support unit will be added to the HIV, Aids and TB Cluster. It seems this is the main body responsible on a day-to-day basis for the implementation of the programme.

The budget for the programme has been calculated using projections for patient loads based on the Actuarial Society of South Africa's models. The programme is envisaged to have treated about 50 000 new people before March 2004, 120 000 new people in the financial year ending March 2005, progressively going up to 550 000 new patients in the year ending March 2009.

Additional staffing costs increase from R20,7-million this financial year to over R1-billion in the year ending March 2009, adding about 22 000 full-time employees to the public health care system.

The nutritional support programme increases from R63-million this year to R798-million in the year ending March 2009. Monitoring of well HIV patients increases from R4-million this year to R249-million for the year ending March 2009. Monitoring of patients on ARVs goes up from R13-million this financial year to R917-million for year ending March 2009. Drug costs rise from R42-million this year to R1,7-billion in the year ending March 2009.

Increased funding for national management of the programme is also set aside, as well as for provincial management. Implementing the infrastructure for the programme (e.g. pharmacovigilance, community mobilisation, research, drug procurement, training, community mobilisation, patient information, etc.) increases from R104-million this financial year to R239-million in the year ending March 2006. Subsequently it drops to R208-million per year. The total programme cost rises from R296-million this financial year to R4,5-billion in the year ending March 2008.

Appendix One: Accreditation Requirements

Directly quoted from pages 98-100 of the report.

1. Presence of a service point project manager, who will supervise programme conduct and expansion. Where practical and effective, a project manager may supervise programme conduct and expansion for more than one service point.

2. Availability of a trained care team on-site with representation of all relevant professions (clinicians, nurses, and counsellors), easy access to trained laboratory, pharmacy and nutritional staff, and links to NGOs and other service providers. The care team should consist of sufficient staff in appropriate ratios to manage the projected number of patients.

3. Implementation and maintenance of current standards of care as provided by the National Treatment Policy Guidelines.

4. Access to care 24 hours a day at the service point, or in the direct vicinity, with coverage relationships explicit to both facility staff and patients.

5. A staff recruitment, training and skills development plan in place for health care workers responsible for HIV and Aids care and treatment (including volunteers and lay counsellors) based on initial needs and projected long-term patient numbers.

6. Appropriate numbers of consultation, treatment and counselling rooms should be available to assure patient confidentiality, based on projected patient numbers.

7. Access to appropriate laboratory services, which have appropriate equipment, trained operators, and an effective maintenance plan, overseen by the National Laboratory Health Service. Adequate specimen preparation protocols should be in place for service points accessing laboratory services outside their own facilities.

8. Secure and adequate pharmacy storage, and sufficient cold-chain capacity, appropriate to handle Schedule 5 drugs.

9. Adherence to drug dispensing Standard Operating Procedures (SOPs) for OI prophylaxis and treatment, and ARVs.

10. Access to patient nutritional status assessment and nutritional support.

11. Existing links with on-site and/or proximal VCT centres, antenatal clinics, TB and STI clinics, TB/HIV demonstration districts, and any other patient referral facilities, to ensure that HIV-positive patients are formally referred to the accredited service point.

12. A PMTCT programme in place for service points providing antenatal care, and a referral system in place for sites without antenatal care facilities.

13. Formal referral systems and links with other operations within the service point (in-patient wards, other clinics, support units) and outside expertise (secondary/tertiary care facilities and sub-specialties, including neurology, ear/nose/throat, ophthalmology, oncology, pulmonary and infectious diseases).

14. Referral systems and linkages with community resources (non-governmental organisations, community-based organisations, faith-based organisations, groups for people living with HIV and Aids, traditional health practitioners, community leaders, industry, and other support organisations) that complete the continuum of medical care and support services.

15. Linkages in place with support organisations and NGOs to ensure continuous care and support in the home and community, including support groups, adherence support, educational activities, bereavement counselling and family support.

16. A system in place to track patients/treatments.

17. A system in place to maintain medical records and to transmit core data to a central data collection point.

18. A system in place to ensure that durable equipment is appropriately inventoried and service and maintenance agreements are in place. Where equipment is needed, the service point shall have a plan for procuring and installing the equipment.

19. 24-hours post-exposure prophylaxis (PEP) access, according to the latest national guidelines.

20. A plan for channelling into the care system HIV-positive blood donors, patients treated with PEP, and prison populations identified as HIV-positive.

21. Established links with the provincial HIV and Aids Unit to coordinate briefing of local officials and to streamline input from local advisory committees.

22. Identification of technical assistance needs in administrative and various other technical areas, including medical training.

23. Enlisting resources to help educate patients, families and communities about the basics of HIV and Aids care and treatment, the role that ARV treatment can play, and the difficulties inherent in lifelong treatment for affected individuals and their families.

Summary derived from a Treatment Action Campaign document

Contacts

Parliament

Phone: ....+27(0)21 403 2911
Fax: ....+27(0)21 461 5372
Post: ....PO Box 15, Cape Town 8000
E-mail: ....info@parliament.gov.za
Website: ....http://www.parliament.gov.za

Presidency

Phone: ....+27(0)12 300 5200
Fax: ....+27(0)12 323 8246
Post: ....Private Bag X1000, Pretoria 0001
Website: ....http://www.gov.za

Phone: ....+27(0)21 464 2100
Fax: ....+27(0)21 462 2838
Post: ....Private Bag X1000, Cape Town 8000

Government Communication and Information System

Phone: ....+27(0)12 314 2911
Fax: ....+27(0)12 325 2030
Post: ....Private Bag X745, Pretoria 0001
E-mail: ....govcom@gcis.pwv.gov.za
Website: ....http://www.gcis.gov.za

Ministries

Ministry in the Presidency

Minister: ....Essop Goolam Pahad
Phone: ....+27(0)12 300 5200
Fax: ....+27(0)12 321 8870
Post: ....Private Bag X1000, Pretoria 0001

Phone: ....+27(0)21 464 2122/2100
Fax: ....+27(0)21 462 2838
Post: ....Private Bag X1000, Cape Town 8000

Ministry of Agriculture and Land Affairs

Minister: .... Angela Thoko Didiza
Phone: .... +27(0)12 319 7236
Fax: .... +27(0)12 321 8558
Post: .... Private Bag X250, Pretoria 0001

Phone: .... +27(0)21 465 7690
Fax: .... +27(0)21 465 6550
Post: .... Private Bag X9087, Cape Town 8000

Ministry of Arts and Culture

Minister: .... Zweledinga Pallo Jordan
Phone: .... +27(0)12 337 8378/8000
Fax: .... +27(0)12 324 2687
Post: .... Private Bag X727, Pretoria 0001

Phone: .... +27(0)21 465 4850/70
Fax: .... +27(0)21 461 1425/4537
Post: .... Private Bag X9156, Cape Town 8000

Ministry of Communications

Minister: .... Ivy Matsepe–Casaburri
Phone: .... +27(0)12 427 8111
Fax: .... +27(0)12 362 6915
Post: .... Private Bag X860, Pretoria 0001

Phone: .... +27(0)21 467 9435
Fax: .... +27(0)21 462 1646
Post: .... Private Bag X9151, Cape Town 8000

Ministry of Correctional Services

Minister: .... Ngconde Balfour
Phone: .... +27(0)12 307 2934/9920
Fax: .... +27(0)12 323 1114
Post: .... Private Bag X853, Pretoria 0001

Phone: .... +27(0)21 462 2314/2316/7
Fax: .... +27(0)21 465 4375
Post: .... Private Bag X9131, Cape Town 8000

Ministry of Defence
Minister: ....Mosiuoa Gerard Patrick Lekota
Phone: ....+27(0)12 355 6119
Fax:..+27(0)12 347 0118
Post: ....Private Bag X427, Pretoria 0001

Phone: ....+27(0)21 787 6070
Fax:..+27(0)21 465 5870
Post: ....PO Box 47, Cape Town 8000

Ministry of Education
Minister:...Grace Naledi Mandisa Pandor
Phone: ....+27(0)12 312 5501
Fax:..+27(0)12 323 5989
Post: ....Private Bag X603, Pretoria 0001

Phone: ....+27(0)21 465 7350
Fax:..+27(0)21 461 4788
Post: ....Private Bag X9034, Cape Town 8000

Ministry of Environmental Affairs and Tourism
Minister: ....Marthinus van Schalkwyk
Phone: ....+27(0)12 310 3611
Fax:..+27(0)12 322 0082
Post: ....Private Bag X447, Pretoria 0001

Phone: ....+27(0)21 465 7240/2
Fax:..+27(0)21 465 3216
Post: ....Private Bag X9154, Cape Town 8000

Ministry of Finance
Minister:..Trevor Andrew Manuel
Phone: ....+27(0)12 323 8911
Fax:..+27(0)12 323 3262
Post: ....Private Bag X115, Pretoria 0001

Phone: ....+27(0)21 464 6100
Fax:..+27(0)21 461 2934
Post: ....PO Box 29, Cape Town 8000

Ministry of Foreign Affairs
Minister: ....Nkosazana Clarice Dlamini-Zuma
Phone: ....+27(0)12 351 0006
Fax: ....+27(0)12 351 0253
Post: ....Private Bag X152, Pretoria 0001
E-mail: ....minister@foreign.gov.za

Phone: ....+27(0)21 464 3700
Fax: ....+27(0)21 465 6548
Post: ....17th floor, Room 1714, 120 Plein St., Cape Town 8001

Ministry of Health
Minister: ....Mantombazana Tshabalala-Msimang
Phone: ....+27(0)12 328 4773/5
Fax: ....+27(0)12 325 5526
Post: ....Private Bag X399, Pretoria 0001

Phone: ....+27(0)21 465 7407/8
Fax: ....+27(0)21 465 1575
Post: ....Private Bag X9070, Cape Town 8000

Ministry of Home Affairs
Minister: ....Nosiviwe Mapisa-Nqakula
Phone: ....+27(0)12 326 8081
Fax: ....+27(0)12 321 6491
Post: ....Private Bag X741, Pretoria 0001

Phone: ....+27(0)21 461 5818
Fax: ....+27(0)21 461 2359
Post: ....Private Bag X9102, Cape Town 8000

Ministry of Housing
Minister: ....Lindiwe Nonceba Sisulu
Phone: ....+27(0)12 421 1311
Fax: ....+27(0)12 341 8513
Post: ....Private Bag X645, Pretoria 0001

Phone: ....+27(0)21 465 7295/7
Fax: ....+27(0)21 465 3610
Post: ....Private Bag X9029, Cape Town 8000

Ministry of Intelligence

Minister:..Ronald Kasrils
Phone: ....+27(0)12 338 1800
Fax:..+27(0)12 323 0718
Post:..................................PO Box 56450, Arcadia 0007

Phone: ....+27(0)21 401 1800
Fax:..+27(0)21 461 5878
Post: ....Private Bag X51278, Waterfront 8002

Ministry of Justice and Constitutional Development

Minister:..............................Brigitte Sylvia Mabandla
Phone: ....+27(0)12 315 1761/3
Fax:..+27(0)12 315 1749
Post: ....Private Bag X276, Pretoria 0001

Phone: ....+27(0)21 467 1700/3
Fax:..+27(0)21 467 1730
Post: ....Private Bag X256, Cape Town 8000

Ministry of Labour

Minister:...................Membathisi Mphumzi Shepherd Mdladlana
Phone: ....+27(0)12 322 6523/4
Fax:..+27(0)12 320 1942
Post: ....Private Bag X499, Pretoria 0001

Phone: ....+27(0)21 461 6030
Fax:..+27(0)21 462 2832
Post: ....Private Bag X9090, Cape Town 8000

Ministry of Minerals and Energy

Minister:..............................Phumzile Mlambo-Ngcuka
Phone: ....+27(0)12 322 8695
Fax:..+27(0)12 322 8699
Post: ....Private Bag X646, Pretoria 0001

Phone: ....+27(0)21 462 2310/11
Fax:..+27(0)21 461 0859
Post: ....Private Bag X9111, Cape Town 8000

Ministry of Provincial and Local Government
Minister: ....Fholisani Sydney Mufamadi
Phone: ....+27(0)12 334 0705
Fax: ....+27(0)12 326 4478
Post: ....Private Bag X804, Pretoria 0001

Phone: ....+27(0)21 462 1441
Fax: ....+27(0)21 461 0851
Post: ....Private Bag X9123, Cape Town 8000

Ministry of Public Enterprise
Minister: ....Alexander Erwin
Phone: ....+27(0)12 431 1000
Fax: ....+27(0)12 342 7224
Post: ....Private Bag X15, Hatfield 0028

Phone: ....+27(0)21 461 6376
Fax: ....+27(0)21 465 2381
Post: ....Private Bag X9079, Cape Town 8000

Ministry of Public Service and Administration
Minister: ....Geraldine Joslyn Fraser-Moleketi
Phone: ....+27(0)12 314 7911
Fax: ....+27(0)12 328 6529/6565
Post: ....Private Bag X884, Pretoria 0001

Phone: ....+27(0)21 467 5120
Fax: ....+27(0)21 465 5484
Post: ....Private Bag X9148, Cape Town 8000

Ministry of Public Works
Minister: ....Stella Sigcau
Phone: ....+27(0)12 337 2255
Fax: ....+27(0)12 325 6380
Post: ....Private Bag X890, Pretoria 0001

Phone: ....+27(0)21 462 4184/7
Fax: ....+27(0)21 461 6962
Post: ....Private Bag X9155, Cape Town 8000

Ministry of Safety and Security

Minister:...Charles Nqakula
Phone: ....+27(0)12 393 2800/3
Fax:...+27(0)12 393 2819/20
Post: ....Private Bag X463, Pretoria 0001

Phone:...+27(0)21 467 7000
Fax:..+27(0)21 467 7033/4
Post: ....Private Bag X9080, Cape Town 8000

Ministry of Science and Technology

Minister: ....Mosibudi Mangena
Phone:..+27(0)12 337 8000/8378
Fax:...+27(0)12 324 2687
Post: ....Private Bag X727, Pretoria 0001

Phone: ....+27(0)21 465 4850/70
Fax:..+27(0)21 4651 1425/4537
Post: ....Private Bag X9156, Cape Town 8000

Ministry of Social Development

Minister: ....Zola Sidney Themba Skweyiya
Phone:..+27(0)12 312 7636
Fax:...+27(0)12 321 2502
Post: ....Private Bag X885, Pretoria 0001

Phone: ....+27(0)21 465 4011
Fax:..+27(0)21 465 4469
Post: ....Private Bag X9153, Cape Town 8000

Ministry of Sport and Recreation

Minister:...Mankhenkesi Stofile
Phone:..+27(0)12 334 3100
Fax:...+27(0)12 321 8493
Post: ....Private Bag X896, Pretoria 0001

Phone: ....+27(0)21 465 5506/9
Fax:..+27(0)21 465 4402
Post: ....Private Bag X9149, Cape Town 8000
Website:...http://www.dsr.gov.za

Ministry of Trade and Industry

Minister: ....Mandisi Bongani Mabuto Mpahlwa
Phone: ....+27(0)12 310 1353
Fax:..+27(0)12 322 7851
Post: ....Private Bag X274, Pretoria 0001

Phone: ....+27(0)21 461 7191/3
Fax:..+27(0)21 465 1291
Post: ....Private Bag X9047, Cape Town 8000

Ministry of Transport

Minister: ....Jeffrey Thamsanqa Radebe
Phone: ....+27(0)12 309 3000
Fax:..+27(0)12 328 3194
Post: ....Private Bag X193, Pretoria 0001

Phone:..+27(0)21 465 7260-4
Fax:..+27(0)21 461 6845
Post: ....Private Bag X9129, Cape Town 8000

Ministry of Water Affairs and Forestry

Minister:...............................Buyelwa Patience Sonjica
Phone: ....+27(0)12 336 8733
Fax:..+27(0)12 328 4254
Post: ....Private Bag X313, Pretoria 0001

Phone: ....+27(0)21 464 1500
Fax:..+27(0)21 465 3362
Post: ....Private Bag X9052, Cape Town 8000

Departments

Department in the Presidency

Director–General: ....Reverend Frank Chikane
Phone: ....+27(0)12 300 5200
Fax:..+27(0)12 323 8246
Post:..Private Bag X1000, Pretoria 0001

Department of Agriculture

Director-General:.. Bongiwe Njobe
Phone: ....+27(0)12 319 6000
Fax:...+27(0)12 321 8558
Post: ....Private Bag X250, Pretoria 0001
Website: ....http://www.nda.agric.za

Department of Arts and Culture

Director-General: ....Itumeleng Mosala
Phone: ....+27(0)12 337 8000
Fax:...+27(0)12 323 8308
Post: ....Private Bag X897, Pretoria 0001
Website:..http://www.dac.gov.za

Department of Communications

Director-General:...........................Mpumelelo Zimande (Acting)
Phone: ....+27(0)12 427 8000
Fax:...+27(0)12 427 8016
Post: ....Private Bag X860, Pretoria 0001
E-mail: ....webmaster@doc.pwv.gov.za
Website: ....http://www.doc.gov.za

Department of Correctional Services

National Commissioner:..Linda Mti
Phone: ....+27(0)12 307 2000
Fax:...+27(0)12 328 6149
Post: ....Private Bag X136, Pretoria 0001
E-mail: ....communications@dcs.gov.za
Website: ....http://www.dcs.gov.za

Department of Defence

Head of Department:....................................January Boy Masilela
Phone: ....+27(0)12 355 6200
Fax:...+27(0)12 347 7445
Post: ....Private Bag X910, Pretoria 0001
E-mail: ....info@mil.za
Website: ....http://www.mil.za

Department of Education

Director-General:...........................Thamsanqa Dennis Mseleku
Phone: ....+27(0)12 312 5911
Fax:...+27(0)12 325 6260
Post: ....Private Bag X895, Pretoria 0001
Website:...http://education.pwv.gov.za

Department of Environmental Affairs and Tourism

Director-General:...Crispian Olver
Phone: ....+27(0)12 310 3911
Fax:..+27(0)12 322 2682
Post: ....Private Bag X447, Pretoria 0001
Website: ....http://www.environment.gov.za

Department of Foreign Affairs

Director-General:...Ayanda Ntsaluba
Phone: ....+27(0)12 351 1000
Fax:..+27(0)12 351 0253
Post: ....Private Bag X152, Pretoria 0001
Website:..................................http://www.dfa.gov.za/department

Department of Health

Director-General: ....Mmathari Kelebogile Matsau
Phone: ....+27(0)12 312 0000
Fax:...+27(0)12 312 0911
Post: ....Private Bag X828, Pretoria 0001
Website: ....http://www.doh.gov.za/index.html

Department of Home Affairs

Director-General:...Barry Gilder
Phone: ....+27(0)12 314 8911
Fax:...+27(0)12 323 2416
Post: ....Private Bag X114, Pretoria 0001
E-mail: ....dha@dbs1.pwv.gov.za
Website:.....................http://www.home-affairs.gov.za/index.asp

Department of Housing

Director-General: ....Mpumi Z Nxumalo
Phone: ....+27(0)12 421 1311
Fax:..+27(0)12 341 2998
Post: ....Private Bag X644, Pretoria 0001
Website:...http://www.housing.gov.za

Department of Justice and Constitutional Development

Director-General: ....Vusi Pikoli
Phone: ....+27(0)12 315 1111
Fax:..+27(0)12 315 1112
Post: ....Private Bag X81, Pretoria 0001
E-mail: ....kkganyago@justice.gov.za
Website:..http://www.doj.gov.za

Department of Labour

Director-General:...............................Vanguard Mkosana (Acting)
Phone:...............+27(0)12 309 4000/5000/1/2/5072//73/74/75
Fax: ....+27(0)12 309 4082/320 2059
Post: ....Private Bag X117, Pretoria 0001
Website:...http://www.labour.gov.za

Department of Land Affairs

Director-General: ....Gilingwe Peter Mayende
Phone:..+27(0)12 312 8911
Fax:..+27(0)12 312 8066
Post: ....Private Bag X833, Pretoria 0001

Department of Minerals and Energy

Director-General:..Sandile Nogxina
Phone: ....+27(0)12 317 9000
Fax:..+27(0)12 322 3416
Post: ....Private Bag X59, Pretoria 0001
Website: ....http://www.dme.gov.za

Department of Provincial and Local Government
Director-General:................................Lindiwe Msengana-Ndlela
Phone: ....+27(0)12 334 0600
Fax:..+27(0)12 334 0603
Post: ....Private Bag X804, Pretoria 0001
Website: ....http://www.dplg.gov.za

Department of Public Enterprises
Director-General: ....Eugene Mohulatsi Mokeyane
Phone: ....+27(0)12 431 1000
Fax:..+27(0)12 431 0139
Post: ....Private Bag X15, Hatfield 0028
E-mail: ....info@dpe.gov.za
Website:............................http://www.dpe.gov.za/dpe/home.asp

Department of Public
Service and Administration
Director-General: ....Alvin Phumudzo Rapea (Acting)
Phone: ....+27(0)12 314 7911
Fax: ....+27(0)12 323 2386/324 5616
Post: ....Private Bag X916, Pretoria 0001
E-mail: ....info@dpsa.gov.za
Website: ....http://www.dpsa.gov.za

Department of Public Works
Director-General:.......................................Themba James Maseko
Phone: ....+27(0)12 337 2000
Fax:..+27(0)12 323 2856
Post: ....Private Bag X65, Pretoria 0001
Website: ....http://www.publicworks.gov.za

Department of Science and Technology
Director-General: ....Robert Martin Adam
Phone:...+27(0)12 337 8297/8001
Fax:..+27(0)12 325 2768
Post: ....Private Bag X894, Pretoria 0001
Website:...http://www.dst.gov.za

Department of Social Development

Director–General: ....Vusimuzi Madonsela
Phone: ....+27(0)12 312 7500
Fax:...+27(0)12 312 7943
Post: ....Private Bag X901, Pretoria 0001
E-mail: ....michaelf@socdev.gov.za
Website:...http://www.welfare.gov.za

Department of Trade and Industry

Director–General: ....Alistair Ruiters
Phone: ....+27(0)861 843 384
Fax:...+27(0)861 843 888
Post: ....Private Bag X84, Pretoria 0001
E-mail: ....contactus@thedti.gov.za
Website:...http://www.thedti.gov.za

Department of Transport

Director–General:...Wrenelle Stander
Phone: ....+27(0)12 309 3000
Fax:...+27(0)12 328 5926
Post: ....Private Bag X193, Pretoria 0001
Website: ....http://www.transport.gov.za

Department of Water Affairs and Forestry

Director–General:.......................................Arnold Mike Muller
Phone: ....+27(0)12 336 7500
Fax:...+27(0)12 336 8850
Post: ....Private Bag X313, Pretoria 0001
Website: ....http://www-dwaf.pwv.gov.za

National Intelligence Agency

Director–General:...Vusi Mavimbela
Phone: ....+27(0)12 427 4000
Fax:...+27(0)12 427 4651
Post: ....Private Bag X87, Pretoria 0001
E-mail: ....info@nia.gov.za
Website: ....http://www.nia.org.za

National Treasury

Director-General: ....Lesetja Kganyago
Phone: ....+27(0)12 315 5111
Fax:...+27(0)12 315 5126
Post: ....Private Bag X115, Pretoria 0001
Website: ....http://www.treasury.gov.za

Secretariat for Safety and Security

National Secretary:..........................Malekolle Johannes Rasegatla
Phone: ....+27(0)12 393 2500
Fax: ....+27(0)12 393 2536/2557
Post: ....Private Bag X922, Pretoria 0001
Website: ....http://www.gov.za/sss/index.html

South African Police Service

National Commissioner: ....Jackie Sello Selebi
Phone: ....+27(0)12 393 5488/9
Fax:...+27(0)12 393 5520
Post: ....Private Bag X 94, Pretoria 0001
E-mail: ....response@saps.gov.za
Website: ....http://www.saps.gov.za

South African Secret Service

Director-General: ....Hilton Dennis
Phone:..+27(0)12 427 6110
Fax:...+27(0)12 427 6428
Post:..Private Bag X5, Elarduspark 0047

Sport and Recreation South Africa

Head:...Denver Hendricks
Phone: ....+27(0)12 334 3189
Fax:...+27(0)12 326 4026
Post: ....Private Bag X896, Pretoria 0001
Website:..http://www.srsa.gov.za

Other Government Institutions

Constitutional Court
Phone: ....+27(0)11 359 7400
Fax:...+27(0)11 403 6524
Post:.....................................Private Bag X1, Braamfontein 2017
Website: ....http://www.concourt.gov.za

Independent Complaints Directorate
Executive Director:..Karen McKenzie
Phone: ....+27(0)12 392 0400
Fax: ....+27(0)012 320 3116/7
Post: ....Private Bag X941, Pretoria 0001
E-mail: ....icdpta@icd.pwv.gov.za
Website: ....http://www.icd.gov.za

South African Management Development Institute
Director-General: ....Bobby Soobrayan
Phone: ....+27(0)12 314 7911
Fax:...+27(0)12 321 1810
Post: ....Private Bag X759, Pretoria 0001
E-mail: ....itumelmo@samdi.gov.za
Website: ....http://www.samdi.gov.za

South African Revenue Service
Commissioner:..Pravin J Gordhan
Phone: ....+27(0)12 422 4000
Fax:...+27(0)12 422 6848
Post: ....Private Bag X923, Pretoria 0001
Website:..................................http://www.sars.gov.za

Statistics South Africa
Statistician General: Pali Lehohla
Phone: ....+27(0)12 310 8911
Fax: ....+27(0)12 310 8500/8495
Post: ....Private Bag X44, Pretoria 0001
E-mail: ....info@statssa.gov.za
Website: ....http//www.statssa.gov.za

Commissions

Commission for Gender Equality
Phone: ....+27(0)11 403 7182
Fax:..+27(0)11 403 7188
Post:...PO Box 32175, Braamfontein 2017
E-mail: ....cgeinfo@cge.org.za
Website:..http://www.cge.org.za

Human Rights Commission
Phone: ....+27(0)11 484 8300
Fax:..+27(0)11 484 7149
Post:...Private Bag 2700, Houghton 2041
E-mail: ....sahrcinfo@sahrc.org.za
Website: ....http://www.sahrc.org.za

Independent Electoral Commission
Toll Free: 0800 11 8000
Phone: ....+27(0)12 428 5700
Fax:..+27(0)12 428 5863
Post: ....PO Box 7943, Pretoria 0001
E-mail: ....iec@elections@org.za
Website:...http://www.elections.org.za

Judicial Service Commission
Phone: ....+27(0)51 447 2769
Fax:..+27(0)51 447 0836
Post: ....Private Bag X258, Bloemfontein 9300
E-mail: ....judsercom@intekom.co.za
Website:......................http://www.gov.za/contacts/bodies/jsc.php

Land Claims Commission
Phone: ....+27(0)12 312 9244
Fax:..+27(0)12 321 0428
Post: ....Private Bag X833, Pretoria 0001
Website: ....http://land.pwv.gov.za/restitution/Default.htm

Public Service Commission
Director General:...............................James Mpumelelo Sikhosana
Phone: ....+27(0)12 328 7690
Fax:..+27(0)12 325 8382
Post: ....Private Bag X121, Pretoria 0001
E-mail: ....info@opsc.gov.za
Website: ....http://www.psc.gov.za

Provincial Governments

Eastern Cape Provincial Government

Premier:..Zisiwe Nosimo Beauty Balindlela
Phone:.......................................+27(0)40 609 2207/639 1415
Fax:...+27(0)40 635 1166
Post: ....Private Bag X0047, Bisho 5605
E-mail: ....premier@otpmleg1.ecape.gov.za
Website:...http://www.ecprov.gov.za

Free State Provincial Government

Premier:..Frances Beatrice Marshoff
Phone: ....+27(0)51 405 5799
Fax:..+27(0)51 405 4803
Post: ....PO Box 20538, Bloemfontein 9300
E-mail: ....focwel127@majuba.ofs.gov.za

Gauteng Provincial Government

Premier: ....Mbhazima Shilowa
Phone: ....+27(0)11 355 6000
Fax:..+27(0)11 836 9334
Post:...............................Private Bag X61, Marshalltown 2107
E-mail: ....mbhazimas@gpg.gov.za
Website: ....http://www.gpg.gov.za

KwaZulu-Natal Provincial Government

Premier:..Joel Sibusiso Ndebele
Phone: ....+27(0)35 874 2004
Fax:..+27(0)35 874 2003
Post:...Private Bag X01, Ulundi 3838
Website:................................http://www.kwazulunatal.gov.za

Limpopo Provincial Government

Premier:...Sello Moloto
Phone: ....+27(0)15 287 6000
Fax:..+27(0)15 291 4808
Post:...........................Private Bag X9483, Polokwane 0700
Website: ....http://www.limpopo.gov.za

Mpumalanga Provincial Government

Premier:...........................Thabang Sampson Phathekge Makwetla
Phone: ....+27(0)13 766 2641
Fax:...+27(0)13 766 2494
Post: ....Private Bag X11291, Nelspruit 1200
Website: ....http://www.mpumalanga.mpu.gov.za

North West Provincial Government

Premier: ....Ednah Molewa
Phone: ....+27(0)18 387 3000
Fax:...+27(0)18 387 3008
Post:.......................................Private Bag X65, Mafikeng 2745
E-mail: ....premnw@nwpg.gov.za
Website: ....http://www.nwpg.gov.za

Northern Cape Provincial Government

Premier: ....Elizabeth Dipuo Peters
Phone: ....+27(0)53 839 8276
Fax:...+27(0)53 831 1894
Post:.......................................Private Bag X5042, Kimberley 8300
Website: ....http://ncwebpage.ncape.gov.za

Western Cape Provincial Government

Premier:...Ebrahim Rasool
Phone: ....+27(0)21 483 4705/6
Fax:...+27(0)21 483 3421
Post: ....Private Bag X9043, Cape Town 8000
Website: ....http://westcape.wcape.gov.za

Political Parties in Parliament

African Christian Democratic Party

Phone: ....+27(0)11 869 3941
Fax:..+27(0)11 869 3942
Post: ....PO Box 1677, Alberton 1450
E-mail: ....acdpnat@iafrica.com
Website: ....http://www.acdp.org.za

African National Congress

Phone: ....+27(0)11 376 1000
Fax:..+27(0)11 376 1134
Post:.......................................PO Box 61884, Marshalltown 2107
E-mail: ....anchq@anc.org.za
Website:..http://www.anc.org.za

Azanian People's Organisation

Phone: ....+27(0)11 336 3551
Fax:..+27(0)11 333 6681
Post: ....PO Box 4230, Johannesburg 2000
E-mail: ....azapo@sn.apc.org
Website: ....http://www.azapo.org.za

Democratic Alliance

Phone: ....+27(0)21 403 2910
Fax:..+27(0)21 461 0092
Post: ....Post Bag 15, Cape Town 8000
E-mail: ....leader@da.org.za
Website: ....http://www.da.org.za

Freedom Front Plus

Phone: ....+27(0)12 322 7141
Fax:..+27(0)12 322 7144
E-mail: ....info@vf.co.za
Website:....................http://www.vryheidsfront.co.za/a/index.asp

Independent Democrats

Phone: ....+27(0)11 337 3515
Fax: ....+27(0)21 532 2095
Call centre: ....+27(0)861 121 344
Post: ....PO Box 10777, Johannesburg 2001
E-mail: ....patricia@id.org.za
Website: ....http://www.id.org.za

New National Party

Phone: ....+27(0)21 461 5833
Fax: ....+27(0)21 461 5329
Post: ....PO Box 1698, Cape Town 8000
E-mail: ....npsenate@mweb.co.za
Website: ....http://www.natweb.co.za

Pan Africanist Congress

Phone: ....+27(0)11 337 2193
Fax: ....+27(0)11 337 6400
Post: ....PO Box 6010, Johannesburg 2000
E-mail: ....azania@sn.apc.org
Website: ....http://www.paca.org.za

United Democratic Movement

Phone: ....+27(0)12 321 0010
Fax: ....+27(0)12 321 0014
Post: ....PO Box 26290, Arcadia 0007
E-mail: ....info@udm.org.za
Website: ....http://www.udm.org.za

Election Results 1994, 1999 and 2004

ELECTION RESULTS 2004

	Eastern Cape	Free State	Gauteng	KZN	Mpuma-langa	North Cape	Limpopo	North West	West Cape
ACDP	0.78%	1.32%	1.61%	1.8%	1%	1.85%	1.23%	1.1%	3.78%
ANC	79.31%	82.05%	68.74%	47.47%	86.34%	68.75%	89.72%	81.83%	46.11%
AZAPO	0.17%	0.34%	0.23%	0.24%	0.19%	0.49%	0.52%	0.27%	0.25%
CDP	0.05%	0.07%	0.16%	0.16%	0.06%	0.06%	0.06%	0.07%	0.17%
DA	7.25%	8.87%	20.33%	10%	7.17%	11.61%	3.81%	5.47%	26.92%
ID	0.84%	0.61%	1.73%	0.75%	0.35%	6.61%	0.19%	0.5%	7.97%
IFP	0.21%	0.43%	2.64%	34.87%	1.03%	0.22%	0.18%	0.29%	0.23%
KISS	0.02%	0.03%	0.03%	0.08%	0.02%	0.06%	0.03%	0.03%	0.06%
MF	0.02%	0.02%	0.05%	1.86%	0.03%	0.03%	0.02%	0.02%	0.04%
NA	0.06%	0.1%	0.12%	0.09%	0.07%	0.1%	0.12%	0.09%	0.16%
NLP	0.02%	0.02%	0.01%	0.04%	0.02%	0.06%	0.03%	0.02%	0.61%
NNP	0.63%	0.82%	0.74%	0.58%	0.43%	7.16%	0.47%	0.43%	9.44%
PAC	0.98%	1.3%	0.81%	0.21%	0.76%	0.43%	0.95%	0.79%	0.46%
PJC	0.07%	0.06%	0.09%	0.1%	0.05%	0.09%	0.07%	0.05%	0.27%
EMSA	0.07%	0.07%	0.03%	0.09%	0.06%	0.09%	0.08%	0.09%	0.07%
TOP	0.04%	0.04%	0.03%	0.08%	0.04%	0.05%	0.05%	0.04%	0.05%
SOPA	0.11%	0.11%	0.07%	0.15%	0.09%	0.07%	0.08%	0.1%	0.04%
UCDP	0.11%	0.66%	0.26%	0.15%	0.16%	0.31%	0.14%	6.53%	0.23%
UDM	8.91%	0.96%	1.01%	0.84%	1.01%	0.42%	1.66%	1.08%	1.85%
UF	0.05%	0.07%	0.11%	0.12%	0.06%	0.05%	0.05%	0.06%	0.03%
VF+	0.28%	2.07%	1.2%	0.34%	1.06%	1.49%	0.52%	1.14%	1.24%

NATIONAL

ACDP	1.6%
ANC	69.68%
AZAPO	0.27%
CDP	0.11%
DA	12.37%
ID	1.73%
IFP	6.97%
KISS	0.04%
MF	0.35%
NA	0.1%
NLP	0.09%
NNP	1.65%
PAC	0.73%
PJC	0.1%
EMSA	0.07%
TOP	0.05%
SOPA	0.1%
UCDP	0.75%
UDM	2.28%
UF	0.08%
VF+	0.89%

PARTY

ACDP	African Christian Democratic Party
ANC	African National Congress
AZAPO	Azanian People's Organisation
CDP	Christian Democratic Party
DA	Democratic Alliance/Demokratiese Alliansie
ID	Independent Democrats
IFP	Inkatha Freedom Party
KISS	Keep It Straight And Simple
MF	Minority Front
NA	Nasionale Aksie
NLP	New Labour Party
NNP	Nuwe Nasionale Party/New National Party
PAC	Pan Africanist Congress Of Azania
PJC	Peace And Justice Congress
EMSA	The Employment Movement Of South Africa
TOP	The Organisation Party
SOPA	The Socialist Party Of Azania
UCDP	United Christian Democratic Party
UDM	United Democratic Movement
UF	United Front
VF+	Vryheidsfront Plus

ELECTION RESULTS 1999

	Eastern Cape	Free State	Gauteng	KZN	Mpuma-langa	North Cape	Northern Province	North West	West Cape
PAC	1%	1.03%	0.69%	0.28%	0.61%	0.64%	1.21%	0.68%	0.50%
GPGP	0.03%	0.03%	0.06%	0.07%	0.02%	0.03%	0.03%	0.02%	0.18%
SOPA	0.03%	0.08%	0.05%	0.09%	0.05%	0.05%	0.08%	0.06%	0.02%
UCDP	0.12%	0.73%	0.21%	0.09%	0.21%	0.25%	0.10%	7.48%	0.11%
UDM	12.88%	1.65%	2.15%	1.29%	1.40%	0.94%	2.57%	1.42%	3.07%
FF	0.31%	1.75%	1.10%	0.20%	1.30%	1.59%	0.53%	1.16%	0.66%
AITUP	0.08%	0.04%	0.03%	0.11%	0.04%	0.12%	0.08%	0.04%	0.09%
ACDP	1.11%	0.92%	1.17%	1.82%	1.10%	1.61%	1.09%	0.90%	3.11%
ANC	73.91%	81.03%	68.16%	39.77%	85.26%	64.40%	89.30%	80.53%	42.62%
AEB	0.18%	0.39%	0.29%	0.20%	0.38%	0.51%	0.37%	0.47%	0.19%
AZAPO	0.13%	0.18%	0.14%	0.15%	0.09%	0.38%	0.49%	0.11%	0.06%
DP	6.38%	5.87%	17.69%	9.76%	4.97%	5.78%	1.69%	3.72%	14.18%
FA	0.19%	0.83%	0.85%	0.30%	0.75%	0.70%	0.37%	0.56%	0.55%
IFP	0.30%	0.45%	3.54%	40.45%	1.41%	0.44%	0.32%	0.45%	0.20%
MF	0.03%	0.03%	0.03%	1.45%	0.04%	0.06%	0.04%	0.03%	0.08%
NNP	3.32%	5%	3.85%	3.96%	2.37%	22.49%	1.72%	2.38%	34.38%

NATIONAL

PAC	0.71%
GPGP	0.06%
SOPA	0.06%
UCDP	0.78%
UDM	3.42%
FF	0.80%
AITUP	0.07%
ACDP	1.43%
ANC	66.35%
AEB	0.29%
AZAPO	0.17%
DP	9.56%
FA	0.54%
IFP	8.58%
MF	0.30%
NNP	6.87%

PARTY

ACDP	African Christian Democratic Party
PAC	Pan Africanist Congress Of Azania
GPGP	The Government by the Green People Party
SOPA	The Socialist Party Of Azania
UCDP	United Christian Democratic Party
UDM	United Democratic Movement
FF	Freedom Front/ Vryheidsfront
AITUP	Abolition of Income Tax and Usury Party
ACDP	African Christian Democratic Party
ANC	African National Congress
AEB	Afrikaner EenheidsBeweging
AZAPO	Azanian People's Organisation
DP	Democratic Party
FA	Federal Alliance
IFP	Inkatha Freedom Party
MF	Minority Front
NNP	Nuwe Nasionale Party/New National Party

Information contained herein from the Independent Electoral Commission of South Africa, The Electoral Institute of Southern Africa and www.electionresources.org

ELECTION RESULTS 1994

	Eastern Cape	Free State	PWV	KZN	East Transvaal	North Cape	North Transvaal	North West	West Cape
ACDP	0.38%	0.33%	0.48%	0.46%	0.34%	0.32%	0.26%	0.25%	0.97%
ADM	0.07%	0.04%	0.03%	0.10%	0.05%	0.05%	0.03%	0.04%	0.02%
AMCP	0.17%	0.19%	0.13%	0.09%	0.20%	0.21%	0.17%	0.20%	0.06%
AMP	0.04%	0.02%	0.18%	0.18%	0.07%	0.08%	0.02%	0.09%	0.74%
ANC	84.39%	77.42%	59.10%	31.61%	81.87%	49.81%	92.73%	83.46%	33.60%
DP	1.24%	0.54%	3%	1.61%	0.42%	1.29%	0.18%	0.37%	4.18%
DPSA	0.04%	0.64%	0.06%	0.05%	0.06%	0.10%	0.04%	0.13%	0.05%
FF/VF	0.65%	3.68%	3.68%	0.46%	3.51%	4.32%	1.51%	3.10%	1.97%
FP	0.03%	0.04%	0.16%	0.09%	0.04%	0.04%	0.02%	0.03%	0.22%
IFP	0.24%	0.62%	4.13%	48.59%	1.59%	0.47%	0.15%	0.45%	0.65%
KISS	0.03%	0.03%	0.03%	0.03%	0.03%	0.07%	0.02%	0.03%	0.04%
LUSO-SA	0.01%	0.01%	0.01%	0.03%	0.02%	0.03%	0.01%	0.02%	0.02%
MF	0.03%	0.04%	0.04%	0.17%	0.04%	0.12%	0.03%	0.05%	0.07%
NP	10.6%	14.53%	27.58%	15.76%	10.27%	41.94%	3.64%	10.10%	56.24%
PAC	1.99%	1.7%	1.25%	0.62%	1.36%	0.97%	1.06%	1.53%	1%
SOCCER	0.03%	0.06%	0.07%	0.06%	0.05%	0.06%	0.03%	0.06%	0.05%
WLP	0.01%	0.02%	0.01%	0.03%	0.02%	0.04%	0.01%	0.02%	0.03%
WRPP	0.02%	0.03%	0.04%	0.03%	0.02%	0.04%	0.01%	0.04%	0.07%
XPP	0.02%	0.05%	0.02%	0.04%	0.03%	0.03%	0.07%	0.04%	0.01%

NATIONAL

ACDP	0.45%
ADM	0.05%
AMCP	0.14%
AMP	0.18%
ANC	62.65%
DP	1.73%
DPSA	0.10%
FF/VF	2.17%
FP	0.09%
IFP	10.54%
KISS	0.03%
LUSO-SA	0.02%
MF	0.07%
NP	20.39%
PAC	1.25%
SOCCER	0.05%
WLP	0.02%
WRPP	0.03%
XPP	0.03%

PARTY

ANC	African National Congress
ACDP	African Christian Democratic Party
ADM	African Democratic Movement
AMP	Africa Muslim Party
AMCP	African Moderates Congress Party
DP	Democratic Party
DPSA	Dikwankwetla Party of South Africa
FF/VF	Vryheidsfront
FP	Federal Party
IFP	Inkatha Freedom Party
LUSO-SA	Luso South African Party
KISS	Keep It Straight and Simple
MF	Minority Front
NP	National Party
PAC	Pan Africanist Congress of Azania
SOCCER	Soccer
WLP	Workers' List Party
WRPP	Women's Rights Peace Party
XPP	Ximoko Progressive Party

List of Contributors

Justin Arenstein is founding editor of the *African Eye News Service* and specialises in investigative reporting on cross-border corruption and social justice issues.

Julia Beffon is sports editor at the *Mail&Guardian*.

Maureen Brady is a freelance writer and sub-editor for *Earthyear* magazine.

Matthew Buckland is editor of the *Mail&Guardian* Online. He is also a columnist for *The Media* magazine and US-based journalism site Poynter Online.

Matthew Burbidge is a journalist on *Mail&Guardian* Online.

Nawaal Deane covers health for the *Mail&Guardian*.

Judith February is head of the Political Information and Monitoring Service at the Institute for Democracy in South Africa, and previously practised law in Cape Town.

Drew Forrest is deputy editor of the *Mail&Guardian*.

Philippa Garson, former editor of *The Teacher*, has written on a range of topics for local and overseas publications and is currently writing articles on Johannesburg for online publishers Big Media.

Julia Grey is editor of *The Teacher*.

Yolandi Groenewald covers land, agriculture and environmental issues for the *Mail&Guardian* and *Earthyear* magazine.

Ferial Haffajee is editor of the *Mail&Guardian*.

Karen Heese is an economist and freelance journalist.

Ufrieda Ho is a freelance journalist.

Lisa Johnston is a sub-editor at the *Mail&Guardian*.

Nicole Johnston, formerly head of print media training at the Institute for the Advancement of Journalism, is assistant editor: training at the *Mail&Guardian* and is involved in labour dispute resolution.

Ronald Monwabisi Kete is a youth development worker, a theologian, and a writer with a keen interest in media and journalism.

Jaspreet Kindra is a freelance journalist.

Matuma Letsoalo is a labour reporter for the *Mail&Guardian*.

Barbara Ludman, a former associate editor of the *Mail&Guardian*, was co-editor of three previous editions of the *A-Z of SA Politics*.

Thebe Mabanga is financial correspondent for the *Mail&Guardian*

Fiona Macleod is environmental editor at the *Mail&Guardian* and editor of *Earthyear* magazine.

Khadija Magardie is a freelance writer and film producer.

Noko Makgato is a journalist with a keen interest in politics and economics.

Mmanaledi Mataboge is a journalist and a producer on SAfm's AM and Midday Live.

Nicola Mawson is a reporter for *Engineering News.*

Marianne Merten is a *Mail&Guardian* journalist covering Parliament and Western Cape politics and current affairs.

Thandee N'wa Mhangwana is a photojournalist from rural Limpopo specialising in social justice and development reporting.

Fikile-Ntsikelelo Moya is criminal justice reporter for the *Mail&Guardian*.

Trish Murphy is a freelance journalist and editor.

Roshila Pillay is a *Mail&Guardian* journalist.

Vicki Robinson is a *Mail&Guardian* journalist.

Ciaran Ryan is a Johannesburg-based freelance writer contributing to several local and international publications on the South African economy.

Pat Schwartz, a former journalist and former director of Wits University Press, is a freelance writer and editor.

Sam Sole is an investigative journalist for the *Mail&Guardian.*

Paul Stober is a deputy editor and political editor of the *Mail&Guardian.*

Rapule Thabane is political correspondent for the *Mail&Guardian.*

Thomas Thale is a journalist who writes for the Johannesburg website, www.joburg.org.za

Mike van Graan is general secretary of the Performing Arts Network of South Africa and a regular columnist for the Friday section of the *Mail&Guardian.*

Wisani wa ka Ngobeni is associate editor of the *Mail&Guardian.*

Index